Contemporary American Economic and Political Problems

Contemporary American Economic and Political Problems

Wesley M. Bagby

Nelson-Hall nh Chicago

Library of Congress Cataloging in Publication Data

Bagby, Wesley Marvin, 1922–
Contemporary American economic and political problems.

Includes bibliographies and index.
1. United States—Economic conditions. 2. United States—Politics and government. I. Title.
HC103.B3 330.973'0926 80–22510
ISBN 0–88229–328–1 (cloth)
ISBN 0–88229–765–1 (paper)

 For information address Nelson-Hall Inc., Publishers, 111 North Canal Street, Chicago, Illinois 60606.

Manufactured in the United States of America

10 9 8 7 6 5 4 3 2 1

To Janice

Contents

Preface

This volume is an introduction to current problems faced by American society—and to the social sciences that analyze them. Its organization is problem-centered and broadly interdisciplinary. It seeks to bring to bear the findings of various social science disciplines on these problems while introducing basic social science concepts and principles. Because it seeks to meet the needs of general as well as specialized students, it emphasizes terminology and methodology somewhat less, and the findings of the disciplines somewhat more than might be found in texts designed primarily for majors in a particular discipline. It puts somewhat more emphasis on the economic basis and the international dimensions of contemporary problems.

Undertaking to write on such a broad range of problems is such an exercise in immodesty that it demands explanation. A number of interests and accidents have combined to give the writer a social science background, whatever its depth, of considerable breadth. These include undergraduate and graduate study of history, economics, psychology, political science, and sociology. Teaching experience has included courses in a small college in sociology, economics, contemporary history, and political science. I also coordinated the basic social science course at West Virginia University. Long experience in teaching freshmen has helped me to understand their difficulties with texts selected for them by professors, and has helped me develop materials palatable to both. Assuming that my readers knew little but could understand much,

I have tried to write a book that is introductory without remaining elementary.

I have sought and received much help in developing this volume. My colleagues at West Virginia University have been generous with their wealth of resources. I want to thank particularly Benedum Professor of Economics William H. Miernyk for a constructive critique of a number of chapters, and Professors John Caruso and Joe Super for reading chapters related to their fields. A number of associates elsewhere performed the signal service of both critically reading chapters and testing them in their social science classes: Don Martin, Aaron Phillips, Mary Petropolis, William Dilgard, John Spears, Daniel Stubbs, and Richard Hughes. Their critiques and those of their students and my students saved the text from many an obscurity and encouraged its ventures beyond blandness into realistic discussion of current issues. Richard Bagby, M.D., critiqued the chapter on health problems. Of course full responsibility for interpretations and errors remains mine. Valuable research and editing assistance was rendered by student assistants Rodney Pyles, David Simpson, Linda Hupp, George Menas, and John McGuire. My wife, Janice, provided helpful criticism, typing, and patient encouragement.

Part 1
Economic Problems

1
Producing and Distributing Goods and Services

What are the basic problems of any economy?
How did modern economic systems develop?
How do economists differ on the best way of meeting modern economic problems?

"The ideas of economists and political philosophers, both when they are right and when they are wrong, are more powerful than is commonly understood. Indeed, the world is ruled by little else."

—Lord Maynard Keynes

"The rules of economics are not working in quite the way they used to."

—Arthur Burns, Chairman of the Federal Reserve Board, 1975

"Economy is the art of making the most of life."

—George Bernard Shaw

The Basic Problems

America has been outstandingly successful in producing and distributing goods and services—until very recently Americans were more plentifully supplied with goods and services than any other people. Nevertheless, our system of production and distribution suffers from many strains, inequalities, and periodic partial breakdowns.

Unfortunately, a conflict-free economy is probably impossible.

The basic problem is that all goods and services can never be plentiful enough to satisfy everyone. Economists agree that with rare exceptions the wants of people for goods and services are practically unlimited. If by some chance a person got everything he wanted, he would immediately develop new wants.

Because wants are unlimited and the means of satisfying them are limited, we are forced to make difficult choices. In order to get some goods and services we must forgo others. In the competition for the scarce supply, some people get more than an equal share and others get less. How such choices are made, how the distribution is determined, and who makes these decisions are the basic issues in any economic system.

Three basic elements enter into the production of goods and services. They are *natural resources,* including soil, stone, ores, timber, and oil; *labor*, of both manual and mental types; and *capital*, including anything of value used in producing and distributing goods and services such as tools, machinery, railroads, warehouses, and shops. The relative value, or price, of any of these three elements varies with its scarcity relative to the supply of the other two.

Organized economic systems began with the division of labor. Men discovered early that they differed in talents, and that frequent repetition of a task increased their skill at performing it. Consequently, they could produce more goods if men specialized in making different goods and then exchanged them. For example, some men made arrowheads better than others. If instead of doing their own hunting and fishing they devoted their time to making arrowheads and traded them for meat hunted by others, their wealth and the total wealth of the tribe would rise. As the amount of such specialization and trade increased, the process of producing and distributing goods and services grew more complex.

THE DEVELOPMENT OF WESTERN ECONOMIES

Men passed through several stages in developing better ways of satisfying their needs and wants. Early men were food gatherers who subsisted on the fruit, berries, nuts, and insects they could find in their natural surroundings. Later, some men invented weapons and traps for killing animals and fish and became hunters and fishermen. Men also learned to tame animals and became herdsmen. Others learned to cultivate food plants and became farmers. As these developments increased the food supply, population density rose, and men congregated in villages where more division of labor was possible. Villages traded with each other for goods of limited geographical distribution such as salt or iron. Such geographical specialization increased as villages found it profitable to devote more of their efforts to producing what their environments permitted them to produce best and exchanging those products for other goods. Some villages grew into cities, conquered surrounding territories, and became empires.

After the collapse of Rome's empire, Europe was overrun by rampaging barbarians, trade was disrupted, and cities shrank to a fraction of their former size. Each village and rural manor was forced back toward self-sufficiency. Later, under the Church's tutelage, some barbarians became more civilized and peaceful. At the same time some nobles subdued others, bringing larger areas under common rule. As trade became safer, towns revived as centers of trade and manufacturing.

We do not know how early in man's development economic folkways took on the force of mores and law. However, the Old Testament sets forth economic rules, and medieval writers concerned themselves with such questions as what prices and rates of interest were just. The division of the crop between knights and peasants was rigidly fixed by custom, law, and religion.

Also, as early as Plato and Aristotle, discussions were under way concerning what actions government could take to increase the wealth and power of the state. As towns revived in Europe, political economists advocated a policy called *mercantilism*. The growth of a city's trade, they said, depended on the reputation of its goods for quality and value. Therefore, the government should closely regulate manufacturing and trade to guarantee high quality. Also, they maintained, the wealth and power of a state depended on its accumulation of gold and silver. Therefore, the state should strive to sell more goods to foreigners than it bought from them—they called such an excess of exports over imports a "favorable balance of trade."

The Industrial Revolution and the Rise of Capitalism

Beginning in England about 1750 a vast change came over the economy of Europe. Men invented a series of power-driven machines that were capable of producing goods that previously had required slow and painstaking work by hand. The changeover from making goods by hand to making them on machines caused such great alterations in the economy that it is called the *Industrial Revolution.*

One result of the Industrial Revolution was the rise of *capitalism,* an economic system in which the production of goods and services is controlled by private owners of capital. Goods are of two general types: consumer goods and capital goods. Consumer goods are those used or consumed to satisfy needs and wants—for example, food, clothing, toothbrushes, and automobiles. Capital goods are those used to make other goods—for example, tools, machinery, iron ore, or warehouses. Owners of capital goods are called capitalists. Because they owned the factories, capitalists could decide what and how many goods to produce and what price to ask for them.

Capitalists denounced mercantilist rules and laws governing production as interfering with the most efficient operation of their factories and the most profitable conduct of their business. Their rising wealth soon gave them the political influence to ignore or abolish such legislation. Thus an economic system developed in which the chief economic decisions were made by individual businessmen for personal gain. This made possible the science of economics which is the study of the behavior of economic systems in which decisions are economically motivated instead of being set by custom or law.

ADAM SMITH ON THE FREE MARKET

Adam Smith is considered the father of modern economics. A Scotsman who reached maturity while the first effects of the Industrial Revolution were being felt, Smith believed that the new developments were leading the way to a vastly superior economic system. In his 1776 book, *An Inquiry into the Nature and Causes of the Wealth of Nations,* he maintained that government regulation of the economy was unnecessary because the economy could better regulate itself. If left free, he said, each man—capitalist or laborer—in self-interest would seek to use his resources, labor, and money in ways that would produce the maximum income. The effect of such unregulated mass selfish behavior would be the most efficient use of the nation's labor and resources. Thus, a nation's wealth would rise most rapidly, he said, when government dropped all economic controls in favor of complete *free enterprise,* a policy also known as "laissez-faire."

Smith believed that the efficient use of economic resources under free enterprise was guaranteed by the natural laws of a free market. By market he meant the hundreds or thousands of buyers and sellers competing throughout the country. A market is free when the government does not regulate it, and when no businessman or group of businessmen controls such a large share of the supply or consumption of any article that they are able to control its price.

In a free market the price of any article would be set by the *laws of supply and demand,* the relationship that exists at any particular time between supply and demand. (Demand means desire plus purchasing power.) An increase in the demand for an article, or a drop in the supply of it, tends to raise its price. Conversely, a drop in demand for an article or an increase in its supply tends to reduce its price. If demand and supply move upward or downward at the same rate no price change results. But if demand rises more rapidly than supply the price will rise, and vice versa. The laws of supply and demand, said Smith, insure that producers will furnish the goods and services that people want to buy, and at the lowest profitable price. For example, if the people's desire for watches exceeds the number of watches available, and if they have the money (demand) to buy them, they will offer to pay more for them. This raises the profit of watchmaking and motivates manufacturers to increase production. When the supply exceeds demand the competition of watchmakers to sell overstocks of watches causes them to cut their prices. They produce fewer watches and less efficient watch manufacturers may go out of business, reducing the supply. If the supply falls below demand, prices rise again and so does production. Thus, in the long run, production automatically adjusts itself to meet consumer demand, and the free market insures the production of as many watches as can be sold at a reasonable profit.

Of course all of this depends on keeping the market free. Its beneficent operation, said Smith, can be destroyed in either of two ways—through government control or through private formation of monopolies. If any one business gains control of the supply of a needed article, it thereby acquires the power to cut production and raise prices, both actions injurious to the economy and the public.

The Labor Problem

The Industrial Revolution eventually brought an undreamed of abundance to mankind, but its first effect on many workers was depressing. It reduced them from independent craftsmen to dependent wage earners. Before the Industrial Revolution skilled workers, called craftsmen, were independent businessmen. A cobbler, for example, would buy leather, thread, nails, and dye, make a pair of shoes with his hand tools, and sell them to a customer. He got whatever profits resulted from shoemaking. After the invention of shoemaking machines, however, cobblers found it difficult to sell expensive handmade shoes, and sank into poverty. Far too expensive for a cobbler to buy, the machines were owned by capitalists who put them in sheds and hired workers to operate them. When cobblers applied for jobs in factories they found that their skill was not needed, and that they had to compete with masses of unskilled workers including women and children.

Wages were low, and living conditions among early industrial workers were miserable. Reports by British parliamentary investigating commissions tell of men, women, and children working fourteen to sixteen hours per day, seven days a week, in poorly lit, unheated textile mills whose air was filled with disease-producing lint and dust; of women harnessed to pull coal cars on their hands and knees through coal mine tunnels; and of children chained to machines to keep them from running away. When workers were injured, became ill or too old to work, or when a depression struck, they were fired and left to shift for themselves. Horrifying amounts of disease, crime, starvation, and stunted growth resulted. The Industrial Revolution had created terrible social problems.

HOW TO HELP THE WORKERS: THE ANSWER OF THE CLASSICAL ECONOMISTS

Many leading economists of the day held that neither private charity nor government action could permanently improve conditions among workers. As followers of Adam Smith, they believed that the economy was most productive when left completely free to operate according to its own natural laws, and that any government regulation, no matter how well intended, interfered with the economy's operation and thereby reduced its total production.

One of these classical economists, Thomas Malthus, formulated what became known as the *Malthusian Law*. Population, he said, increases more rapidly than the food supply. Therefore, if many people are not killed by war and disease, some must starve. Naturally, such starvation would occur among the poor.

Another classical economist, David Ricardo, formulated what

he called the *iron law of wages*. Wages, he said, were the price of labor and, under a free economy, were determined by supply and demand. If wages rose, workers would marry earlier and rear more children. When the number of workers exceeded the number of available jobs, wages would fall until some of them starved. Thus the iron law was that wages would fluctuate between slightly above and slightly below starvation levels. No wonder political economics came to be called the "gloomy science"!

Some people, however, refused to accept these conclusions. Humanitarians, for example, including religious and charitable groups, persisted in giving free milk to hungry children and demanding laws to prevent overworking of women and children. Such measures relieved some suffering but did not solve the problem.

Robert Owen, an enlightened English manufacturer, tried to introduce profit sharing into capitalism. He proved that he could make good profits while providing workers with improved working conditions and higher wages, but he was not able to persuade many of his fellow capitalists to adopt his methods.

How to Help the Workers: The Socialist Answer

Some economists who disagreed with the classical economists were called *socialists*. Agreeing with Ricardo that labor was the source of wealth, they argued that working people were impoverished because they received only a fraction of the wealth they produced. The lion's share was taken by capitalists because they owned the machinery on which goods were made. The proposed solution of the socialists was to give the machines to the workers and thereby enable them to enjoy the wealth they produced. Of course, if a factory were given to one worker he would stop working and be a capitalist. Therefore, they said, the factories must be given to groups of workers. Because they advocated group, or social ownership, they were called socialists.

Socialism, of course, was not a new idea. Primitive tribes had owned land in common as had many agricultural villages. A form of socialism was advocated in Plato's *Republic*. Among early Christians, according to the Bible, "no one said that any of the things which he possessed was his own, but they had everything in common." However, after much discussion and experimentation, most postindustrialization socialists concluded that the most practical plan was ownership by all of the people, through their government, of all factories and other means of production and distribution. Thus, socialism came to mean an economic system in which production and distribution are controlled by government.

Socialists rejected many of the arguments of classical economists. They denied that free enterprise was more productive than socialism. Under free enterprise, they said, producers wasted economic resources in fighting each other for sales. Also, they said, most capitalists were more interested in making money than in making goods and sometimes cut production in order to raise prices. Thus, they said, capitalism was an "economy of scarcity" which almost never produced at full capacity, and underwent recurrent depressions. If the government owned the factories, they said, it would run them at full capacity and thus provide more jobs and wealth. They claimed that socialism would even reduce crime and war, because much crime was caused by capitalism's inequitable distribution of wealth, and many wars were caused by the competition between capitalists of different nations for markets and raw materials.

KARL MARX AND COMMUNISM

In a broad sense "communism" means "any system of social organization in which goods are held in common." In this sense it is synonymous with socialism. However, in its modern sense, *communism* means "a doctrine and program based upon revolutionary Marxian socialism as developed by N. Lenin and the Bolshevik party." To understand it one must examine Karl Marx's type of socialism, how it was changed by Lenin, and how it developed in the Soviet Union.

Karl Marx (1818–1883) became history's most controversial and influential economist. The son of a prosperous German lawyer, he earned a doctoral degree and, forced to leave Germany, went to England where he studied and wrote in the library of the British Museum.

Marx's economic concepts were interwoven with political theories on how to put socialism into effect. He denounced other socialists as impractical idealists who taught that capitalism could be abolished by convincing enough people that socialism was better. That was foolish, said Marx, because capitalists controlled the press, churches, schools, and government and could not be forced or persuaded to surrender their wealth and power. Marx claimed that he, in contrast, had discovered the natural laws that governed economic and historical development. In every period of history, he said, men who owned property forced those who did not to work for them. This caused class conflict which eventually destroyed the society and produced a new one. A class struggle between nobles and a rising middle class had destroyed feudalism and produced capitalism, he said, and, in turn, a struggle between capitalists and workers would destroy capitalism and produce socialism.

In 1848, Marx and his collaborator, Friedrich Engels, then both in their twenties, published their *Communist Manifesto,* a pamphlet outlining their program and calling on workers to put it into effect. During its "rule of scarcely one hundred years," the bourgeoisie (by which they meant mostly businessmen, bankers, and industrialists) had "accomplished wonders." It had destroyed feudalism, and created "more colossal productive forces than have all preceding generations together." But it had also created "the modern working class" who were "daily and hourly enslaved by the machine, by the foreman, and above all, by the individual bourgeois manufacturer." This class (the "proletariat") would grow in numbers, as small businessmen and farmers were "swamped in the competition with large capitalists." When it became an "immense majority," it would take control of the government and the factories. Thus, they concluded, capitalism inevitably would produce socialism. Marx later wrote the multivolume *Das Kapital* (Capital) in an attempt to prove scientifically the soundness of his theories.

Normally, Marx expected, capitalists would use violence rather than surrender their power and, therefore, the workers would need to use violence to achieve a socialist revolution. However, violence might not be necessary in democratic countries "where the worker may attain his object by peaceful means." Arguing that nations were the creatures of capitalists, he called for displacing them with a worldwide brotherhood of workingmen.

Marx's ideas strongly influenced most socialists. After his death, his followers organized political parties in several countries, called "Socialists" in some countries and "Social Democrats" in others. They formed Germany's largest single party, and won a share of political power in almost every West European country. However, as they matured they tended to become less revolutionary and more interested in reforming capitalism than in overthrowing it.

THE FAILURE OF MARX'S PREDICTIONS

Had Marx's predictions come true, the first country to have a communist revolution would have been the one with the most advanced capitalism. In fact, no industrialized country adopted communism except those occupied by Russian armies in World War II. What was his mistake?

Marx assumed that a few big capitalists would take all of the property and reduce the vast majority of the people to poverty. This did not happen. The continued growth of democracy gave political power to the common man and led governments to adopt policies that benefited him. No advanced country gave its capitalists a completely free rein. Instead, governments enacted laws designed to prevent any small group of capitalists from gaining control of the entire economy. Thus protected, small businessmen remained numerous and, together with a growing number of professionals (doctors, lawyers, teachers, etc.), preserved a large middle class.

In addition, many businessmen decided to improve conditions among workers in efforts to prevent them from becoming Communists. Joining with humanitarians, they adopted a *New Liberalism* which called for government economic regulations to protect labor. With their support, labor won enactment of laws limiting hours of work, raising wages, providing free schools, retirement pensions, unemployment insurance, and welfare. Partly financed by income taxes, these measures helped to maintain a wide distribution of income, promoted economic growth, and limited the severity of depressions. As workers won more benefits from the economy they became less susceptible to communist appeals. Marx had not foreseen that free enterprise could become so humanitarian. Only in underdeveloped countries ruled by reactionaries did Communists gain wide popular support.

LENIN AND COMMUNISM IN RUSSIA

Russia was an underdeveloped country. Its economy was primarily agricultural, a few nobles owned most of the land, and most of its people were illiterate peasants. Many young people wanted to overthrow its undemocratic regime. A Social Democratic party was organized in 1898.

Vladimir Ilyich Ulyanov (1870–1924), a lawyer who adopted the name Lenin, ranks second only to Marx as the creator of modern communism. Adding to, and changing, Marx's theories in some respects, he put them into practice in Russia. He argued that it was not necessary to wait years for capitalism to develop in Russia to prepare the way for communism, but it was possible to move directly from feudalism to communism. This would require, he said, a small party of disciplined revolutionaries dedicated to overthrowing the Tsar and seizing power in the name of the workers.

Lenin received his opportunity to put his theories into practice when the government of the Tsar collapsed because of its incompetence and defeats in World War I. The middle-class leaders of the parliament (Duma) wanted to postpone basic reforms until the end of the war, but Lenin called for immediate peace and the gift of all land to peasants and of all factories to workers. His program appealed to workers, soldiers, and peasants, and he won support in their elected committees called "soviets." In November 1917, under Lenin's leadership, the soviets took over the government. In the ensuing civil war with the "whites," Lenin's "reds" benefitted from peasant hostility to landlords and from nationalistic resentment of foreign intervention in behalf of the whites. By 1920 Lenin and his followers controlled Russia.

World war, civil war, and communist innovations left Russia's economy in ruins. Lenin was forced to retreat. His 1921 New Economic Policy, while retaining government control of large industries, restored free enterprise in small business and farming. By 1928 production had recovered to prewar levels.

After Lenin died in 1924, he was succeeded by Joseph Stalin who introduced a series of *five-year plans* designed to build up Russia's economy. Pushing construction of industry with as reckless a disregard of human costs as if Russia were at war, he forced peasants to combine their small plots of land into large collective farms and to furnish food, at low prices, for the government to export to pay for machinery. Many starved. By 1940, at frightful human cost, the five-year plans had raised Russia's industrial production to second in the world.

The Soviet economy was devastated by World War II but made a rapid recovery and narrowed somewhat the large gap between its production and that of America. However, its growth rate was slower than that of Japan. The Soviets adopted economic reforms which seemed to move the economy more in the direction of capitalistic free enterprise, and even adopted some features of profit-

and market-oriented economies. In the late 1960s a U.S. Congress economic committee concluded that the Soviet Union was abandoning some communist practices in favor of more practical techniques copied from free enterprise.

DEVELOPMENTS IN FREE ENTERPRISE SYSTEMS

While the production of the Soviet economy climbed, the output of the American economy also rose—at a somewhat slower percentage rate, but still enough to preserve a massive lead. The growth rate of the economies of Western Europe was nearer to that of the Soviet Union, and the growth rate of Japan was higher still.

The economies of Western nations did not seem to be in danger of being converted to communist ones, but they had a full quota of other problems. Even in periods of prosperity the economy of the United States was plagued by chronic unemployment. Inflation became more persistent. Everywhere free enterprise economies continued to be disrupted by recessions and depressions which periodically idled much of their productive capacity.

America departed substantially from free enterprise by enacting laws to regulate the economy in the interest of workers and consumers. The freedom of the market seemed to be even more endangered by big business. In one respect, some economists feared, the predictions of Marx were coming true: control of the economy was concentrating into fewer hands, and freedom of the market was being constricted as huge corporations eliminated competition in their respective fields.

The most widely read economist of the 1970s, John Kenneth Galbraith, called the teams of experts whose combined knowledge was needed to manage great corporations "technocrats," and said that our economy was becoming a "technocracy." Furthermore, he said, the federal government could no longer be counted on for effective regulation because corporations and government were merging into a partnership. Other economists argued that the growth of giant labor unions had created another form of monopoly.

Of course America had never relied entirely on a free market to direct its economic activities. Government, for example, purchased about one-fourth of all goods and services. Churches and social and charitable organizations also produced and distributed goods and services. Furthermore, where natural monopolies such as railroad and power companies existed, government regulation was near total, and government regulations also had a growing impact on decisions made in the free enterprise sector. The government, some thought, was becoming almost an equal partner in every large corporation. Our economy was, Ambassador Henry Cabot Lodge told the UN, no longer a "capitalist" economy, but had become a "mixed economy."

Interestingly, while the free market was being squeezed by big corporations and government controls, its value as a regulator of economic activities was gaining new respect in socialist countries. Yugoslavia and Poland restored a free market in agriculture. In the Soviet Union, economic planners, despairing of successfully adjusting production to consumer tastes from government bureaus in Moscow, established a degree of decentralization and the market control of the production of consumer goods.

Socialist and free enterprise economies had opposite problems. In socialist economies the principal problem was to produce enough high quality goods and services. Selling them was not difficult—lines of buyers formed wherever they were available. Because the government controlled both prices and wages it could easily adjust demand to absorb the existing supply either by raising wages or cutting prices. Capitalist economies, on the other hand, excelled at producing great quantities of high quality goods. Nevertheless, they seldom produced to the limit of their physical capacity because they had difficulty in selling all that they were capable of producing. Their growth was retarded by a chronic insufficiency of effective demand. Socialism's principal shortcoming was in production; free enterprise's principal shortcoming was in its inability to distribute all that it could produce.

Each kind of economic system borrowed from the other. Economists debated how much farther economic systems based on such contradictory theoretical principles could move toward convergence.

In the 1970s economic thought was in a state of flux. Some of the old ideas seemed to be inappropriate to new economic problems, and predictions based on them regarding employment and inflation proved to be wide of the mark. In 1971 the chairman of the Federal Reserve Board told Congress that "the rules of economics are not working in quite the way they used to." Apparently, our economic system was more easily understood when it was freer from monopolistic and governmental controls and when economic decisions were made for economic reasons in a relatively free market. In the 1970s it became more difficult to separate economic from political and social problems. Thus, a broad multidisciplinary approach seemed to be necessary to gain a realistic understanding of the ways in which Americans produced and distributed goods and services.

Let us now turn from this short general overview to a closer look at some of the leading problems of the American economy.

Questions

1. What hard choices does the scarcity of goods and services make necessary?
2. What are the three basic elements needed for economic production and what determines the relative price of each?
3. What developments contributed to the growth of specialization and trade?
4. What policies did mercantilists advocate concerning government regulation and trade?
5. Explain how the laws of supply and demand bring about an increase or a decrease in production of an article. How do they protect consumers against overcharging?
6. How did the industrial revolution change the status of workingmen?
7. Why did classical economists believe that government measures to improve conditions among workingmen were unwise?
8. Why, according to the socialists, did workers receive less than their fair share of profits? What solution did they propose?
9. How did the ideas of Marx differ from those of other socialists? How did Lenin's ideas differ from those of Marx?
10. In what ways did Marx's predictions prove to be fallacious? Why?
11. What seemed to be the most difficult problems of free enterprise economies?
12. In what ways did socialistic and free enterprise economies seem to borrow from each other?
13. How has the work of professional economists become more difficult than it was in the past?
14. Define or identify: geographical specialization, capitalism,

socialism, Adam Smith, free market, Malthusian Law, iron law of wages, New Liberalism.

Suggested Reading

Galbraith, John Kenneth. *The New Industrial State.* 2d ed. New York: Houghton-Mifflin, 1972.

More readable than one might expect of a book on modern corporations and their relationship to the government. Adequately covers the subject and gives new interpretations.

Heilbroner, Robert L. *The Worldly Philosophers: The Lives, Times, and Ideas of the Great Economic Thinkers.* Rev. ed. New York: Simon and Schuster, 1967.

Suitable as an introduction for the general reader. Well organized and written in an entertaining style in nontechnical language. Its organization by chapters on individual economists or closely related groups of them makes it useful for reference.

President of the United States. *Economic Report of the President, Together With the Annual Report of the Council of Economic Advisers.* Washington, D.C.: United States Government Printing Office, issued annually.

Contains the Administration's view on the state of the economy and the Council of Economic Advisers' ideas on the problems the economy faces and the policies needed to meet them. Useful graphs and tables present the latest information on many aspects of the economy.

United States Department of Commerce. *Do You Know Your Economic ABCs?* Washington, D.C.: U.S. Government Printing Office, 1970.

A well-prepared series of booklets giving simplified explanations of various aspects of the American economy. One explains the concept of the gross national product, another the balance of payments, and others measurements of economic growth, the role of profits, the role of patents, and marketing. Readable, well illustrated, and with well-presented statistical data.

2

Problems Arising From Industrial Growth and Business Consolidation

What enabled America to achieve the world's largest industrial production?
What effect did the consolidation of business have on free enterprise and democracy?
Should the federal government regulate business?

"The business of America is business."
—President Calvin Coolidge

"The power of a few to manage the economic life of the nation must be diffused among the many or transferred to the public and its democratically responsible government."
—President Franklin D. Roosevelt

"It is the continuing policy and responsibility of the Federal Government . . . to coordinate and utilize all its plans, functions, and resources for the purpose of creating and maintaining . . . useful employment opportunities."
—the Full Employment Act of 1946

How Did America Achieve Industrial Supremacy?

In the nineteenth century American industry grew more rapidly than that of any other nation. By 1894 we were the world's leading producer of manufactured goods, a lead we seemed sure to preserve at least into the 1990s. This rapid industrial growth gave America the world's highest standard of living and made it the world's most powerful nation. It also produced rapid social and political changes that created new problems. Some of these problems, including the agricultural revolution and labor problem, are discussed elsewhere. This chapter examines the question of why America's industry grew so rapidly, and the problems caused by the rise of big industry and big business.

In the 1970s, when America's industrial growth was faltering, it seemed particularly important to Americans to understand the reasons for earlier successes. Why did America's industry grow more rapidly than the industry of any other country in the late nineteenth and early twentieth centuries? Nineteenth-century America was blessed with an abundance of natural resources, but so were other nations. The capital with which to build railroads, factories, and other productive facilities was less plentiful in America than in Europe. Labor was also in relatively short supply. But in one respect America exceeded all other nations at the time—in the size of the market. Other countries had larger populations, but nowhere else was wealth so widely distributed, thus giving the people the ability to buy so many manufactured goods. Our government was more democratic and its policies were more favorable to the common man. Because farm land was cheap or free here, the common man had an opportunity to become a landowning farmer. Partly because of such opportunities to become farmers, Americans had to be paid higher wages to induce them to work in factories. The government gave the people free education which enabled more of them to improve their skills and abilities. Consequently, America had numerous landowning farmers and well-paid factory workers with incomes that enabled them to buy manufactured articles. This made America the world's largest market for manufactured products. Attracted by this unequalled opportunity to sell goods, European as well as American investors supplied the capital to expand America's industry.

America's shortage of labor and vast size gave us special economic problems. We were quick to adopt labor-saving and distance-overcoming devices invented here and elsewhere. The development of railroads helped to solve the problem of economically transporting heavy and bulky loads over long distances not served by rivers or canals. By enabling industrialists to ship goods throughout the country they made it possible to build large factories where production costs were low instead of many smaller factories in different parts of the country. American factories were usually larger and more efficient than European factories.

The basic material of modern industry is steel, and America led the world in steel production from 1890 to 1971.

The assembly line also reached its highest development in America. By manufacturing parts with such precision that they were identical and interchangeable—a technique developed earlier by Eli Whitney—Henry Ford could divide the assembly of automobiles into hundreds of simple tasks. As an overhead conveyer moved the frame of an automobile between rows of workers, each fitted a different part to it. Constant repetition gave them incredible skill and speed, and cars rolled off the end of the assembly line at the rate of one per minute. This efficiency so reduced Ford's costs that he could price his cars low enough for the average man to afford (pun intended) and thereby sell them by the millions.

The Industrial Revolution continues to accelerate. An apparently endless stream of labor-saving inventions flows from research laboratories. A recent phase of the revolution is *automation,* the use of electronic computers to direct complex machines to perform tasks formerly handled by men on assembly lines. Some assembly lines are now operated by one or two men who merely push buttons at control panels, and automation of entire factories seems to be in prospect.

The Rise of Giant Corporations

America's spectacular industrial growth was led by an able group of businessmen including Cornelius Vanderbilt and E. H. Harriman (railroads), John D. Rockefeller (oil), Andrew Carnegie (steel), Henry Ford (automobiles), and J. P. Morgan (banking). Their methods were sometimes ruthless, but as a group they contributed much to the growth of America's wealth and power. They also destroyed their competitors, merged many companies into giant corporations, and concentrated the control of large sections of the American economy into a few hands.

This concentration was aided by the growing use of a form of business organization known as the *corporation.* Previously, an owner or part owner of a business was personally responsible for all of the debts of the business. If his company went bankrupt, his personal car, home, or other possessions might be seized to pay its creditors. The corporation, on the other hand, had limited liability, and its owners risked only the amount of money that they invested in the business. Consequently, more people were willing to invest in a corporation even when they were unable to keep a close watch over its affairs. This enabled industry to attract thousands of investors and to amass huge amounts of capital.

For example, if a businessman wanted to build a $1 million bicycle factory, he might offer 100,000 shares of stock for sale at $10 each. Each share represents ownership of 1/100,000 of the company, and gives its owner the right to cast one vote in meetings of its stockholders. Some investors might buy several thousand shares, others hundreds, and some only one. If the corporation earns profits it might distribute them as dividends, perhaps $1 or more per year, to the owners of each share of stock.

The rise of large corporations brought many economic benefits. It eliminated much wasteful competition between rival salesmen and advertisers. Large corporations could afford the latest machinery and equipment, and their large-scale production permitted a more efficient division of labor. They could make better use of by-products. A big meat packer, for example, could sell all of the meat from a steer for less than he paid for the steer, and make his profits from the hide, hair, bones, and scraps that are used to make glue, soap, violin strings, and fertilizers.

Because large corporations are more efficient and have all of the legal rights of individual businessmen plus an unlimited life span, they grew to enormous size, either by buying out many small businesses or forcing them into bankruptcy. As a result, 80 percent or more of the production of such important goods as oil, sugar, salt, whisky, matches, and lead came under the control of single corporations.

After the enactment of the 1890 Sherman Anti-Trust Act the federal government broke up some of the more monopolistic corporations into smaller corporations, but this did not halt the general trend toward concentration of the control of the economy into fewer hands. The share of manufacturing assets controlled by the two hundred largest industrial corporations rose from less than half in 1950 to more than 60 percent in 1973. In a recent year the twenty or fewer largest companies in each field produced the following percentages of these goods:

Cigarettes	100
Synthetic fibers	100
Automobiles	99
Telephone and telegraph equipment	99
Aircraft	99
Tires	99
Photographic equipment	99
Computers	97
Soap and detergents	86
Organic chemicals	85
Radio and TV receivers	85
Steel	84
Oil	84
Plastics	79
Drugs	71

And these figures by no means revealed the full extent of the concentration of economic control. The antitrust laws blocked the merging of competing corporations, but not of companies in different fields. This permitted the rise of giant "conglomerates" which brought under one management many companies that manufactured unrelated types of goods. In 1979, 227 corporations reported sales of $1 billion or more each. The 1976 profits of General Motors were nearly $3 billion, and the profits of Exxon were $4.3 billion. In 1979 American Telephone and Telegraph reported profits of $5.7 billion. Moreover, a small group of men sometimes controlled several big corporations. A 1978 study found that twelve of America's largest corporations were closely connected through sixty-one interlocking directorates. Also, large banks, through their power to grant or withhold capital and their power to vote the stock held in trust by them, had much control over the affairs of many corporations.

The Supreme Court ruled that corporations were "persons" and thus entitled to all of the property rights of any citizen. Unlike individual businessmen they did not have limited life spans, but could go on expanding and accumulating wealth indefinitely. Some of them employed more people and spent more money than the largest American states, and only seven of the world's nations had larger budgets than American Telephone and Telegraph.

Most Americans had little power to bargain with such corporations. They found it necessary to pay whatever price the corporations asked if they bought from them at all, and those who sold supplies to them had no choice but to accept the price they offered. Those who felt unfairly treated by big corporations found it difficult to win court cases against corporation lawyers with the financial resources to appeal and delay indefinitely.

As corporations grew larger and older, an increasing separation of ownership of them and control of them occurred. At first some of them, including Standard Oil, Carnegie Steel, and Ford Motors, were personally directed by their principal owners. More typically, however, they were owned by thousands of stockholders who did not have the time or information required to operate them. Such corporations were directed by groups of professional managers who might or might not own significant shares of the corporations, but who were usually able to keep themselves in control indefinitely.

When a corporation was managed by its principal owner one could assume that it would be operated for the purpose of producing the largest possible profit for its owner. But non-owning professional managers might have different priorities. Their interest in preserving and extending their personal power might cause them to give higher priority to the corporation's growth, which would put more people under their command, justify salary increases, and raise their economic and political influence. Of course, they also sought to make high profits to forestall stockholder revolts, to demonstrate success, and to strengthen the corporation. However, they might be less interested in paying higher dividends than in ensuring the corporation's survival and enlargement.

The development of the techniques of modern advertising gave corporations more control of the market for their products. They were no longer limited to producing for pre-existing needs and wants, nor were they at the mercy of possibly fickle shifts in consumer preferences. Modern advertising gave them a means of arousing new wants in people and of keeping demand high. For example, clothing and automobile manufacturers could confidently rely on their ability to convince sizeable proportions of the population that their latest models made all previous styles obsolete. New soaps, breakfast foods, and toys could be sold in predictable ratios to the money spent on advertising them. Thus, within limits, corporations could sway popular tastes and preferences to their purposes.

The Effect of Business Consolidation on Free Enterprise

The trend toward concentration of control of the economy into fewer hands threatened to change the fundamental character of the American economic system. The case for free enterprise rests on the belief that government regulation is unnecessary and undesirable because, if left unregulated, a free enterprise economy automatically will produce at the lowest possible prices the largest possible supply of the goods and services wanted by the people. It does so, its advocates say, because it is automatically self-regulated by the laws of supply and demand. Thus, a free market assures that natural resources, labor, and capital will be used efficiently.

But a free market exists only where there are so many competing sellers and buyers that no one of them can control prices but, instead, are forced to sell and buy at prices set by the laws of supply and demand. Only when the market is uncontrolled can it be relied on to protect consumers against overcharging and ensure the efficient use of labor and resources.

Freedom of the market can be destroyed by government if it seizes the means of production and distribution and establishes socialism, or if it imposes excessive economic controls. Businessmen were highly alert to this threat, and quick to denounce any move in that direction. However, government was not the only threat. In their search for higher profits, businessmen themselves tended to eliminate competitors and to move toward monopoly or oligopoly. A monopoly exists when one corporation or business group secures control of the entire supply of a product. This blocks the operation of the law of supply and demand.

The effect on the public can be devastating. When the monopoly controls a product considered by the public to be a necessity such as salt, sugar, steel, or oil, it can raise prices far above the level that would prevail if competition existed. The monopoly practically has the power of private taxation.

In a free market, when the supply of an article exceeds the demand for it, competing sellers cut prices in efforts to stimulate sales. A monopoly, on the other hand, can choose to restrict production to the amount it can sell for the price it asks. Such a decision to cut production denies the public the benefit of lower prices, reduces or holds down employment, and thereby depresses the market for other goods and services.

Because monopoly is so destructive to free enterprise and so harmful to the public interest, great efforts were made to prevent its formation. In England any attempt to form a monopoly was called a "conspiracy in restraint of trade," a punishable crime. In America state legislatures passed antimonopoly laws, but they proved to be ineffective because large corporations were too powerful for state governments to control. In 1890 the United States Congress enacted the Sherman Anti-Trust Act which made an attempt to establish a monopoly a federal crime, and entitled anyone injured as a result of such an attempt to triple damages. Congress later made it illegal for corporations to buy the stock of competitors, to place their directors on the directing boards of competing corporations, or to enter into exclusive sales contracts designed to destroy competitors.

Armed with these laws, the federal government forced several huge corporations, including Standard Oil, American Tobacco, and United States Steel, to dissolve themselves into several smaller companies. As a result the amount of actual monopoly was probably less in 1980 than it had been in 1900. Nevertheless, as we have seen, the control of the supply of some goods and services did pass into the hands of small numbers of corporations.

A situation in which nearly all of the supply of a commodity is controlled by a few companies is called an *oligopoly*. The corporations that comprise such oligopolies often cooperate almost as closely as if they comprised a monopoly. They have what has been called a "shared monopoly." They may continue to compete in advertising, quality, and service, but they no longer compete in pricing. When they cannot sell all of their products, they do not cut prices as they would if they were competing in a free market but instead limit production to what can be sold at the price they desire. Their prices are not set by competition or supply and demand. In 1974, for example, when sales of automobiles dropped more than 25 percent, the automobile companies raised prices by an average $1,000 per car.

Sometimes oligopolistic price-fixing takes illegal forms. In 1961, for example, the executives of America's largest electrical equipment companies were convicted of prearranging the prices they offered in supposedly secret competitive bids. Their illegal price-fixing defrauded the government and public of millions of dollars. On conviction, seven officials were jailed and twenty companies were fined. A Congressional investigation also found widespread price-fixing in the drug industry, and three drug companies were convicted.

An absence of price competition may also result from an informal, even unspoken, understanding that could not be proven in court. In large sections of the economy the prices charged by the large companies that comprise oligopolies are identical and are raised in unison by supposedly competing companies.

In 1974 the Federal Trade Commission estimated that if such highly concentrated industries were broken up, their prices would fall by at least 25 percent. One member of the FTC charged that price-fixing in the steel industry alone cost consumers at least $1.3 billion a year and that in the entire economy "prices set by collusion rather than competition" resulted in overcharges of "$10 billion or more per year."

Obviously, the continuing restriction of the freedom of the market through the formation of oligopolies can be highly damaging.

The Effect of Business Consolidation on Democracy

The economic power of corporations translates almost automatically into political power. (Some political scientists have concluded that whoever controls a nation's economy normally controls its government.) Leaders of large corporations and oligopolies sometimes amassed more power than was held by state governors or U.S. senators, power not given to them by vote of the people and, therefore, not democratic power. Such power enabled them to extract special favors from the government and to block the passage of laws desired by the majority of the people. At times their amassing and exercising of such great political power seemed to be undermining the functioning of our democratic system.

They could scarcely avoid much of this political power even if they tried. Heads of corporations were often besieged on all sides by people asking them to assume leading roles in all kinds of community and state affairs. It would be almost impossible for the huge DuPont corporation to avoid political impact on the small state of Delaware or for Consolidation Coal to stay out of politics in West Virginia.

One of the most effective means of acquiring political power is by financing the campaign expenses of political parties and candidates. The dangers to our political system of allowing corporations with unmatched financial resources to do so was so obvious that Congress passed laws barring them from making political contributions. But the laws were poorly enforced, and Congressional investigations revealed that in 1972 dozens of corporations made illegal gifts to several candidates, particularly to the Committee to Reelect President Nixon. Some corporate contributions could also be made legally. For example, a corporation might give its executives bonuses with the understanding that they would be passed on to candidates as "private" political contributions. Or they might provide goods and services to political candidates on credit and later cancel all or part of the debt. They could have the public news media that they owned show the candidate in a more favorable light than his opponents.

The success of big corporations in exercising political power revealed itself in many ways. Some corporations succeeded in getting special provisions written into the tax laws largely exempting them from taxes. Some continued to pollute the environment despite antipollution laws. They secured tariffs and import quotas that blocked the importation of competing goods. They influenced foreign policy, particularly in regard to smaller underdeveloped countries about which the general public had little information. Probusiness national administrations usually relaxed federal regulation of business, cut taxes on corporations and upper income groups, and restricted welfare spending for the poor.

Somewhat offsetting these tendencies was the apparent development of more sense of social responsibility by corporate leaders. Showing more concern for their public image, they published expensive advertisements aimed at justifying to the public their activities and views. Many of them contributed large sums from corporate treasuries to education and other community activities. Some learned that their long-term interests were better served by low tariffs than high ones. Corporations also grew increasingly interested in efforts to assure the stability of future business conditions in order to assure the profitability of investing huge sums in plant expansion or developing new products. Of course assured future sales required assured future markets and this gave corporations a long-term if dimly recognized interest in policies designed to raise the income of America's consumers.

In an earlier period of American history other private groups existed which could effectively check and balance the power of corporations. The economy contained large numbers of farmers, small businessmen, and self-employed persons, who as a group possessed formidable economic and political power. However, the growth of corporations diminished their relative numbers. The independent druggist and grocer, for example, became rare. The number of farmers declined until by the 1980s they made up less than 5 percent of the population. Labor unions became a powerful counterbalancing force, but they grew less rapidly after World War II than did the corporations. In the late 1960s and early 1970s challenges came from consumer and environmental groups. In addition, the economic downturn and high inflation after 1973 prompted scholars to make a searching reexamination of the American economy.

Government Regulation of Business

Three possible government approaches to the problems raised by the consolidation of business control were: (1) seeking to break up monopolies and oligopolies and to revive competition, (2) accepting consolidation as inevitable, while outlawing the more damaging practices of big business, and seeking to supervise and regulate it in the public interest, or (3) taking over ownership of all or a part of an industry, as advocated by socialists. Because of devotion to free enterprise, the third alternative was never seriously considered by most Americans, but efforts were directed along the lines of the first two.

In the early stages of government intervention, the chief hope seemed to be to restore competition. The Sherman Anti-Trust Act of 1890 outlawed attempts to create monopolies and set fines and imprisonment for those convicted of doing so. More importantly, it gave those injured by the large corporations' attempts to create monopolies the right to collect triple damages. However, the courts were staffed with conservative judges, and convictions were difficult to obtain. Not until the Theodore Roosevelt administration (1901–1909) were any large corporations split. "Teddy the Trust-Buster" took the lead in dissolving several trusts, and this policy was carried on under his successors, William Howard Taft and Woodrow Wilson.

The results of trust-busting, however, were less than had been hoped. By dissolving some large companies into a number of smaller ones it restored some elements of competition. But it seldom restored much competition—the different parts of dissolved trusts continued to cooperate. Dissolving a trust was about as easy as "unscrambling an egg," exclaimed President Roosevelt. Also, the consolidation of business control into fewer hands continued more rapidly than trusts could be dissolved. Trust-busting helped prevent the formation of complete monopolies, but it did not succeed in restoring competition or the freedom of the market.

Another proposal for preserving competition was to remove the tariff on goods produced by oligopolies and thus expose them to the competition of foreign firms. This could benefit consumers. Low-cost German and Japanese automobiles, for example, gave American consumers a wider choice and stimulated American companies to produce competitive small cars and sell them at smaller profits margins than larger cars. On the other hand, the steel industry and others succeeded in getting Congress to put import quotas on cheaper foreign-made steel to protect the industry against foreign competition and enable it to raise steel prices.

As the shortcomings of trust-busting became evident, emphasis shifted to the second approach, government regulation. Congress outlawed corporate practices that damaged the public welfare such as the use of harmful substances in food and medicines, misleading labels and advertising, unsanitary methods in packing meat, and child labor. The federal government also set maximum hours and minimum wages, and made it illegal for businessmen to discriminate in hiring workers or in serving customers because of their race or sex. It required corporations to furnish full information on their financial condition when they offered stock for sale, to contribute to old age and unemployment insurance, and to recognize and bargain with labor unions. In 1972 President Nixon temporarily imposed wage and price controls.

REGULATORY COMMISSIONS

Congress established special governmental commissions to enforce the laws against monopoly and bad business practices. Some businesses such as the utilities supplying water, gas, electricity, and telephones were natural monopolies because it was not practical for more than one company to construct pipes or wires to compete for business. Where conditions prevented competition, governments had long resorted to regulation to safeguard the public interest. American state governments established regulatory commissions to supervise public utilities, and in 1887 the first such federal agency, the Interstate Commerce Commission, was established by Congress to regulate railroads.

Federal regulatory commissions ordinarily consisted of from

three to nine men appointed by the president and confirmed by the Senate. The law specified that they must include members of both political parties. To give them some independence they were appointed for comparatively long terms, seven to twelve years, and their terms ended at different times so that they could not all be appointed by any one president. Because one of their functions was to decide whether particular actions by corporations violated the law, they were described as quasi-judicial. If they found a particular practice by a corporation to be in violation of a law they could order it to stop, but corporations had the right to appeal their decisions to the courts.

Among the more important semi-independent, quasi-judicial regulatory agencies set up by the federal government were the Interstate Commerce Commission (1887) for the purpose of regulating railroads and, later, other means of interstate transportation; the Federal Reserve Board (1913) designed to supervise and regulate banks; the Federal Trade Commission (1914) to supervise corporations and enforce the laws against adulteration of foods and drugs, false advertising, and formation of monopolies; the Federal Power Commission (1920) to regulate interstate electric and gas companies; the Federal Communications Commission (1934) to supervise interstate telephone, radio, and television transmission; and the Securities and Exchange Commission (1934) to regulate the stock market. Government regulation of the economy tended to become ever more detailed. Railroads, for example, needed government permission to raise or lower their rates, to reduce or discontinue service, or even to go out of business.

Many reformers were disappointed by the performance of the independent agencies in defending the public interest. In 1969 investigations revealed that some members of agencies, including the ICC and FTC, were on chummy terms with the corporations they regulated and even allowed corporation executives to pay their travel expenses. Many former members of these commissions were given high-paying jobs after they left government service by the industries they had supervised—a practice having the appearance of a "deferred bribe." Apparently, the confrontation between a government regulatory commission and the great corporations was an unequal contest. The commissioners were on small government salaries while corporations controlled great wealth that gave them countless ways of rewarding their friends including jobs, investment tips, or law or insurance business for the friends or relatives of a commissioner.

In some cases it appeared that regulatory commissions were more protective of the industries they were supposed to police than of the public. Economist John Kenneth Galbraith said that many of them had become "an arm of the industry they are regulating." *Time* magazine reported that the ICC acted "more like a mother hen than a watchdog." In 1974 the FTC chairman charged that "most regulated industries have become federal protectorates." They benefited, he said, from regulations intended to reduce competition and to raise their profits, "hidden regulatory subsidies" which cost consumers $16 billion annually in transportation alone.

Even when the commissions took action against big business law violators the penalties they imposed were mild. Often they were merely arranged "consent decrees," promises by corporation executives not to repeat the illegal acts. None of the electrical equipment executives who were convicted in 1961 of defrauding the government and public of millions of dollars received a jail sentence of more than thirty days. Their maximum fines of $50,000 were relatively small sums to large corporations. In 1975 antitrust violations were made felonies with maximum jail sentences of three years and maximum fines of $100,000 for individuals and $1 million for corporations.

Among other reforms proposed were laws to prevent former corporation officials from serving on commissions regulating their former firms, and to bar commission members from taking jobs after retirement in the industries which they had regulated. In 1974 President Ford urged the creation of a "National Commission on Regulatory Reform," to act as a watchdog on the watchdogs. Probably, however, there was no substitute for a public opinion sufficiently aroused to secure the appointment of men dedicated to the public interest and to inform itself on at least the general trend of commission decisions.

THE DEBATE ON GOVERNMENT REGULATION

Many businessmen resented the growing government regulation. They charged that it violated their right to do as they pleased with their private property, prevented them from operating their businesses efficiently, and amounted to "creeping socialism." Federal controls were multiplying to the point, they charged, that enforcing them would require a government bureaucracy so huge and powerful as to threaten an inefficient dictatorship over all of American life. Financing such a huge bureaucracy, they said, would require taxation so high as to take most profits, remove the incentive to invest, and destroy private initiative and enterprise. Economic freedom, they maintained, was essential to the preservation of political freedom.

Advocates of federal regulation, on the other hand, argued that factories were of a class of property that was not private in the same sense as a man's toothbrush or automobile. Instead, they said, it was semipublic in nature like a sidewalk which might be privately owned but legally open to the public. Public carriers such as airplanes and buses, for example, although privately owned, are required by law to recognize the public's right to ride without discrimination. Furthermore, they maintained, business corporations were licensed by the state, and the public had a legitimate interest in their operation.

If left unregulated, advocates of regulation maintained, larger companies would eliminate their competitors. Consequently, only government regulation could preserve what was left of free enterprise.

Some kinds of federal regulation were welcomed by business. The government protected industry from foreign competition by tariffs and quotas. It made loans to businessmen and subsidized the shipping, aircraft, and cotton industries. The Patent Office protected rights to inventions. The Bureau of the Census, the Office of Business Economics, and the Bureau of Labor Statistics collected information on production, employment, prices and other aspects of the economy and aided business planning. The foreign service searched for opportunities for sales and investments abroad. On occasion the armed forces guarded businessmen and their property overseas. Most of the billions spent for research and development, which produced many business opportunities, was provided by the federal government.

Most businessmen also accepted the necessity of federal intervention to prevent corporations from destroying competition. Some businessmen hoped that if the government succeeded in at least partly preserving a free market other types of federal controls could be avoided. In any case it seemed certain that further destruction of market freedom would inevitably be followed by more government regulation.

THE RISE OF MULTINATIONAL CORPORATIONS

In the 1970s the question of regulating large corporations was made more complicated by the rapid rise of multinationals—corporations that expanded their foreign investments to the point that they conducted a large part of their business in other than their home countries.

Most of the early multinationals, such as Exxon, Anaconda Copper, and United Fruit, were engaged in extracting natural resources from other lands. After World War II more of them built or bought factories abroad for manufacturing such goods as chemicals, electronics, automobiles and computers. By 1972, two hundred large American corporations were multinationals, including General Motors, DuPont, Boeing, International Business Machines, Ford, Chrysler, Goodyear, General Electric, Honeywell, Trans World Airlines, Xerox, Kodak, First National City Bank, International Telephone and Telegraph, Western Electric, and U.S. Steel. Direct U.S. foreign business investments (not including bonds, or stocks of foreign corporations) rose from $12 billion in 1950 to $149 billion in 1977. Of this, 38 percent was in manufacturing and 22 percent in petroleum. Americans invested more in European countries than in other areas, including Canada and Latin America.

What caused corporations to expand so vigorously abroad? One motive was to obtain the advantage of selling their products on the other side of tariff and quota walls. For example, computers exported from America to France were subject to French import taxes. However, IBM could avoid paying these taxes by manufacturing computers in France. It might also specialize in the kind of computers preferred by the French and provide quicker repair service on them. Also, as an added incentive, American corporations were not required to pay U.S. taxes on the profit they earned abroad unless they brought it back to America. Sometimes the country in which they invested did not require them to pay taxes for the first five years or so. Low foreign wages attracted some American companies, and some of them manufactured goods abroad for sale in America.

Labor unions protested that the construction of factories abroad by American corporations exported American jobs, adding to unemployment in America. Studies by the Tariff Commission confirmed that such investments did cause the loss of some jobs, but not as many as the unions claimed. Other critics charged that the investment of dollars abroad caused a deficit in our balance of payments. However, this was partly offset by the flow of profits to America. Others feared that multinationals had outgrown the checks on their power by labor unions, consumer groups, and even the federal government.

The multinationals also had strong defenders. In 1973, President Nixon said: "American investment abroad . . . has meant more and better jobs for American workers, has improved our balance of trade and our overall balance of payments, and has generally strengthened our economy."

The effect of multinationals on international economics and politics is examined in a later chapter.

In conclusion, the growth of industry brought more changes in the life of the average man than any other development of the past two centuries. Multiplying wealth, it enormously raised the standard of living and made America the wealthiest and most powerful nation on earth. More change is in store for the future. The problem of adapting political and social practices and attitudes to rapid economic change is at the root of much controversy in America and the world.

The next two chapters will examine the impact of the growth of industry on agriculture and labor. In a later chapter we will turn our attention to the problems involved in avoiding depressions and maintaining economic growth.

Questions

1. Why did industry grow more rapidly in America than in other countries?
2. List economic advantages resulting from the consolidation of industry.
3. What is a free market? How does it determine prices? How does it determine what shall be produced? How does it protect consumers from being overcharged?
4. Define: tariff, monopoly, oligopoly, free enterprise, corporation, and by-product.
5. How did the growth of huge corporations endanger free enterprise?

6. How did the growth of oligopolies endanger democracy?
7. What measures has the government taken to preserve free enterprise and competition?
8. In what way does an oligopoly behave differently from a monopoly? In what way is its behavior frequently similar?
9. What regulations does the government impose on "natural monopolies"?
10. List the controls that the government imposed on corporations.
11. Give reasons why regulation of big business through federal regulatory agencies has been less successful than reformers hoped.
12. What are the arguments for and against government regulation of business?
13. Why does it make a difference whether a corporation is directed by its owner or by a professional manager?
14. In what ways can corporations use their power to the disadvantage of the majority of citizens?
15. What were the economic advantages to a corporation of becoming multinational? What were the economic effects of multinationals on America's economy?

Suggested Reading

Barber, Richard J. *The American Corporation: Its Power, Its Money, Its Politics*. New York: Dutton, 1970.

In a lively style for the general reader, this book tells what business is up to, how economic power has concentrated, its ties with universities, and its increasing interdependence with government.

Douglas, Paul H. *America in the Market Place*. New York: Holt, Rinehart and Winston, 1966.

A former United States Senator gives the arguments for lowering the tariff.

Evans, Trevor, and M. Stewart. *Pathway to Tomorrow: The Impact of Automation on People*. Elmsford, N.Y.: Pergamon Press, 1970.

Friedman, Milton and Rose. *Free to Choose*. New York: Harcourt Brace Jovanovich, 1980.

A penetrating discussion of our economic problems and a lively and provocative defense of private enterprise as opposed to government intervention in the economy.

Galbraith, John K. *The New Industrial State,* 2d. ed. New York: Houghton-Mifflin, 1972.
Well written account which deals with the question of who manages the modern American economy. Shows the growing power of groups of experts, which he calls technocrats, and how their motives are different from those popularly supposed.

Kefauver, Estes. *In a Few Hands.* New York: Pantheon, 1965.
The Senator who headed a Senate investigation into industrial monopolies discusses the work of the committee and what it discovered concerning monopolistic practices in the drug, automobile, bakery, and other industries.

MacAvoy, Paul W. *The Crisis of the Regulatory Commission: An Introduction to a Current Issue of Public Policy.* New York: W. W. Norton, 1970.

Schriftgiessar, Karl. *Business and the American Government.* New York: David McKay, 1964.

Shapiro, Harvey D. "The Multinationals: Giants Beyond Flag and Country," *New York Times Magazine,* March 18, 1973.
An excellent short description and interpretation of their growth and consequences.

3
The Impact of Modernization on Agriculture

What caused the decline of farmers?
What were the effects of federal farm programs?
What is the future of agriculture?

"*The farmer wants, has earned, and deserves more freedom to make his own decisions. The nation wants and needs expanded supplies of reasonably priced goods and commodities.*"

—President Richard M. Nixon

"*I think the outlook for the farmer will be bright for some time to come. For the consumer, the outlook is not as hopeful.*"

—U.S. Agriculture Department expert

"*I am incapable of understanding why the federal government should provide large amounts of subsidized water to a farmer in an arid region to grow a water-intensive crop like rice or cotton, when we at the very same time pay farmers, in other areas of the country where these crops would grow easily, not to grow them.*"

—Congressman George Miller

Why Farmers Declined in Numbers and Prosperity

America is the world's leading producer and exporter of farm products. In 1970 with 5.5 percent of the world's population, we produced 12 percent of its farm products. We are by far the chief source of exportable food for the world's rapidly growing population.

The Europeans who immigrated to the area that later became the United States established a society comprised mostly of farmers. They learned much from the American Indians who were excellent agriculturalists and cultivated a number of crops then unknown to Europeans including corn, sweet potatoes, peanuts, beans, tomatoes, squash, and pumpkins. Land was plentiful, and governments either gave it to settlers or sold it at very low prices. This enabled the common man to acquire land, and consequently America had less abject poverty than any other country. The resulting wide distribution of wealth also contributed to social and political democracy.

Many Americans regarded a democratic society of independent landowning farmers as the ideal society. Farming, they felt, kept men close to nature, physically healthy, and gave them opportunities to be creative. The necessity for saving and hard work developed their character, and land ownership, they said, made them responsible and patriotic citizens. They feared that the rise of industries and cities might change the nature of society. The young Thomas Jefferson hoped that America would remain a land of family farms and be spared the turmoil, filth, and immorality that he saw in Europe's cities.

Early American farmers tended to be self-reliant and to ask little from the government. Largely self-sufficient, a typical farmer produced grain, vegetables, fruit, and meat for his family, constructed his own buildings, and made his own furniture, while his wife made thread and cloth, and sewed the family's clothes. A part of his crop was sold for money to buy the few necessities that he could not make himself. In later generations men would imagine that the self-sufficient farmer had an ideal life, forgetting his enormous labor and low standard of living.

Because land was abundant and cheap, early farmers made little effort to conserve it. Clearing trees from a field, they planted crops on it every year until the soil's fertility was exhausted and then abandoned it to clear a "new ground." This practice produced crops at small expense, but it amounted to mining the soil of its fertility, a practice that later generations would call "land butchery." A chief concern of modern agricultural programs is to encourage farmers to adopt methods that conserve the soil and restore it to agricultural usefulness.

The Industrial Revolution which spread to America after 1800 was accompanied by an agricultural revolution, the application of machinery and science to farming. The cotton gin, the steel plow, and horse-drawn mowers, rakes, reapers, and cultivators lightened human labor. The use of improved seeds and livestock and of chemicals raised production. Improved transportation and the growth of cities enlarged available markets, and subsistence farms gave way to commercial farms which concentrated on growing one or two crops for sale. Farm output more than tripled every forty years. In 1800 the labor of eight farmers was required to grow enough food and fiber for ten people; by 1980 one farmer could produce enough for sixty people.

As farm production climbed, farm prices fell. Only large farms which made efficient use of machinery prospered. Attempts by farmers to meet their problems by organizing, electing state governments, and establishing cooperatives could not reverse their steady decline. The basic problem was that the nation needed fewer farmers.

Industrial workers outnumbered farmers by 1890. Farmers comprised 60 percent of the nation's population in 1860, 30 percent in 1920, and only 3.6 percent in 1977. Their political power dropped along with their numbers and, under the rising influence of bankers, manufacturers, and organized labor, government policies became less favorable to farmers.

The rise of huge manufacturing corporations put farmers at a further disadvantage. Farmers had too little economic power to bargain effectively with such giants and usually were forced to accept the price they were offered for their crops and to pay what corporations asked for manufactured goods. The return on a farmer's labor averaged less than half that of non-farm workers.

Small family farms were particularly hard hit. Between 1940 and 1970 the number of farms fell by more than half. Of the 2.8 million farms still existing in 1973, the Agriculture Department listed 1.2 million as too poor to survive. Their operators kept them afloat only because they held other jobs, or because they received pensions. By 1979 the number of farms fell to 2.3 million.

For many of the remaining small farmers life was hard. Their work days were long and their responsibilities were unremitting. Their housing, educational opportunities, and access to medical care were inferior. And life in the country had few social or cultural advantages.

FARM ORGANIZATIONS

Farmers, of course, made many efforts to improve their condition. One of the early approaches was to put pressure on state legislatures to pass laws to help farmers. Many of these laws, however, were declared unconstitutional by the Supreme Court. Furthermore, giant trusts proved to be too large and powerful for state governments to control.

To strengthen their hand in bargaining with big business, many farmers organized *cooperatives*. They joined together to combine their crops and their orders for such things as fertilizer and tools because they could secure better prices by buying and selling in large quantities. Operating like corporations, they distributed profits to members. Many succeeded—in 1970 nearly eight thousand farmer co-ops did more than $19 billion in business, and five out of every six farmers used them in one way or another. But helpful as they were, they did not get at the root of the farmer's problem.

Farmers also organized for political pressure. The National Grange (600,000 members) and the American Farm Bureau (3.1 million members) were basically conservative and wanted to hold federal controls on agriculture to a minimum. The National Farmers' Union (300,000 members), on the other hand, contained more small farmers who favored government price supports and crop controls. The NFU also organized farm strikes that withheld farm products from the market in the hope of being offered better prices. In Congress, representatives of farm states formed a Farm Bloc to promote farm interests, and special groups of farmers, such as the milk producers, formed powerful lobbies and made large political campaign contributions.

FEDERAL AID FOR FARMERS

Although farmers were a dwindling minority, they were still numerous enough to tilt the balance between political parties in elections. Consequently, nearly every politician was careful to praise agriculture, and nearly every president proposed a program to help them.

Most early federal agricultural programs were designed to help farmers increase production. In the Lincoln administration, the federal government made large gifts of land to states to enable them to establish agricultural and mechanical colleges, and the Wilson administration began contributions to the salaries of public school agricultural teachers and county farm agents. The Department of Agriculture still provides many such services. Its Agricultural Research Service maintains experimental farms and laboratories for improving plants, livestock, chemical fertilizers, and for combatting plant and livestock diseases. The Farm Credit System makes loans to farmers and cooperatives. Another credit service, the Farmers Home Administration (FHA) makes loans and grants to help buy farms, improve housing, build community recreational facilities, water distribution and sewage systems, conserve soil and water, and recover from floods, drought, or other disasters. The Federal Crop Insurance Corporation insures crops against natural disasters. The Rural Electrification Administration lends money to farmers' cooperatives to build electric power lines to remote farms.

However, the price support program is the principal federal means for assisting farmers. With the coming of the 1929 Great Depression prices received for farm products fell unbelievably low. In this emergency the Hoover administration bought and stored large quantities of farm products in an effort to raise their prices. After 1933, President Franklin Roosevelt greatly expanded this program.

The announced goal of the price support program was to bring farm prices up to *parity,* by which was meant the same relationship between prices received by the farmer for his crops and the prices paid by him for supplies and consumer goods that prevailed in the 1910–1914 period of relative prosperity for farmers. However, this goal was elusive and, even counting various government payments, total farm income in 1978 was only 70 percent of parity.

Moreover, the price support program created serious new problems. The higher prices gave farmers an incentive to increase the size of their crops. To maintain prices the government was forced to buy and store enormous quantities of farm products which by 1960 amounted in value to more than $9 billion. Just to store them cost more than $400 million annually. Price supports also reduced the sale of farm products to low-income groups in America and abroad, added to the cost of welfare programs, and raised the cost of food to American consumers by $4.5 billion a year (1972).

In the 1950s the federal government maintained the price of cotton at 32.5 cents per pound. Because we produced half of the world's supply of cotton, this kept its world price high which gave farmers in Brazil, Mexico, Egypt, Pakistan, and Turkey an additional incentive to increase their production. Consequently, exports of American cotton fell and our share of the world's cotton production dropped from one-half to one-fifth by 1969.

A second major type of farm program was acreage limitation. Many economists considered the farm income problem to be the result of overproduction and they maintained that farmers would never receive fair prices until they reduced the size of their crops. Because cutting production was the method used by big business to maintain prices, it was considered compatible with America's economic system. No farmer produced so large a share of a crop that a reduction by him would raise its price. Therefore, acting individually a farmer could maintain his income amid falling prices only by growing larger crops. To make it possible for farmers to restrict production, President Roosevelt inaugurated a program of paying them to plant fewer acres in certain crops. Soon the practice developed of making price supports conditional on the farmers' agreement to reduce acres planted. However, acreage reduction cut the size of crops less than was hoped. By using more machinery, fertilizer, insecticides, and irrigation, farmers grew larger crops on fewer acres thus adding to the cost of price supports and the size of the stocks stored by the government.

However, the problem of reducing the government's huge stored surpluses of farm products was solved. A 1954 law established the "Food for Peace" program under which we shipped surplus farm products to countries that needed but could not afford to buy them. Particularly large shipments of wheat were made to India. One of the most successful ways of distributing it in Latin America was to give free lunches to school children, which improved both their health and their school attendance. By 1975, the United States had supplied $20 billion in food and fiber under this program to one hundred countries. In the 1970s Food for Peace tended to become less of a charitable or surplus disposal program than a means of supplying aid for Cold War purposes to such countries as South Vietnam and Egypt.

Various programs were also established to distribute surplus food to America's needy. The federal government gave surplus foods to states for use in public school lunchrooms and for distribution to families on welfare. The "Food Stamp" program to allow low-income families to buy surplus foods at a discount expanded rapidly. These programs, assisted by a rapid rise of farm exports, reduced the government's stockpile of surplus foods to a manageable problem. In the Nixon administration this aspect of farm price supports was dropped.

INCONSISTENCIES IN FEDERAL FARM PROGRAMS

Over the years serious contradictions developed in federal farm programs. Some of them counteracted the effects of others. While paying farmers to grow less, the government continued to spend large sums on research and education to help them grow more. While paying farmers to take land out of production, it also spent millions to irrigate new farmland. Price supports raised the cost of living and of government programs to help the poor and to increase farm exports. The people were forced to pay higher taxes which were used to raise their grocery bills.

These programs were frightfully expensive. In 1970 the federal government spent $7.4 billion on agriculture, an amount equal to half of all farm profits for that year. State and county governments spent additional large sums.

Farm price supports were originally adopted as a welfare measure to "encourage, promote, and strengthen the family farm." However, most of the money did not go to the rural poor or to family farms. In 1970, 46 percent of the nearly $4 billion in subsidies went to fewer than 5 percent of the farmers. Twenty-three farms received more than $500,000 each and one of them received $4.4 million. Thus most of the money went to the big farms whose competition was helping to destroy small family farms.

The farm programs also aggravated the severity of social problems. For example, by 1969 the government was paying farmers to keep sixty million acres of crop land idle. This forced many farm workers off the land. When they moved into cities in a search for jobs, they added to overcrowding, unemployment, and other urban problems.

Federal farm programs also troubled the consciences of many Americans. While the government was cutting food production and raising food prices, millions of people in America and abroad were not getting enough to eat. In 1968 a Citizens' Board of Inquiry found widespread malnutrition and even starvation among the poor in America. Abroad, more than half of mankind regularly went to bed hungry, and in some countries the death of large numbers from malnutrition was common. Under these circumstances, paying farmers to grow less allowed our enemies to charge us with putting profits above human life.

In 1949 former Secretary of Agriculture Charles Brannan proposed what was known as the "Brannan Plan." In order to raise the supply of food and lower its price, he said, the government should allow farmers to grow as much as they desired and sell it for whatever price it would bring on the market. If the government wanted to maintain farm incomes it could then do so by paying farmers the difference between their selling price and the parity price. It could also set an upper limit on the amount paid to any one farmer. However, the Brannan Plan was defeated by the opposition of wealthy farmers who enjoyed large government payments and of conservatives who feared that the kind of payments proposed by Brannan might be extended to other areas of the economy.

One explanation for the persistence of contradictory farm programs lay in the nature of the behavior of government bureaus. Once a program is established it becomes very difficult to abolish it. The government workers who staff it, the politicians who head it, and the farmers who benefit from it all put pressure on Congress to keep it in existence. Consequently, it is easier for Congress to set up a new program to counteract its effects than to abolish the old one. Between 1950 and 1970 while the number of farmers fell by half, the number of Agriculture Department personnel rose from 84,000 to 125,000.

Of course, the root of the farm problem is the existence of more farmers than are needed. If America could achieve full employment and provide enough jobs in business and industry to employ surplus farmers there would be no need to subsidize them.

THE AMERICAN FARM SYSTEM IN THE 1970S

Despite the decline of small farms and the entry of large corporations into farming, the family farm remained the dominant type of farm. Many small farmers could not sustain themselves and a frequently heard saying among them was "get big or get out." However, many farmers succeeded in securing the capital required to enlarge their land holdings and buy the machinery needed to farm efficiently. As late as 1970, a farmer and members of his family performed most of the work on 95 percent of America's farms. However, the other 5 percent produced two-fifths of all farm products sold.

In 1979 America had 2.3 million farms. Their average size was over four hundred acres. A farm was defined as a piece of land,

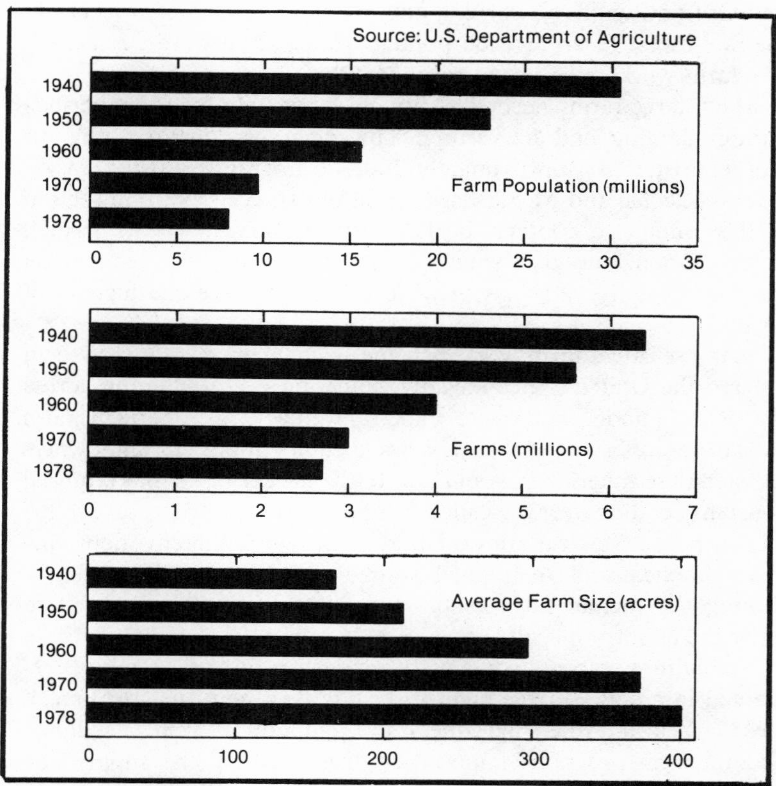

Fig. 3.1. **Changes in Farming.** (U. S. Bureau of the Census, 1977)

an "economic unit," with a product worth at least $1,000 annually. This included many part-time farmers. Seventy percent of all farms had total sales of less than $20,000 per year, and the average operator of one of these small farms got 80 percent of his income from an off-farm job. At the upper end, the 162,000 farms that grossed $100,000 or more annually accounted for more than half of all farm sales.

Many farms employed day laborers. The hired farm labor force in 1970 numbered 2.5 million. With wages averaging $1.42 per hour, they were the lowest paid group of workers in America and their income was substantially below the poverty level. Not until 1969 were even large farms required to pay them a minimum wage. In 1977 hired farm workers averaged $2.87 per hour. A few farm worker unions existed, and the efforts of Cesar Chavez to unionize and improve working conditions among farm workers in the Southwest received wide popular support. However, relatively few farm workers belonged to unions.

Many large farms needed additional labor only for short periods during planting and harvesting. This need was met by migrant workers. In 1970 approximately 200,000 migrants, mostly blacks, Puerto Ricans, and Mexicans, rode in old trucks from one section of the country to another to plant lettuce, harvest wheat, or pick apples. Often housed in small unsanitary shacks, they secured on the average only 120 days of work for a 1967 average income of $1,083.

Many seasonal farm workers came from Mexico. Many of them entered the United States illegally, sometimes by swimming across the Rio Grande, and were called "wetbacks." American farm workers complained of their low-wage competition, but landowners claimed that Americans would not do the harder tasks that required constant bending over, so-called "stoop labor." Congress prohibited the entry of Mexican farm laborers in 1965 thereby depriving many Mexicans of their chief source of income and creating a shortage of menial farm labor. But Mexicans still continued to enter the country illegally.

Agriculture, more than any other sector of the economy, remained in a state of free enterprise; but even here the freedom of the market and the ruggedness of competition were declining. Federal farm programs imposed controls on both the supply and demand. Also market competition among purchasers was diminishing. In a recent year, for example, three tobacco companies bought all of the tobacco, three canning companies bought more than half of the plums, pears, and peaches, and ten meat packers bought more than half of all cattle. An average farmer could not bargain with such giants—he was forced to accept whatever prices they offered him.

Large food-merchandising corporations were extending their control over farming in other ways. Some of them bought vast amounts of land and became "vertical corporations" which controlled the production and sale of food from seed to consumer. Other big corporations gave farmers contracts to grow crops and to sell the entire production to the corporation for a prearranged price.

The farmer's share of the dollars spent by consumers on food was 52 cents in 1952; it was 38 cents in 1974. Net farm income (profits) reached a peak of $19 billion soon after World War II, but then declined and remained almost constant for more than twenty years after 1950 at $12–17 billion. The return on a farmer's labor averaged less than half that of nonfarm workers.

One kind of farm income that was not included in the usual figures on farm income was the farmer's capital gain on his land holdings. In the 1960s and 1970s the price of farm land rose at a more rapid rate than inflation. This greatly eased the financial problems of many farmers who left farming—even a small farmer whose sales totalled less than $20,000 a year could often sell his farmland for as much as $200,000.

The trend toward fewer, larger farms continued. From 1960 to 1979 the number of farms declined from 4 million to 2.3 million, while the average size of farms rose from 297 to nearly 450 acres. To enter farming on a sufficiently large scale to be competitive required capital of several hundred thousand dollars.

Farm Products in Foreign Trade

America exports more farm products than does any other country. In 1979 the products of approximately one-third of our farm acreage were sold abroad supplying about one-sixth of world agricultural exports. In 1973 our percentage of world exports of wheat was 44 percent, of corn for grain 76 percent, and of soybeans 85 percent.

America was also a large importer of agricultural products, particularly of tropical crops such as coffee, rubber, cocoa, bananas, and tea that we did not grow ourselves. Our farm exports, however, greatly exceeded our farm imports—in 1978 the excess of farm exports over imports was more than $14 billion. We badly needed these earnings to offset the rising cost of imported oil.

Like America, the European Economic Community (EEC) subsidized agriculture and maintained artificially high prices on farm products. As a part of this policy it restricted the importation into Europe of cheaper American farm commodities. Our resentment of such restrictions caused one of our principal controversies with the EEC nations.

Europe bought more of our farm products than any other geographical region, but Japan bought more than any other single nation. Her 1972 purchases of American farm products totalled approximately $1.5 billion. Russia was second with $1.2 billion, mostly in emergency purchases of wheat. In 1973, China bought more American grain than any other country.

A New Era for American Agriculture?

Beginning in 1972, American agriculture experienced a wave of prosperity unprecedented in peacetime, bringing a sharp change in federal farm programs and in the outlook for the future. The change began when the Russians quietly bought $1.1 billion of wheat, corn, and soybeans, the largest single agricultural purchase in history. This included about one-fourth of America's 1972 wheat crop. So accustomed had Americans become to thinking that our major problem was to dispose of farm surpluses that the federal government assisted the Russians to make the purchase with nearly $1 billion in credits and subsidies, and the Agriculture Department put new restrictions on the planting of wheat for the next year.

At the same time other events contributed to a shortage of farm products in America. Other nations increased their buying of American farm products. Anchovies disappeared for a two-year period from Peruvian waters cutting off the supply of the fish meal which had been used in many parts of the world as a protein-rich food for livestock. Bad weather reduced harvests in India, sub-Saharan Africa, and East Asia. Devaluation of the American dollar reduced the price of American goods to foreigners. Farm exports soared from $6.7 billion in 1970 to $32 billion in 1979.

As a result the prices that farmers received for their crops rose sharply. In little more than a year the price of wheat jumped from $1.80 to $5.00. From less than $17 billion in 1971, farm profits rose to $19.7 billion in 1972 and $33 billion in 1973, and slipped back to only $24 billion in 1976. The per capita income of farm families reached near equality with nonfarm families.

As shortages developed and prices soared, the federal farm programs that held down production seemed completely inappropriate. President Nixon opposed them and seized the opportunity to dismantle them. He ordered the sale of remaining government-held surplus stocks, suspended export subsidies, and cut from 60 million down to 20 million the number of acres that farmers were paid to keep idle. The 1973 farm law substantially enacted the Brannan Plan. It continued price supports but eliminated all acreage controls and payments for reducing acres planted. The government allowed farmers to sell for whatever they could get on the market and then sent them checks for the difference between their selling prices and "target prices." Such checks were limited to a maximum of $20,000 per farmer. Subsidy payments to farmers dropped below $1 billion in 1975.

The new farm program met some of the objections to the old one. It curbed the practice of paying farmers to grow less while many people went hungry. It also ended expensive government buying and storage of surplus crops. It changed the method of maintaining farm income to one that did not raise prices to consumers and, therefore, did not reduce the sales of food by artificially pricing it above the reach of the hungry. However, it left unanswered the question of whether farmers should be subsidized by the government at all. If the government guaranteed that the prices of one industry would not fall below a given level, why should it not do the same for all industries? Why should citizens be taxed for the purpose of giving money to private businessmen?

Farmers answered that other industries were already subsidized—through tariffs, quotas, direct government payments, depletion allowances, and fast tax write-offs—and therefore, that farm price supports were no more than the farmer's fair share of the subsidies being handed out to every interest. But was this not a better argument for removing the unfair subsidies to other industries?

Another defense of subsidies was that they had been in effect for many years and that farmers had based their business plans on them. But, it might be asked, does one acquire a property right to a subsidy?

It was also argued that spending government money to keep small farmers in the countryside was a better form of welfare payment than letting them go bankrupt and add to the nation's unemployment problem. But most price support payments went to big farmers who did not need welfare payments and these subsidies helped them force small farmers out of business.

Agriculture department spokesmen claimed that continuation of price supports was necessary to encourage farmers to expand production. If they were worried about a possible catastrophic collapse of prices they might not expand production as much. However, some economists believe that the economic laws of a free market are sufficient to assure adequate farm production.

How permanent was the farmer's newfound prosperity? The surge of 1972–1975 was caused by the unusual simultaneous occurrence of a number of shortages. Farm profits slipped from $33 billion in 1973 to $24.3 billion in 1975 and $20 billion in 1977. This drop in income brought such a wave of farmer protests and strikes that the Carter administration returned to the old practice of paying farmers to take land out of production. Price supports and subsidies were raised again, and the maximum payment to an individual farmer was raised to $40,000. To qualify for these subsidies farmers were required to set aside more than 20 percent of their wheat acreage and 10 percent of their corn lands, for a total of about 24 million acres. Government payments to support farm income shot back up to $8 billion in 1978 when farm profits were $25 billion. By 1979 profits were back up to $33 billion.

A number of long-term trends seemed to promise that the demand for American farm products would continue to be strong. One was the rapid growth of the world's population. Furthermore, rapid economic progress in many parts of the world was giving more people the ability to pay for food. Japan bought nearly $4.2 billion of American farm products in 1979. Other developing countries, including South Korea, Taiwan, and Venezuela, greatly expanded their purchases. Improving relations with the Soviet Union and Communist China opened new markets. The rise in the price of oil and other commodities raised the purchasing power of the countries that produced them. The rising consumption of meat in developed countries increased the demand for American feed grains. A depression in America, or bumper crops abroad, might temporarily reduce sales, but it seemed certain that the long-term demand for American farm products was upward.

Questions

1. What were the distinctive characteristics of early American farmers?
2. What caused farmers to lose political power?
3. What government policies were unfavorable to farmers?
4. Why did the farmer's share of the food dollar decline?
5. What kind of farmers were most frequently forced out of business?
6. What steps did farmers take to improve their economic and political power?

7. What new form of federal farm aid did the Hoover administration begin?
8. What nonfarm problems are made worse when farmers are forced out of farming?
9. What are the arguments for and against farm price supports?
10. What is the long-term farm problem? Why?
11. Define: parity, wetback, FHA, Rural Electrification Administration, "Food for Peace."

Suggested Reading

Bishop, C. Franklin. *World Hunger: Reality and Challenge.* Independence, Mo.: Herald House, 1969.

Heady, Earl O. *Primer on Food, Agriculture, and Public Policy.* New York: Random House, 1968.
Criticizes federal farm programs for treating the symptoms of farm problems rather than their causes. Concludes that we have too many farmers.

Milliken, Max F., and David Hapgood. *No Easy Harvest.* Boston: Little, Brown, 1968.

United States Department of Agriculture. *Fact Book of United States Agriculture.* Washington, D.C.: U.S. Government Printing Office.
A convenient annual booklet that gives the latest information on the output, finance, and general condition of agriculture and rural America. Designed as a general reference for the nonspecialist.

4 Problems in Labor-Management Relations

Why did workers form unions?
What are the causes of conflict between labor and management?
What policies should the government follow regarding industrial conflict?

"Employees have as clear a right to organize and select their representatives for lawful purposes as (management) has to organize its business and select its own officers and agents."

—United States Supreme Court, 1937

"The question of our day is this: in an economy capable of sustaining high employment, how can we assure every American who is willing to work the right to earn a living?"

—President Lyndon B. Johnson

"All of us in management must resolve to make every effort to work in close cooperation with our employees and with the union leadership to meet the legitimate needs of the changing American work force, remembering always that we have more in common than in conflict."

—Richard C. Gerstenberg,
Chairman of General Motors, 1972

Why Workers Organized Unions

One of the oldest continuing problems in America, and in other countries, is the conflict between businessmen and workers. This often erupts into strikes that affect the public. This chapter discusses the organization of unions, the subjects of conflict between labor and management, the process of collective bargaining, the development of government policy on this problem, and current trends and issues.

The rise of modern industry changed the status of the workingman from that of an independent craftsman to that of a hired factory hand. It made him dependent on getting and keeping a job in a factory, and made his standard of living dependent on the wage paid by his employer. Decisions concerning his comfort and safety in the factories and his working hours were made by management. If he felt himself abused he had little chance of remedy through a man-to-man appeal because he had no contact with the factory's owner which was often a large and impersonal corporation. He could not force concessions from management by threatening to quit—usually many men were waiting to take his job.

On the other hand, if a large group of workers joined together to make a request they were more likely to get respectful attention. An employer could hardly fire them all without loss to himself. Consequently, some workers began organizing unions in American cities about the time that the Constitution was adopted.

What did labor unions demand? In general, they wanted more money, more job security, better working conditions, and more leisure. They wanted a comfortable and healthful working environment. They wanted to be consulted on decisions which affected them. They also sought the enactment of laws that protected their right to join unions and to strike, that provided public education for their children, and made other groups pay their share of taxes.

In their efforts to secure these goals unions used two general approaches. One was *direct action*—putting pressure directly on employers. The second was *political action*—seeking to elect prolabor men to office or otherwise influence the government to adopt prolabor measures. We will first examine the controversies involving direct action.

INDUSTRIAL WARFARE

Owners of factories and businesses considered the organization of unions and the demands that they made to be outrageous violations of the system of free enterprise and private property rights. Instead of complaints and demands, they felt that they deserved appreciation for providing workers with jobs, and they looked upon unions as conspiracies to raise the price of labor. No one was compelled to work for them, they said, and if workers did not like their jobs they were free to go elsewhere. They insisted that workers were not competent to make business decisions, but that, to avoid bankruptcy, those responsible for the success of the business must be allowed to direct its operation. In 1902, George F. Baer, President of the Coal Operator's Association, was thus quoted on his refusal to recognize a union: "The rights and interests of the workingman will be cared for, not by the labor agitators, but by the Christian men to whom God in His infinite wisdom has given the control of the property interests of this country."

When employers refused to yield to demands or persuasion, organized workers fell back on their reserve weapon, the *strike*—a mass refusal to work until their demands were met. Leaving their machines, they would *picket*—march in front of factories carrying signs designed to win public support and to persuade other workers not to take their jobs. Sometimes they also called on the public to *boycott*—to refuse to buy the products of the offending company.

A strike, like all warfare, damaged both sides. A long strike exhausted workers' savings, put them in debt, and caused their families to suffer. They hoped that the strike would confront the factory owner with such large losses that he would find it cheaper to agree to their demands. Sometimes, if they remained united and determined, they succeeded. However, many strikes failed and workers either lost their jobs or were forced to go back to work under the old conditions.

Employers, of course, had means of fighting against unions. Sometimes, they refused to hire a new man unless he first signed an agreement not to join a union, which agreement labor called a *yellow dog contract.* If they discovered a man trying to organize a union they might fire him as a troublemaker and put his name on a *blacklist* which they circulated to keep him from getting a job in another company. Sometimes they set up *company unions,* which they could control, and required workers to join them instead of labor-controlled unions. Sometimes they punished workers by closing the plant, which was called a *lock-out.* At other times they hired non-union men, called *scabs,* to take the jobs of strikers, and brought in large numbers of armed guards, *goons* or *strike-breakers,* to protect the scabs from pickets.

At first the public was hostile to strikers. Strikes meant disorder, inconvenience to the public, and sometimes violence. People considered factories to be private property which owners had a right to operate as they saw fit. If a worker was not satisfied, they thought, he should seek another job. It was illegal for businessmen or craftsmen to form *combinations in restraint of trade* (as associations for the purpose of raising prices were called) because they violated free enterprise and raised the cost of living. Labor unions, also, were considered to be prohibited by this law, and police helped to suppress them. Eventually the courts ruled that the laws against restraint of trade did not apply to labor unions.

Even after unions became legal, strikes remained illegal and companies could collect damages from unions for strike losses. Employers could also secure injunctions against strikes. (An injunction is a judge's order forbidding a planned act that might inflict damages for which adequate compensation could not be collected later because the offender has insufficient funds.) To secure an injunction, an employer would swear before a judge that a union was about to call a strike that would cause him irreparable losses. If convinced, the judge would order the workers not to strike. If they struck in defiance of the injunction they would be guilty of contempt of court and subject to fines and imprisonment.

THE RISE OF NATIONWIDE UNIONS

The first unions were local and small. Sometimes they joined together into city or state federations of unions in order to gain influence and give each other mutual support. After the Civil War workers attempted to unite these unions into a nationwide federation.

The first two attempts, the National Labor Union and the Knights of Labor, failed—perhaps because they attempted too many things. The National Labor Union set up cooperative stores and factories and attempted to establish a new political party, the failure of which caused its collapse. The Knights of Labor admitted not only skilled and unskilled workers but also farmers, small businessmen, and social reformers; and it sought an income tax and government ownership of railroads and public utilities. When its enemies succeeded in convincing the public that it was dangerously radical, the more conservative unions withdrew from the organization.

As the Knights of Labor declined, skilled workers joined the American Federation of Labor (AFL), under the presidency of Samuel Gompers. The AFL had strictly limited membership and goals. Only skilled workers could join. It was a federation of *trade unions* in which workers in a certain craft, such as bricklaying, joined together even though they worked in different industries. It was conservative and supported capitalism; it merely sought to get labor a larger share of the profits. Relying mainly on direct action, it used boycotts and strikes to win higher wages, shorter hours, and better working conditions. It restricted its political activity to supporting individual Democratic or Republican candidates "to defeat labor's enemies and reward its friends." Under this formula the AFL prospered and reached a membership of 2 million by 1914.

The AFL was a loose federation of more than one hundred unions, the largest of which were national craft unions such as the Typesetters or Ladies Garment Workers. *National unions,* in turn, were made up of hundreds of factory unions called *locals,* each of which retained a large measure of self-government. This form of organization enabled the national directors to concentrate on nationwide policies, while leaving most of the problems in individual factories to be handled by the locals.

Before 1933 the federal government was usually hostile to labor, but the Great Depression led to the election of Franklin D. Roosevelt, whose New Deal program favored labor. The 1935 Wagner Act, the most prolabor law, outlawed measures, such as the blacklist and company union, used by management to prevent workers from forming unions. The act also established a three-man *National Labor Relations Board* (NLRB) to enforce these provisions. When requested by 30 percent of the workers, the NLRB would hold elections in factories to determine which union the workers wanted to join. Under this law's provisions, union membership soared from 2.5 million in 1933 to 11.5 million by 1941, and unions gained economic and political power.

But labor was not united. Most AFL unions admitted skilled workers only, while some union leaders wanted to enroll unskilled workers. To do so required formation of a different type of organization, an *industrial union,* which enrolled all of the workers in an industry, top to bottom, skilled and unskilled. Some of the older craft unions objected. They wanted the electricians in the automobile industry, for example, to belong to the Electricians' Union instead of the United Automobile Workers. In 1936 angry craft unions expelled industrial unions from the AFL, whereupon the expelled unions formed the Congress of Industrial Organizations (CIO) under the presidency of John L. Lewis. He succeeded in organizing unions in America's strongest industries—the automobile, steel, and electrical equipment industries—which had crushed every previous attempt to unionize their workers. By 1941 the CIO had almost as many members as the AFL.

THE GROWTH OF UNIONS IS CHECKED

After World War II the government became less favorable to labor. A wave of nationwide strikes, some of which threatened to endanger the public's health, strengthened management's argument that unions had become too powerful. In a move to trim their power, Congress passed the 1947 *Taft-Hartley Act*. This act outlawed the closed shop (which permitted employers to hire only union members). It allowed the union shop (in which non-union men can be hired on the condition that they join the union) only if approved by the workers in a secret ballot. Furthermore, it authorized state governments to outlaw the union shop and require the *open shop* (under which workers do not have to join unions to hold jobs). It forbade unions to force workers to join unions against their will, or to charge excessive initiation fees. It outlawed *featherbedding* (paying workers for work no longer needed). It required union officials to take an oath that they had never been Communists, compelled unions to make annual public financial reports, and forbade unions to contribute union funds to political campaigns.

The Taft-Hartley law also required unions to give sixty days' notice before a strike. If the strike might endanger the nation's health or welfare, the president could postpone it an additional eighty days while a president's board of inquiry investigated the facts and the workers voted by secret ballot on whether to accept management's latest offer. If these measures failed to produce a settlement the president could refer the problem to Congress for action.

John L. Lewis denounced the Taft-Hartley law as a "slave labor" law, and President Truman vetoed it; but a Republican Congress passed it over his veto. Under its provisions, twenty states passed laws outlawing the union shop, commonly called "right to work laws." Unions fought unsuccessfully to repeal the Taft-Hartley Act, particularly Section 14b which empowered states to outlaw the union shop.

The honesty of union leaders was important to unions, employers, and the public. Unfortunately, unscrupulous men sometimes won election to union office and used their position to steal union funds or collect bribes from employers in return for signing contracts which were unfair to labor. To combat such practices, the unions adopted codes of ethics that barred men with criminal records from holding union office, forbade any business dealings between union officials and employers, and set strict controls on the handling of union funds. Several unions that failed to comply with this code were expelled from the AFL-CIO.

When a Congressional investigation found that corruption still existed in some unions, Congress passed the 1959 Landrum-Griffin Act. It required unions to adopt constitutions that guaranteed free speech at union meetings and elections by secret ballot at least every five years. It required all payments by companies to union officials to be reported, and barred persons convicted of crimes from holding union office for five years after completing their sentence. These measures were partially effective, and were followed by a trend toward the election of well-trained administrators to union office. However, recurring scandals such as the 1977 revelation of Teamsters Union retirement fund loans to organized crime figures caused public concern. Realizing that disunity weakened labor's influence, labor leaders worked to reunite labor into one large union. In 1955, the AFL and the CIO merged to form the American Federation of Labor and Congress of Industrial Organizations (AFL-CIO). George Meany, president of the AFL, became president of the combined unions, and Walter Reuther, president of the CIO and United Automobile Workers, became first vice president. This brought all major unions, except for the railroad brotherhoods, into one household.

But unity was hard to maintain. In 1957 the AFL-CIO expelled its largest single union, the Teamsters (originally drivers of horses and mules, but now mostly truck drivers), for unethical practices by its leadership. Vice President Walter Reuther also wanted greater efforts to unionize unskilled workers, to end racial discrimination, and to promote other welfare goals. In 1968 he led the United Automobile Workers, the nation's second largest union, out of the AFL-CIO. He soon formed an alliance with the Teamsters Union, called the Alliance for Labor Action. With a combined membership of 3.5 million, the two unions announced that they would work for guaranteed work and income, free university education, consumer protection, and antipollution programs.

After World War II the growth of union membership slowed. Total membership was 20 million in 1977. Union growth was

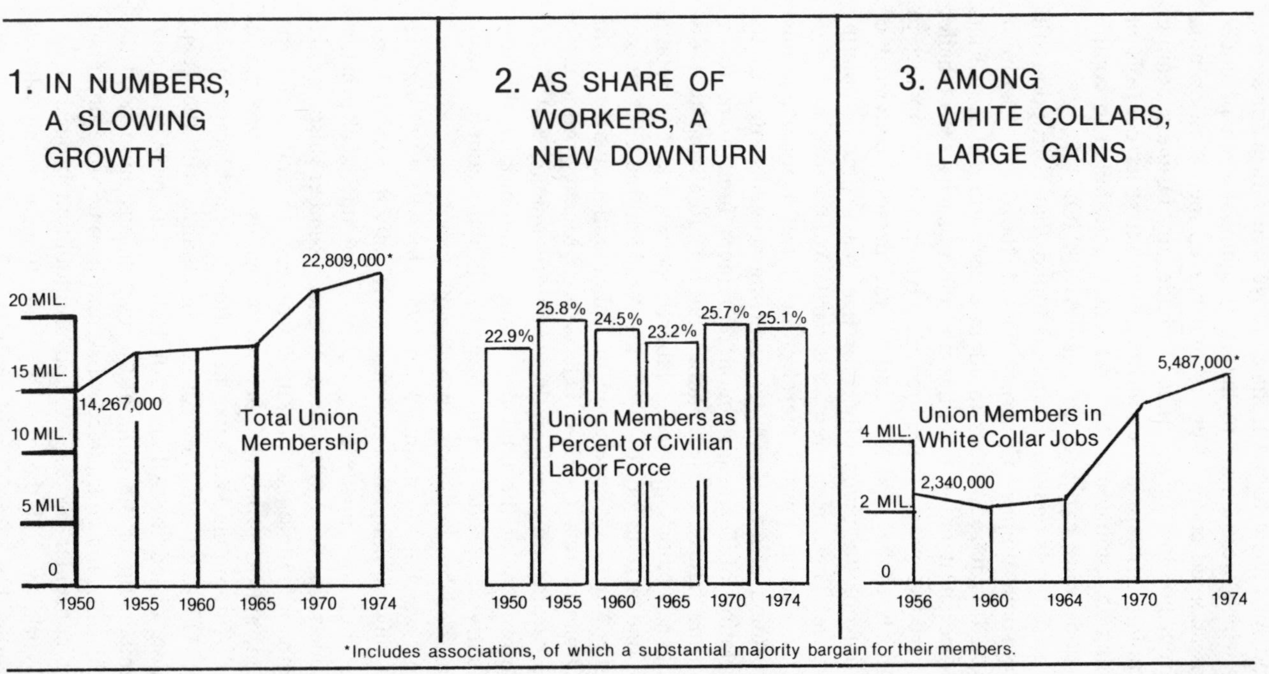

Fig. 4.1. **Facts about Unions.** (U. S. Department of Labor, 1976)

slower than the growth of the labor force, and the percentage of non-farm workers who belonged to unions dropped from 36 percent in 1945 to 24 percent in 1977.

Several factors help to explain this setback to the unions. Most large industries had already been unionized, and organizing small factories was more difficult. Ninety percent of manufacturing corporations with twenty-five hundred or more employees were unionized as compared to only 55 percent of those with one hundred or fewer employees. Also, automation reduced the number of blue-collar workers (manual, factory, or other workers who wear rough work clothes on the job). The new jobs were mostly for white-collar workers (who work in regular street clothes), and in 1956 for the first time their number surpassed that of blue-collar workers. White-collar workers were less willing to join unions —in 1965 only 10 percent of them were union members in contrast to 57 percent of blue-collar workers. The Taft-Hartley Act also added to the difficulty of organizing unions, particularly in the twenty states that outlawed the union shop.

Another factor retarding union growth was the reluctance of some unions to admit members of minority groups. Race hostility tends to be higher among working people, who look upon members of minorities as economic rivals. However, some gains were made. Federal and state governments put pressure on unions working on government projects to admit more minority members. In 1972, 20 percent of new members enrolled were nonwhite, and 13 percent of all construction trade apprentices were black.

One of the handicaps of the unions was that much of the public blamed them for inflation. When unions forced wages up, it was argued, they raised production costs and made it necessary for industry to raise prices. Union replies, that wage increases had been more than offset by increases in labor productivity (the goods and services produced per worker), were not as well understood or did not carry conviction.

In the post World War II era labor's real income rose less rapidly than the average of other groups. Wage increases lagged behind productivity and also failed to keep pace with inflation. From 1965 to 1969, while the average real income of other groups rose 12 percent, the real income of workers declined. In the ten years from 1967 to 1977 the weekly take-home pay of an average nonsupervisory production worker scarcely rose from $83.38 to

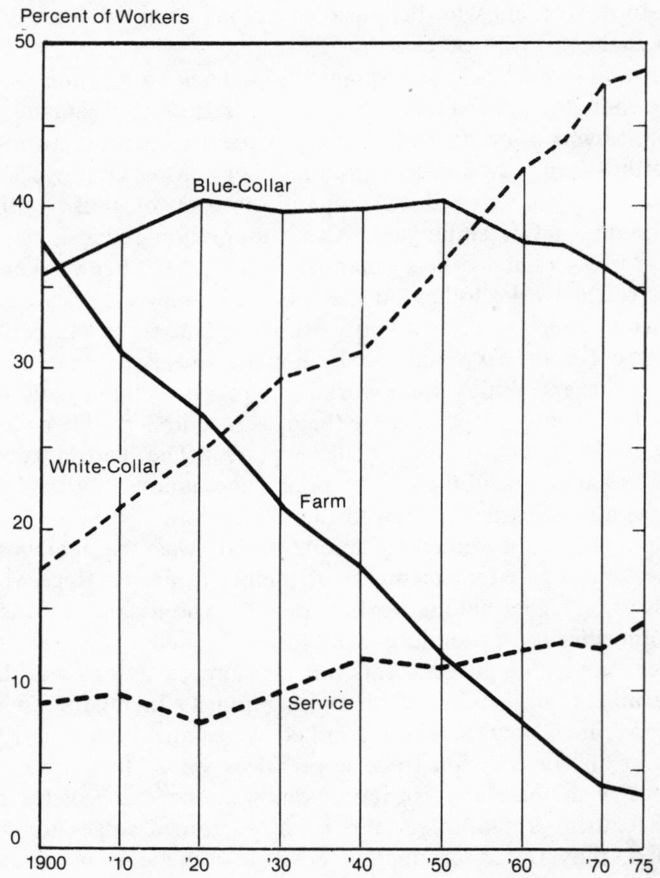

Fig. 4.2. **Occupational Distribution of the Labor Force.** (U. S. Bureau of the Census, 1976)

$85.72—a total of $2.34 a week (in 1967 dollars). In 1980 it fell below the 1967 level.

COLLECTIVE BARGAINING

The term *collective bargaining* means simply negotiation between management and unions (workers collectively). Over the years customs and laws have given collective bargaining certain fairly regular procedures. In union meetings, the workers decide what provisions they want included in the new labor contract. Meanwhile management prepares its proposals. Then representatives of the two sides meet in bargaining sessions which sometimes grow loud and long. Sometimes an impartial person is called in as a *mediator* to help arrange compromises on disputed points. The Federal Mediation Service can furnish experienced mediators for this purpose if requested. If the two sides reach agreement (they do 98 percent of the time) a contract for the next one to three years is signed. It is then submitted to the workers for a vote of acceptance.

A typical labor contract covers many subjects. It sets the rate of pay per hour. It fixes the number of hours in the work week and provides for extra pay for workers who are required to work over-

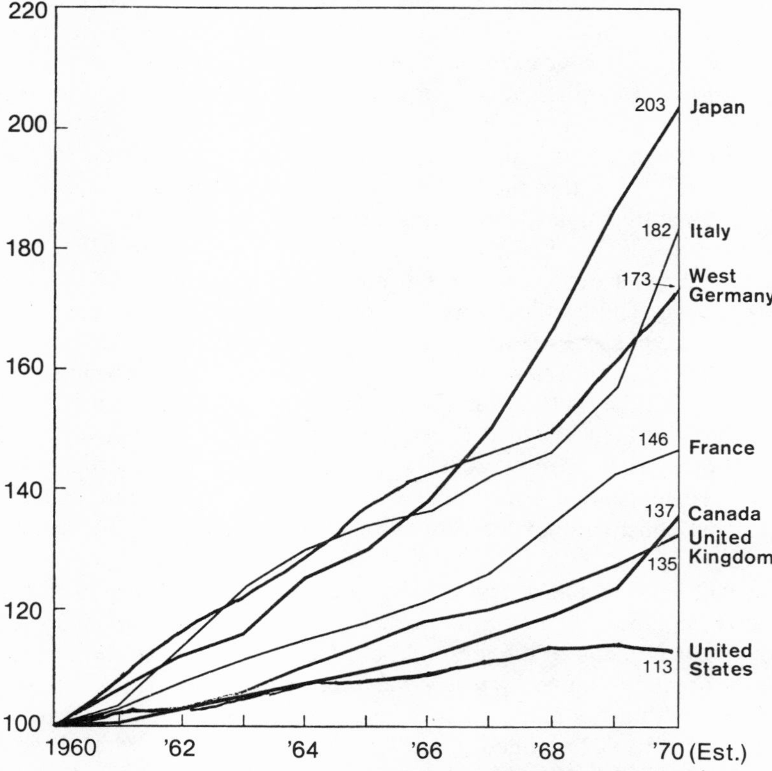

Fig. 4.3. **Index of Real Average Hourly Earning of Wage Workers in Manufacturing.** In the 1960s real wages rose more rapidly abroad than in America. (Council on International Economic Policy, 1971)

time, at night, on weekends, or on holidays. In 1980 the contracts of over half of union workers contained *escalator clauses* which provide automatic wage increases as the cost of living rises.

Contracts also specify the *fringe benefits* that workers receive in addition to wages. These usually include company contributions to Social Security, retirement pensions, insurance, and paid vacations and holidays. More than 90 percent of blue-collar workers have company-supported health and welfare plans. These fringe benefits are taxed less heavily than wages; they give workers more financial security; and they give experienced workers more incentive to stay with the company. Fringe benefits more than quadrupled between 1948 and 1975, at which time they amounted to 35 percent of total employment costs.

Sometimes the most emotional disputes arise over *work rules*. Management feels that it must be allowed to run the plant as it thinks best in order to meet its obligations to stockholders to make a profit and to customers to produce a high quality product at low cost. To do this, it insists, it needs freedom to hire and fire workers, reassign work, and introduce new machinery. Workers, on the other hand, feel that they have a right to be consulted on decisions that affect them, and they seek guarantees against unfair treatment, unreasonable demands, and elimination of their jobs. Over the years they succeeded in getting more work rules included in their contracts. These rules usually protect workers against excessive punishment and establish procedures for workers with grievances to get a hearing. They often give coffee breaks and wash-up time. Sometimes they specify the speed at which assembly lines move, the number of men assigned to a given job, and the amount of work expected from each worker. They usually give those who have worked longer for a company *seniority rights* which entitle them to first consideration for promotion and to be the last to be laid off.

Automation sharpened the issue of job security. When workers were replaced by new machinery, unions sometimes insisted that workers be kept on the job and paid for work that they did not do —a practice known as *featherbedding*. When featherbedding was outlawed, unions made other adjustments. Realizing that otherwise coal could not be mined cheaply enough to compete with oil and gas, the United Mine Workers agreed to allow mechanization of coal mining in return for higher wages and a 40 cents per ton contribution to a welfare and retirement fund for miners. Other unions, including telegraph operators and longshoremen, accepted automation on the condition that machines replace workers only as they were transferred to other jobs or retired. Some companies paid workers bonuses to retire early. The AFL-CIO suggested that work be spread among more men by shortening the work week to thirty-five hours.

In some industries the number of employees fluctuated widely, and many workers had jobs only part of the year. In order to give them more income security, Walter Reuther proposed that each worker be paid a *guaranteed annual wage* regardless of the number of days that he was allowed to work. In 1967 Ford, General Motors, and other companies agreed to make payments to laid-off workers that, including their unemployment compensation, would equal 95 percent of their regular take-home pay.

Another hotly contested labor-management issue is *union security*. Unions prefer a *closed shop,* a contract provision which specifies that no one except union members can be hired to work in the plant. Management prefers an *open shop,* under which workers are not required to be union members. A closed shop, managers argue, prevents them from employing better qualified men and violates the freedom of the workers. Unions regard the open shop as unfair because nonmembers receive the same benefits as union members whose union dues pay the costs of the fight for better wages, hours, and working conditions. Labor leaders regard such nonunion men as "free riders." Furthermore, labor argues, unless all workers are union members the union cannot speak for them in bargaining sessions nor assure management that all will comply with the agreed-upon terms. A compromise arrangement is the *union shop* under which management may hire nonunion men, but they are required to join the union within a short time after being hired. The Taft-Hartley Act outlawed the closed shop, but unions usually succeeded in winning the union shop except in the twenty states that outlawed it.

Can Strikes Be Prevented?

If labor and management cannot agree on contract terms, the workers may vote to strike. In most unions this requires a two-thirds vote plus the approval of the union's national president. The law requires them to give sixty days' notice of a strike and allow the Federal Conciliation Service an opportunity to adjust the dispute. If this fails, the workers walk off their jobs and picket the plant. Most states require pickets to keep moving and forbid them to touch anyone, to trespass on company property, to use abusive language, or to block the entrance to the plant.

During the strike, attempts to arrive at a settlement continue. Sometimes both sides submit the dispute to an impartial third party, a process called *arbitration*. Some strikes drag on for months. Fortunately, however, most of them are settled within a few weeks, and in recent years they have caused the loss of less than .3 percent of work time.

Most labor contracts forbid any strike for the duration of the contract and require all disputes concerning interpretation of the contract to be submitted to arbitration. Strikes in violation of contracts are illegal. Strikes that do not have the approval of union leaders are called *wildcat strikes*.

When strikes involve big corporations and big unions they can cause enormous economic losses and endanger the health and safety of the public by depriving it of essential goods and services. A prolonged railroad or coal strike, for example, would soon paralyze much of the nation's economy. Therefore, the American people increasingly expect the federal government to act when such strikes occur.

In a free country the government cannot force men to work against their will, but it can help to end the strike. In an emergency the president can seize and operate a plant with troops. In 1963 Congress virtually compelled both sides in a railway dispute to accept the decision of the government's arbitration board. And the president can mobilize public opinion behind a proposed settlement. Although he had no specific authority to do so, President Johnson suggested the terms that he thought both sides ought to accept to settle a steel strike—and they accepted them.

Compulsory arbitration has been suggested as a means of avoiding strikes, particularly in industries of major national importance. This requires all labor-management disputes to be submitted to an impartial arbitration board and requires both sides to accept its decision. It has been adopted by Australia and a few other countries. However, many experts believe that it is better to allow labor and management to compromise their differences with as little government interference as possible. Most congressmen regard compulsory arbitration as inconsistent with free enterprise, and both labor and management oppose it. Thus the strike, although increasingly hemmed in by legal restrictions, continues to be labor's weapon of last resort.

SHOULD GOVERNMENT WORKERS JOIN UNIONS?

By the 1970s government had become the nation's largest and fastest growing business. It employed 11.9 million workers in 1977, one of every six. Increasingly, government employees demanded the right to organize unions and bargain collectively on grievances, working conditions, wages, and hours. Traditionally such attempts were strongly resisted, even outlawed on the basis that no group had the right to organize for the purpose of extorting money from the government.

Concessions, nevertheless, were made. By 1977 thirty states had laws giving government employees the right to organize and negotiate with local and state governments. In 1962 President Kennedy, calling it unjust to deny government employees rights that private employees were encouraged to assert, directed federal agencies to recognize unions. Responsible unions, he said, might improve the efficiency of government agencies. As a result, unions of government employees grew rapidly. By 1975, 4 million public employees, local, state, and federal, belonged to unions.

Public employees, however, were not conceded the right to strike. Most state and local governments specifically prohibited it. Government employees, it was argued, could not be given the right to strike without thereby giving them the right to extract additional taxes from the public and, in the case of firemen and policemen, to endanger the public safety. Others argued that strikes by government construction workers, janitors, garbage collectors and clerks would be no more dangerous than strikes in private industry. Furthermore, they claimed, if government workers had effective means of remedying their grievances their efficiency would improve.

In any case, public employees did strike. School teachers took the lead. Their incomes were lower than those of any other profession; they were seldom consulted on decisions that affected them; and they were saddled with menial clerical and police duties. When years of genteel complaints proved ineffective, many of them overcame their aversion to unions and launched a series of strikes that often succeeded in winning higher salaries and improved working conditions. Many strikes were also called by trash collectors, janitors, and hospital workers.

LABOR'S POLITICAL POWER

Thus far we have examined only one of the approaches by which labor sought to achieve its goals—direct action—putting pressure directly on employers. A second strategy was political action designed to secure the passage of laws beneficial to workingmen. Union labor has always been in a minority, and not a wealthy minority. Usually its legislative proposals were enacted only if they won support from farmers or the middle class. After the Civil War the federal government was strongly probusiness. Huge corporations became so powerful that labor was unable to force them to accept unions. In this period labor suffered many defeats.

Some discouraged workers came to feel that neither collective bargaining nor political action could improve their condition. Convinced that big business controlled both economy and government so completely that labor could not receive fair treatment, some of them became Socialists or Communists. Followers of Karl Marx joined with other groups to form the Socialist party of America under the leadership of Eugene Debs. Only if the government owned America's mines, factories, and railroads, Debs argued, could labor get a fair wage, consumers get fair prices, and democracy be preserved. In 1912 nearly a million Americans voted for him for president. Debs also helped organize the Industrial Workers of the World, a radical union that called for the destruction of capitalism and its replacement by socialism. Although its membership was small, it aroused much alarm.

Many businessmen feared that if nothing more were done to counteract the rise of revolutionary radicalism than forcible suppression, the workers would become more radical. Hostility to capitalism could be more effectively reduced, they argued, by giving workers a larger share of its benefits. Abandoning their belief in completely free enterprise, they began advocating laws to improve the incomes and living conditions of workingmen. With their support, labor achieved many of its legislative goals between 1900 and 1917. Reducing the tariff and adopting an income tax shifted a part of the burden of financing the federal government from the poor to the wealthy. Railroads were forced to lower their rates; some of the larger corporations were broken up; and more money was spent for public education. Meanwhile, state governments outlawed child labor, improved working conditions for women, forced employers to pay damages to injured workers, and raised safety and health standards in factories and mines.

After World War I, the government was less friendly to labor, and both union membership and labor's share of the national income declined. But the Great Depression brought a return to prolabor policies under President Franklin D. Roosevelt's New Deal, which included enactment of the Wagner Act, Social Security, and laws setting minimum wages and maximum hours.

The years following World War II saw another period of antilabor legislation including the Taft-Hartley Act and the Landrum-Griffin Act. In the 1960s, however, several prolabor programs were adopted: more federal aid to public education; Medicare, and new programs to train workers and reduce unemployment.

Although American labor did not organize a labor party, it was politically active. Regular union funds could not be contributed to political campaigns, but the AFL-CIO Committee on Political Education (COPE) collected voluntary contributions from union members to support prolabor candidates. In 1968 labor spent an estimated $4 million in local, state, and national elections. Unions supported the Democratic candidate for President in 1960, 1964, and 1968, but backed a few prolabor Republicans for the United States Senate and other offices. In 1972 the AFL-CIO refused to endorse Senator George McGovern, the liberal Democratic candidate for President, and most union members seem to have voted for President Nixon. In 1976, most unions were back in the Democratic camp and their political action committees raised large campaign funds for the Democrats.

Unions also maintained legislative representatives, or lobbyists, in Washington. There, they testified before Congressional committees and provided Congressmen with facts, figures, and arguments that supported labor's position on laws under consideration. The labor lobby was considered to be one of the most influential in Washington.

Thus labor, by direct action and by political action, achieved many of its economic and political goals. Some skilled workers achieved incomes that enabled them to move into suburbs and buy expensive homes among doctors and lawyers. Many of them shared middle-class interests and attitudes, and almost none of them was radical. A 1967 poll found that many union members would not even admit that they belonged to a union and were losing interest in labor's traditional goals such as unemployment compensation and minimum wages. Instead, they were worried about high taxes and the possible decline in the value of their homes if their neighborhoods were integrated.

Interestingly, unions themselves became increasingly capitalistic. The accumulation of funds in union treasuries and in welfare and pension funds gave them great financial resources. They invested in housing projects and corporation stocks and acquired ownership of office buildings and even large banks. They employed news commentators, published newspapers and magazines and, in general, engaged in many activities which formerly were restricted to corporation executives.

WORKER JOB DISSATISFACTION

In the 1970s many observers saw evidence of growing worker dissatisfaction with routine type jobs. In the automobile industry, where the assembly line was prevalent, absenteeism rose 100 percent in a decade. A government study blamed dissatisfaction with "dull, repetitive, seemingly meaningless tasks, offering little challenge or autonomy" for much absenteeism, alienation, alcoholism, drug addiction, crime, mental disorders, and premature death among workers.

In attempts to give workers a greater sense of satisfaction and accomplishment, hundreds of companies adopted "enrichment" programs. In some cases they discontinued assembly lines and gave the task of assembling articles to teams of workers who could divide up the work as they chose. This worked well in some plants, such as the Volvo automobile plants in Sweden. In others it brought a slight loss of production and was disliked by workers.

Some observers considered the concern with worker dissatisfaction with routine jobs to be exaggerated. Only about 2 percent of American workers had assembly line jobs and some polls showed that they were more satisfied than white collar workers. For some, not having to think about what they were doing was an advantage. Many of them did not expect much more from a job than security and the money with which to enjoy other activities. Some labor leaders suspected that enrichment programs were management tactics to increase labor productivity and reduce the number of jobs. The Gallup Poll showed that worker dissatisfaction had declined significantly since 1949 and that eight out of ten Americans were satisfied with the work they performed.

However, the results of enrichment programs did seem to show that asking workers to participate more in the design and management of their jobs had positive results. Benefits included higher production, better quality, and significantly less waste and spoilage.

Despite their many disputes, the long-run best interests of labor and management coincide in many ways. It is to labor's best interest to have business operate efficiently and profitably so that it can expand and provide more and better jobs. It is to management's best interest to pay wages sufficient to recruit and retain able workers. Satisfied workers are more productive, and well-established unions tend to be more reasonable and more interested in helping to make the business profitable. In some industries the trend is for management to consult more fully with labor on decisions concerning the operation of the plant and to share profits with workers through payment of bonuses and gifts of stock in the company.

Strikes make news, but the most impressive fact about American labor-management relations is the degree of peaceful cooperation that is achieved. Really long strikes are rare; 98 percent of collective bargaining agreements are concluded without strikes; and strikes cause the loss of only 0.3 percent of working time. This successful cooperation is one of the major factors in our development of the world's most productive economy and highest standard of living. Many of the remaining labor problems would be easier to manage if America could achieve full production and employment, but that is the subject of a following chapter.

Questions

1. Why did labor originally form unions?
2. By what means do unions put pressure on employers?
3. List three measures that management uses against unions.
4. How did the Wagner Act aid unions?
5. What restrictions did the Taft-Hartley Act place on unions? How did it seek to reduce the number of strikes?
6. What causes disputes between unions?

7. What guarantees have been provided for ethical conduct and democratic government in unions by the unions themselves? By the federal government?
8. Why has the growth of union membership slowed in recent years?
9. What is meant by "collective bargaining"? What subjects does a typical labor contract cover?
10. What measures do unions propose to give workers greater job security?
11. Should the government outlaw strikes?
12. Should government employees be allowed to join unions? Should they have the right to strike? Give reasons for your answers.
13. Why did some workers become Socialists? How strong did the socialist movement in America become?
14. What social reforms were advocated by labor?
15. What changes have occurred in the political and social views of union members? Why?
16. Give the evidence for and against the proposition that dissatisfaction with jobs is rising.
17. Define: collective bargaining, strike, picket, boycott, yellow dog contract, blacklist, company union, lockout, injunction, closed shop, union shop, open shop, featherbedding, right to work laws, seniority, escalator clause, fringe benefit.

Suggested Reading

Dulles, Foster Rhea, *Labor in America: A History,* 3d rev. ed. New York: Crowell, 1966.

The most readable short history.

Galenson, Walter, *Primer on Employment and Wages*. New York: Random House, 1966.

An introductory account of contemporary problems concerning labor, wages, and unions.

Greenstone, J. David, *Labor in American Politics*. New York: Alfred A. Knopf, 1969.

Discusses the role of labor as a dominant factor within the Democratic party.

Kennedy, Robert, *The Enemy Within*. New York: Harper and Row, 1960.

A former labor investigator discusses the menace of labor racketeers.

Larid, Donald and E. C., *How to Get Along with Automation*. New York: McGraw-Hill, 1964.

A simple and readable account of the advantages and disadvantages of automation and what we must do to adjust to it.

Widick, B. J., *Labor Today: The Triumphs and Failures of Unionism*. Boston: Houghton-Mifflin, 1964.

Emphasizes the changes that have occurred in modern unions such as their becoming big business themselves. Short profiles of modern labor leaders.

Work in America. Report of a Special Task Force to the Secretary of Health, Education, and Welfare. Cambridge: Massachusetts Institute of Technology Press, 1973.

A study of worker discontent with jobs, with recommendations on what management can do to make jobs more challenging and satisfying and thereby increase production and worker loyalty.

5

Maintaining Economic Growth

What causes depressions and recessions?
What promotes economic growth?
Should America seek a higher rate of economic growth?

"That America shall succeed in getting out of the rut of slow economic progress while unemployment is high and rising is in the interest of the world and not only America. Indeed, as I see it, it is the most important problem in the world today."

—Gunnar Myrdal

"The chief problem confronting our economy . . . is its unrealized potential—slow growth, under-investment, unused capacity, and persistent unemployment."

—President Lyndon B. Johnson

"The consumer's main problem is a shortage of income and the businessman's main problem is a shortage of consumers. If the government gives consumers the income it will solve the businessman's problem, too."

—Arthur M. Oken, Former Chairman of
the Council of Economic Advisers

The Importance of Growth

America's economy has demonstrated impressive capacity to produce unequalled quantities of goods and services. In 1967 we had almost a third of the world's railroads, two-thirds of its automobiles, half of its trucks, almost half of its radios, and we produced a third of its electricity and a fourth of its steel. With only 6 percent of the world's population, we owned half of its wealth.

Despite past successes, America's economic growth rate has lagged behind that of most other industrialized nations since World War II. Unemployment has been a persistent problem. We have had no major depression since the 1930s, but recessions (mild depressions) occurred in 1948–49, 1953–54, 1957–58, 1960–61, 1969–72, 1974–75, and 1980.

Because national power is largely a function of economic production, the slowness of economic growth eroded the basis of America's world leadership. The world's second largest economy, that of the Soviet Union, produced less than 60 percent as much as America's in 1977, but its growth rate exceeded ours nearly every year since World War II, and narrowed our once great lead in national strength. Soviet leaders claim that surpassing America in economic production would prove that their system was superior. Indeed, if they succeed, the people of much of the world may decide that communism is the better way of achieving the higher standard of living that they desperately want. Thus, for reasons involving America's material well-being, national strength, and ideology, maintaining economic growth ranks among its more crucial problems. (We will examine the ideas of those who question the value of unrestrained growth later in the chapter.)

ECONOMIC CYCLES

Recent history gives us reason to hope that economists and statesmen have learned enough about economics to avoid the terrible depressions that plagued our economy before World War II. Nevertheless, an examination of the causes of depressions can contribute to understanding some of the difficulties in maintaining economic growth.

America's economy, like other free enterprise economies, has ups and downs that seem to move in a cycle, like the rim of a wheel, through four phases: boom, decline, depression, and recovery. The top phase, a *boom,* is a period of high business activity. Sales of the products of farms and factories soar. Production rises and more workers get jobs, giving them money to further raise retail sales. Corporation profits and dividends rise. In expectation of continued high and rising sales businessmen buy to build up their inventories of goods. Industrialists build new factories, warehouses, offices, and stores, creating more jobs and sales. Some of the growth in consumer sales and business investment is financed with borrowed money. Often demand for goods and services becomes so great that prices rise excessively.

However, when consumers reach the limit of their credit their rate of buying slows, particularly for the "big ticket" items such as houses and automobiles. When retail sales lag behind production, many items pile up on shelves and in warehouses until inventories of unsold goods become excessive. When this happens, merchants order fewer goods, manufacturers cut production, businessmen cancel plans to expand, cautious bankers lend less money, profits and dividends fall, and workers get fired. The prices of stocks in business corporations drop sharply. The loss of wages and salaries further cuts retail sales. In the resulting *decline,* factories continue to cut production and fire more workers, causing sales to fall sharply in a vicious downward spiral.

In a *depression,* businesses and banks go bankrupt with resultant loss of savings and investments. However, bankruptcy also cancels much of the burden of accumulated debt and helps reduce production costs. Prices fall to a level at which stocks of goods can be sold. As inventories of some goods are depleted, production revives, workers are rehired, and their wages fuel a rise in sales. Regaining confidence, businessmen invest in new businesses and factories, creating more jobs and adding to demand. This period of *recovery* often develops into another boom, completing the cycle.

The Great Depression

Beginning in 1837 the American economy had severe depressions on an average of every fifteen years, but the worst of these was the Great Depression (1929–1940). In early 1929 economic conditions seemed excellent—on the surface. The 1920s had seen a business boom in which our gross national product (GNP) had risen at an average annual rate of nearly 5 percent.

Looking back, however, we can see that the prosperity of the 1920s did not reach large sections of the people. Farm prices remained low and the farmer's share of the national income dropped. Wages rose so slowly that labor's share of the national income fell. Therefore, the ability of farmers and workers to buy did not keep pace with the economy's ability to produce.

High profits gave high incomes to businessmen, and they spent freely for consumer goods. However, American industry is constructed to produce on such a large scale that only a mass market can absorb all of its products. The sale of a million high-priced automobiles, for example, cannot keep our automobile industry in full production. It must sell ten million cars or else close down some of its factories. Its prosperity, therefore, depends on the ability of ordinary farmers and workers to buy automobiles.

Because the income of consumers did not rise as rapidly as production, the rising output of goods and services could be sold only through a generous extension of credit. But credit could not be expanded indefinitely, and after consumers had borrowed their limit their buying slowed to the level of their incomes. Falling retail sales in the summer of 1929 dimmed the prospects of business profits and caused prices of shares of stock in corporations to drop sharply. The bottom seemed to fall out. Industrial production fell by half, putting more than one-fourth of the labor force out of work. As corporation profits fell from $9 billion in 1929 to a loss of $6 billion in 1933, stocks valued at $87 billion dropped to less than $19 billion.

The depression's impact on individual lives was devastating. Great fortunes disappeared overnight. Middle-income families lost homes and cars to banks, while their sons dropped out of college to search hopelessly for jobs. In Kentucky, unemployed miners cooked weeds; in Chicago, unemployed men fought for garbage. Half of America's families were forced to seek public welfare assistance. The birthrate dropped so far that in America in 1940 there were fewer children under the age of ten than there had been in 1930. The Great Depression was the worst disaster that had yet struck our nation.

Bewilderingly, all this suffering occurred while stores and warehouses bulged with food and goods, factories stood idle, and labor begged to work. "Plenty is at our doorsteps," said President Franklin D. Roosevelt in 1933, "but a generous use of it languishes in the very sight of the supply." Why?

Economists developed varying theories on the causes of depressions, and the question is still much debated and imperfectly understood. Some maintained that depressions were a normal part of inevitable business cycles and that the economy would recover automatically if the government did not interfere. Others blamed the Great Depression on maladjustments in international trade, on the excessive use of credit, on overproduction, on overspeculation in stocks, or on loss of business confidence. However, most economists eventually rejected these theories on the grounds that they mistook symptoms for fundamental causes.

A widely accepted explanation of the cause of depressions was put forth by the British economist, John Maynard Keynes. He attributed it to inadequate consumer demand resulting from over-concentration of purchasing power (the money supply) into few hands. This could be solved, he said, only by corrective government action. At first his ideas were considered by many conservatives to be subversive of free enterprise, but were later accepted even by such a staunch conservative as President Richard Nixon. The analysis made by Keynesian economists was roughly as follows:

America was unexcelled in ability to produce goods and services, but had difficulty with its system of distributing goods and services. The capacity of the economy to produce exceeded the capacity of the people to buy. Some economists called this "overproduction," but we never produced more of all kinds of goods and services than the people needed or wanted. More accurately the problem was "underconsumption" caused by the fact that people who wanted them did not have enough money to buy them.

In the 1920s much of the nation's wealth became concentrated into a relatively few hands. While business profits were high and the savings of business and upper income groups tripled, many low and middle income people exhausted their savings and sank deeply into debt. Why did this concentration of money occur?

One reason why more money accumulated in the hands of the wealthy was that great corporations grew and absorbed small businesses and acquired the power to charge high prices for their products, to pay low prices for farm products and raw materials, and to hold down wages. At the same time, the federal government was controlled by men who believed that the best policy was to reduce taxes on business and hold wages down in order to raise business profits. Cutting federal spending by half, they reduced taxes on the wealthy, such as income and inheritance taxes, but raised the tariff which added to the profits of favored industries at the expense of consumers. By enlarging profits, these policies, they maintained, would induce businessmen to invest accumulated money in new factories, expand production, and give jobs to the poor.

Why did these policies fail to produce the predicted prosperity? Apparently business and government leaders assumed that no direct government measures were needed to assure a growing market for America's rising production of goods and services. They assumed that spending by businessmen to build new factories and the wages the new jobs paid would expand the income of consumers sufficiently to enable them to buy the products of the new factories. This was known as "Say's Law." Keynes agreed that such investment did expand the market, but, he said, unfortunately not quite enough to absorb all the goods that the new factories could produce. Consequently, over the years the ability of businessmen to produce tended to outrun the ability of the people to buy. And, when unsold goods accumulated, businessmen would stop building new factories no matter how deeply taxes and wages were cut. When capital investments dropped, construction workers lost jobs, which further reduced the market, unsold goods piled up, and production and employment sunk in a downward spiral into the Great Depression.

When the stock market crashed, President Herbert Hoover was in the first year of a four-year term. Unlike earlier presidents, he took responsibility for leading the nation back to economic health. He upped spending on public works and loaned money to banks and corporations. But he made less effort to maintain wages and farm income, and he blocked any spending of federal money for direct welfare payments to the poor. The continued decline of the economy insured his loss of the 1932 election.

Franklin D. Roosevelt took office in March, 1933, at the low point of the depression. He increased government spending, mostly for a large variety of welfare programs designed to assist low-income groups, and raised the necessary money through higher income and corporation taxes, and by borrowing. He cut taxes on the poor and raised taxes on the rich. He was the first president to spend federal funds for direct welfare payments to the poor. He lifted farm income by price supports and raised labor's income through minimum wage and maximum hours laws, Social Security, and encouragement of unions. The economy partly recovered.

During World War II, which we entered in 1941, government spending and taxes soared to new highs, and our government and allies bought all of the food and war materials that the economy could produce. The effect of this unlimited market on economic growth was astonishing. Wages rose, unemployment vanished, and women and old people flocked to work in factories and shipyards. Even with 11 million men subtracted from the civilian labor force by the armed services, we almost doubled industrial production between 1940 and 1945.

New Deal reforms and the war brought about a wider distribution of income. The percent of total personal income received by the upper 5 percent of families fell from 30 in 1929 to 18 in 1947 as the percent received by the lowest 40 percent rose from 12.5 to 16. During the war workers and farmers paid their debts and accumulated savings and emerged from the war with large reserves of purchasing power. The resulting high postwar demand for goods and services encouraged capital investment. The GNP expanded at an average rate of 3.7 percent between 1950 and 1965, raising the American standard of living far above any previously known.

Growth after 1961 was particularly impressive. In the longest sustained economic advance in our history, production rose steadily and with hardly a pause between 1961 and 1969. Our GNP rose by one-third, creating 10.5 million new jobs, more than doubling profits and lifting 18 million Americans out of poverty.

Can America Have Another Depression?

Despite our prosperity, our rate of economic growth remained below that of several other countries. We failed to achieve full employment even when business was booming, and our economy suffered six recessions between 1947 and 1978. While we grew at a rate of 3.7 percent, Western Europe grew at 6 percent, the Soviet Union at 7 percent; and Japan at nearly 12 percent annually. America's share of the world's production declined from approximately 50 percent in 1945 to 24 percent in 1976.

Some economists attributed the sluggishness of our growth to the persistence of the gap between productive capacity and consumer purchasing power. During most of the postwar era, farm income did not rise and labor income lagged behind labor productivity. While one group of Americans, mostly with high incomes, raised their savings to record levels, another group sank deeper into debt. Consumer debt, excluding mortgages, soared from $5 billion in 1944 to 237 billion in 1978. Total personal debt rose from $38 billion in 1946 (one-fourth of after tax annual income) to $1,364 billion in 1979 (three-fourths of after tax annual income). Thus, the high rate of sales was being sustained partly by consumer spending in excess of consumer income and would

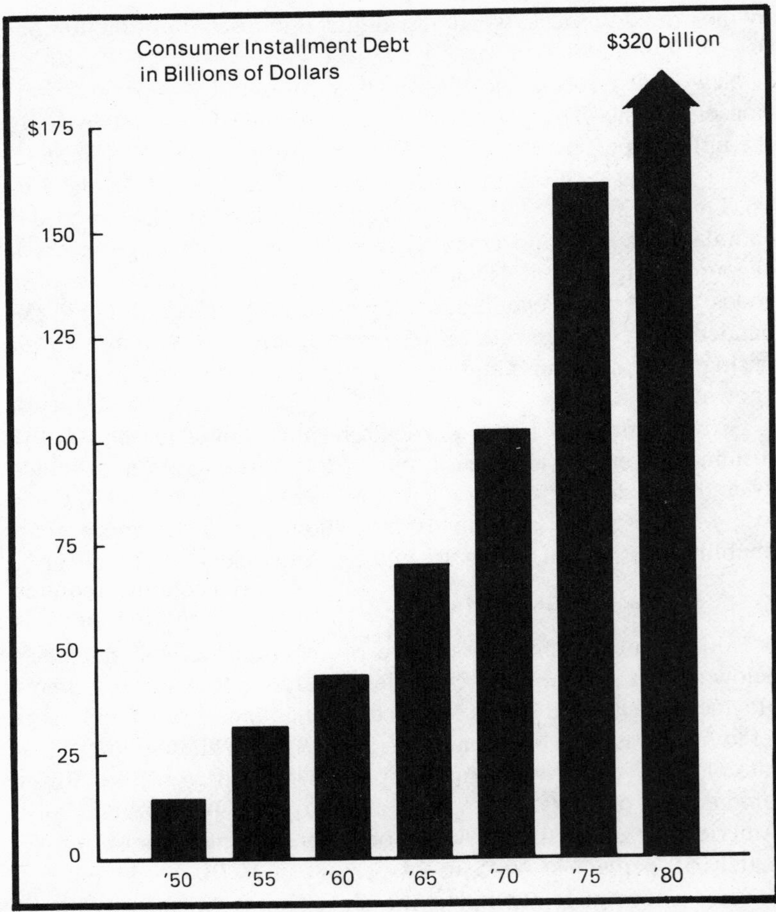

Fig. 5.1. **Consumer Installment Debt.** Consumer debt rose rapidly after 1950 not only in total amount but also as a percentage of consumers' income.

necessarily decline to the level of consumer income or below when consumers accumulated all the debt they could make payments on.

On the other hand, the economy had acquired new safeguards against depressions. These included a number of *built-in stabilizers* including unemployment insurance, guaranteed annual wages, old age pensions, and disability pensions which maintained some consumer income even during periods of high unemployment. Government spending remained high in depressions. Farm price supports maintained farm income, and federal-state welfare programs put a floor under the incomes of many citizens. Also, when incomes fell, income tax collections took less money out of the economy. These built-in stabilizers helped to prevent incomes from falling as abruptly and as far as they had in 1929.

Furthermore, despite continued preference for free enterprise, there was broad new agreement that private businessmen could not prevent wide fluctuations in total spending and that, therefore, the federal government should play an active role in combatting recessions. The 1946 Employment Act pledged the government to manage its spending, taxing, and monetary policies with the aim of achieving full employment, and established a three-man Council of Economic Advisers to help the president make plans to achieve that goal. In the event of a severe economic downturn, the government was generally expected to take vigorous counter measures.

What Factors Contribute to Economic Growth?

In order to achieve a rapid growth rate, any economy requires adequate supplies of three essential elements. The first need is natural resources: soil, water, timber, coal, oil, gas, iron, and others. America is relatively abundantly blessed with natural resources. Our problem in this area is merely to follow policies that do not exhaust our domestic supplies or endanger our imports of essential nonrenewable natural resources such as oil and iron.

A second essential element is the labor to transform resources into desired goods. Historically, America has had a shortage of labor, but in the twentieth century the shortage became a surplus. Even at the peak of our 1969 boom we were unable to provide jobs for 3.5 percent of those who wanted to work and, in most recent years, we have had an even larger labor surplus.

A third essential is capital. This means the money needed to build factories, railways, and warehouses, to open mines, and to equip all of these. As our technology advances, the amount of capital needed to develop the new machinery and materials rises rapidly. Nevertheless, America has been extraordinarily successful in accumulating capital. Capital in the 1970s was so plentiful that real annual interest rates (allowing for the effects of inflation) averaged only 2 or 3 percent. We even export capital for investment in other countries.

Economic growth is also largely dependent on the skill of business management. Some managers are *entrepreneurs,* the economic leaders who decide what products are needed, make plans to build factories, raise the necessary capital, and organize production. They are deservedly highly honored and rewarded in American society. Management's responsibility for organizing production includes providing equipment, machines, and raw materials, employing and training workers, using labor and machinery efficiently, adjusting production to demand, and distributing and selling products. America has no serious deficiency in this area—our management is among the most efficient and progressive in the world.

A fifth factor essential to production is an adequate market. No matter how well a free economy is supplied with resources, labor, capital, and management skill, it will knowingly produce only the goods and services that it can sell at a profit. Furthermore, unless nearly all of the goods currently produced are being sold, entrepreneurs will not risk their capital to expand production. America has surmounted the problems of providing plenty of the other essentials of economic growth, but our businessmen seldom have a market large enough to absorb all of the goods and services they are capable of producing. In its 1969 report to the president, the Council of Economic Advisers stressed the market's importance:

> When aggregate [total] demand matches supply capability, resources are fully utilized and production equals the economy's potential. If aggregate demand should fall short of supply capability, part of the output that the economy is capable of turning out would not be produced.

The level of economic activity is determined by total spending—called *aggregate demand.* This includes three kinds of spending. Private consumer spending for goods and services is nearly two-thirds of aggregate demand. A second kind, government spending, accounted for 20 percent of total spending in the 1970s. A third component is capital investment—the spending by business and investors on facilities to modernize and increase the capacity to produce goods and services.

Fluctuations in economic activity, the business cycle, are fluctuations in total spending. Of the three kinds, government spending is most stable. Much of it is fixed and unavoidable, such as interest on the public debt and Social Security benefits, so that it drops little if any as the economy enters a decline. Consumer spending is more variable, and in periods of unemployment and uncertain economic prospect it may drop significantly, particularly for luxury goods and durable goods such as television sets, automobiles, and new houses. But capital investment is the most volatile of all. When businessmen are convinced that the prospects for larger sales are bright, they may scramble to enlarge and improve their production facilities. However, if they lose confidence that sales will rise, they may cancel or postpone expansion, sharply cutting aggregate demand and possibly triggering a recession.

Thus, the problem of preventing depressions is largely the problem of avoiding sharp drops in investment spending or, if that cannot be done, offsetting its effects with simultaneous increases of other kinds of spending to maintain aggregate demand. Of course, as long as consumer buying is rising and seems likely to continue to rise, investment spending will also be high.

How Can the Government Help Sustain Economic Growth?

The federal government has several means, or "tools," that it can use to influence total spending and therefore the level of total economic activity. One of these is *monetary policy*. The federal government has a monopoly of the power to create money, to coin and print it, and can increase or decrease its supply at will. However, coins and currency play a relatively minor role in modern American business transactions; most payments are made by bank check. Also much business expansion and many consumer purchases are financed by bank loans. By making loans, banks increase the money supply and spending. The federal government can raise or lower the amount of money that banks lend, a power it exercises through its Federal Reserve Board (FRB). By requiring banks to raise interest rates or to hold a larger part of their money in reserve, or by borrowing their money itself, the FRB can reduce private bank loans and thus cut the money supply and total spending. On the other hand, if it so desires, the FRB can, by reversing the above measures, increase the amount of credit available to business and consumers.

Most economists agree that when the economy is facing a slowdown or recession, the Federal Reserve Board should adopt an "easy money" policy and make more credit available in order to stimulate higher rates of investment and consumption. On the other hand, when economic activity is high and prices rise rapidly in undesirable inflation, they believe that the FRB should adopt a "tight money" policy and "cool off" the economy by restricting credit and thereby investment and consumer spending. So used, they say, monetary policy can help to stabilize the economy at high employment levels.

However, monetary policy is difficult to apply effectively. Its impact is not fully felt for several months (possibly one or two years), and it must be applied early and in just the right amount to achieve the desired results. Human judgments on proper timing can be off. In 1968 the Chairman of the Joint Economic Committee of Congress charged that "the Federal Reserve Board has a record of deepening almost every recession or depression we have suffered in the last thirty years by reducing the money supply," and "has often excessively increased the money supply to fan the flames of inflation when the economy has been booming." Also, fighting inflation by upping interest rates is partly self-defeating because higher interest itself raises most business costs. Furthermore, raising interest rates transfers money from those who owe money to those who lend money, usually from low-income to high-income groups, and unfairly penalizes some industries, such as home building. The "monetarist" school of economists urges that the FRB not manipulate the money supply, but confine itself to expanding the money supply at a steady rate, perhaps 5 percent annually.

A second tool by which the federal government can affect the level of economic activity is *fiscal policy,* the way that it manages its taxing and spending. A rise in government spending raises total spending. On the other hand, taxes extract money which taxpayers might otherwise spend for goods and services. A tax increase, therefore, reduces total demand and a tax cut tends to raise spending.

Fiscal policy is dependable in its effects, but is also difficult to apply effectively. Like monetary policy it is far more effective when used quickly, before a recession or inflation is allowed to gather momentum. A small increase in government spending may halt a downturn if applied early enough, but much more spending may be needed to bring us out of a recession once it develops. However, it is politically difficult to raise or lower taxes or spending quickly. Even after the spending has been authorized by Congress, it sometimes takes months or years to let contracts and get construction of dams or highways started. Also, it is expensive to halt construction of a dam or highway when the economy is entering a boom and inflation. It is even more difficult to persuade Congress to moderate an inflationary boom by raising taxes.

When President Kennedy wanted to expand total demand he knew that he could not get Congress to vote a sufficient increase in federal spending. Therefore, he asked for a tax reduction even though the government was already expecting an $8 billion deficit for the year. The tax bill of 1964, which cut taxes by $11.5 billion, was a clear example of adjusting fiscal policy to accelerate economic expansion, and some economists gave it credit for the subsequent rise in the growth rate.

But soon after taxes were cut, deeper involvement in the war in Vietnam sharply raised government spending. The result was a rapid inflation that by 1969 was cutting the value of the dollar by 7 percent a year. When President Johnson recommended a small tax increase to check inflation, Congress took more than a year and a half to comply.

Because of the difficulty of getting Congress to respond quickly enough to make fiscal policy a reliable tool for heading off recessions or inflations, the Council of Economic Advisers in 1969 recommended that the president be empowered to raise or lower by 5 percent the withholding of income tax from paychecks. This would enable him to make quick changes in the amount of money in the hands of consumers. He already had such limited authority to adjust tariff rates.

The Debate on Government Economic Policy

If America were well equipped with natural resources, labor, capital, and management, why did not our economy grow more rapidly? The answer seems to be that economic growth requires not only capacity to produce; it requires a growing ability on the part of the people to buy more goods and services. Unless additional goods can be sold at a profit, businessmen will not produce them.

Most economists, both liberal and conservative, agree with the analysis to this point. They further agree on the value of putting accumulated capital back to work by investing it in new factories to expand production and provide new jobs. Both recognize that upper income groups tend to save money which, if not reinvested, accumulates as idle savings. And they agree that investors are most likely to risk money to build new factories when the prospect of profit is brightest. But they disagree on which government policies best improve the prospect of profits. Many conservatives argue that the best contribution that the government can make is to hold down wages, raw material prices, and business taxes in order to reduce business costs and thereby raise profits. By making investment more rewarding, they say, these policies induce businessmen to expand productive facilities. The new jobs thereby generated give workers added income that provides the necessary growth of consumer purchasing power. This policy was followed during the 1920s. Many liberals, on the other hand, insist that no matter how low taxes, costs, and wages are, businessmen cannot be induced to build new factories unless they are first convinced that the products of such factories can be sold. A larger market is the indispensable requirement, they say, and furthermore it must be created first, before additional investments will be made. Thus, while conservatives give priority to cutting government spending and reducing taxes on upper incomes, liberals seek first to raise consumer incomes.

Which of these policies was followed by the nations that grew more rapidly than America? Their taxes were higher. In 1977 the percentage of the GNP taken by national, state, and local taxes was 30 in America, 38 in Italy, 38 in West Germany, 39 in France and 53 in Sweden. They spent smaller percentages of their GNPs on defense, and much larger percentages on welfare measures which raised the income of the poor. Sweden, which achieved the highest standard of living in Western Europe, had both the highest taxes and the highest social spending. A group of economists who were assigned to discover why America was growing less rapidly than Europe, concluded that the only important problem in America was insufficient consumer demand.

In the light of such evidence, a growing number of American businessmen came to favor government measures to widen the distribution of purchasing power. The *Wall Street Journal* praised old age pensions, unemployment insurance, and farm price supports as "built-in stabilizers." In 1969 the Republican administration of President Nixon proposed to remove income taxes from many low-income families, and to provide a guaranteed annual income for all Americans who were willing to work.

Obstacles to Economic Growth

Economic growth is made more difficult by the increasing effort required to extract natural resources such as iron, copper, and coal. Earlier miners mined the ores that were most accessible, and it has become necessary to seek them at ever greater depths in ever more inaccessible locations. Offsetting the decreasing returns, of course, are technological developments that cut the cost of mining and shipping minerals. We can now drill for oil, for example, at depths that were impossible fifty years ago. Also, our greater wealth gives us the means to pay higher costs.

Expenditures for military purposes are nonproductive. Modern weapons are expensive, and the large armed forces maintained by some nations absorb so much of their national production as to leave little for economic expansion. The nation that achieved the highest rate of economic growth between 1950 and 1980 was Japan whose constitution forbade her to maintain armed forces.

Labor unions sometimes resist the introduction of more efficient machinery or work rules or restrict the training of new workers in their craft. Oligopolies cut production instead of prices when sales of their product decline and thereby deny consumers the benefit of lower prices, add to unemployment, and retard economic growth. And some of the measures used by governments to combat inflation have the effect of retarding growth.

The Causes of Inflation

America's economic growth is much affected by popular concern over inflation and by the measures the federal government uses to combat it. Everyone experiences inflation, and a 1978 public opinion poll found that it was the chief cause of public concern, but public discussion reveals that the people hold many conflicting opinions regarding its causes, effects, and relationship to economic growth.

As is the case with many economic issues, views on inflation are affected by emotion, self-interest, political preference, and psychological influences. Some commonly expressed views are that inflation is caused by certain price rises, particularly of widely used commodities such as steel or oil, the forcing up of wages by labor unions, or dimly understood underlying forces that are largely beyond human control.

Economic groups tend to blame inflation on competing economic groups. Farmers point to the rising prices of the things they buy, and urban dwellers cite rising food prices. Workers argue that rising prices justify their demand for higher wages to maintain their standard of living.

Many businessmen believe that inflation is caused by the action of labor unions that force producers to pay higher wages and thus raise production costs and force producers to raise prices. Therefore, they maintain, the way to prevent inflation is to hold down wage increases, and only if a large number of unemployed persons are waiting to take their jobs can workers be restrained from making excessive demands. One economist developed the Phillips Curve to show that inflation can be held in check only if unemployment is at least 4 percent, and President Nixon's Council of Economic Advisers warned that efforts to reduce unemployment below 5 percent would cause high inflation.

Some economists blame the persistence of inflation through both boom and recession on the power of the oligopolies that dominate

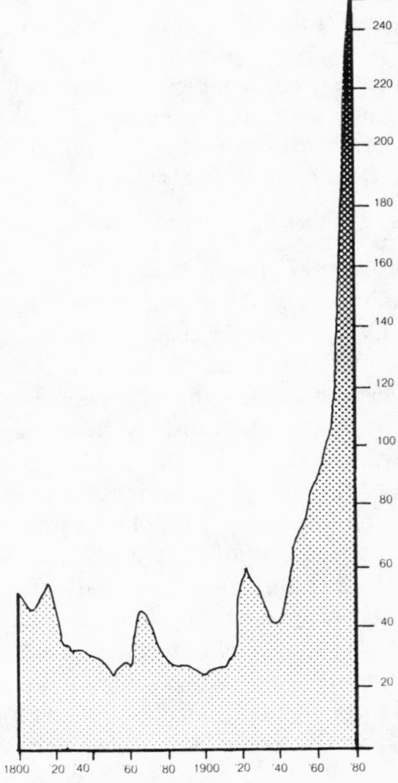

Fig. 5.2. **Consumer price index.** In America, wars have brought sharp inflation—as can be seen in the peaks during and shortly after the War of 1812, the Civil War, World War I, and World War II—while periods of peace have been periods of deflation. The value of the 1942 dollar was approximately the same as the value of the 1800 dollar. Only after World War II did we experience continuous inflation. (U.S. Bureau of the Census, 1977)

America's leading industries to set prices independently of supply and demand. When a recession reduces demand for automobiles, for example, the automobile companies do not cut prices but reduce production. Sometimes they even raise prices in periods of falling demand.

However, most such public discussion touches only the symptoms and not the fundamental causes of inflation. Inflation is by definition a rapid rise in the quantity of money relative to the supply of goods and services available for purchase. An effect of inflation is a rise in the general level of all prices including the price of labor.

What causes inflation? The answer, of course, is whatever causes the money supply to expand. Inflation cannot occur without an upsurge of the money supply, and a disproportionate upsurge makes price rises inevitable. Contrary to a popular view, in the absence of money expansion a price hike on an individual product, or group of products, cannot cause inflation. If the price of oil, for example, goes up and people spend more money for gasoline they will have less money to spend on other things. The consequent drop in the demand for other goods and services will cause their prices to fall and hold down the average price level. Only an expansion of the money supply permits the average of all prices to rise.

What causes the money supply to rise? Some ancient countries used gold stamped into coins by kings. Some kings "debased" the coinage by reducing the size of coins or mixing lead with the gold. But this usually caused the value of the coins to fall and prices to rise. An increase in the gold supply can also mean inflation. When Spain seized large stocks of gold from the Indians of Latin America in the sixteenth century the resulting increase in the quantity of gold caused a general price rise in Europe.

In modern times money creation is a monopoly of government. The invention of paper money made it easier for governments to increase the money supply and led to spectacular inflation. In 1923 a French invasion and occupation of the principal industrial regions of Germany drastically cut the tax income of the German government. To pay its bills it printed new paper money. As the volume of money rose, its value fell and prices soared to one trillion times their former level. A similar printing press inflation occurred in China during and after World War II.

When their spending exceeds their incomes, governments can

create new money to pay their bills. Government spending is popular, but taxes are unpopular, so politics tends to make governments spend more money than they collect in taxes. A private individual in this position would find it necessary to raise his income or cut his spending. Unlike individuals, governments have the power to create new money and are tempted to print additional money rather than cut spending or raise taxes.

Another reason why modern governments expand the money supply is to raise total spending and thus stimulate the economy as an antirecession measure.

THE EFFECTS OF INFLATION

In its effects inflation hurts some groups, helps some, and scarcely affects others.

A decline in the value of money hurts persons on fixed money incomes. For example, a retired person who lives on a $400 per month pension finds that it will buy fewer and fewer things. His

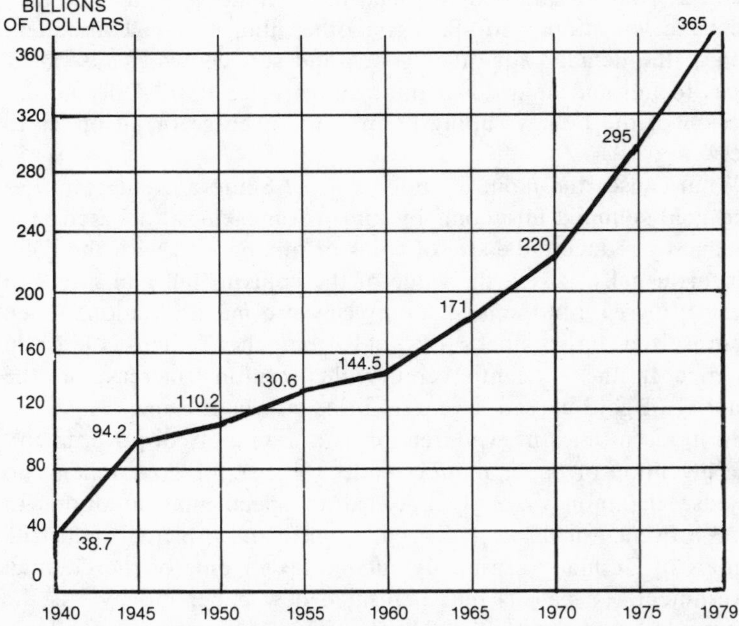

Fig. 5.3. **Money Supply, 1940–1979.** After World War II, the money supply rose at a more rapid rate than the GNP. This was particularly true after 1965, when the sharpest inflation occurred. (Historical Statistics of the U. S. Survey of Current Business)

monetary income remains unchanged, but his real income falls. The same is true of persons who live on income from bonds or insurance policies. Inflation also hurts those whose assets are of a fixed money value such as bonds, insurance policies, or savings deposits.

On the other hand, inflation helps those who owe money. By reducing the value of the money they owe, and usually raising their wages and salaries, it makes it easier for them to pay their debts. A 10 percent inflation amounts to a 10 percent cancellation of all debts. It helps the government by reducing the relative size of the government's debt and making it easier for the government to pay interest on it and to borrow more.

Many groups in society are largely unaffected by inflation. It neither hurts nor benefits most wage and salary earners because it usually raises both prices and wages. Nevertheless, psychological factors cause the unaffected groups to resent inflation bitterly. They regard the rise in their income to be merited, do not attribute it to inflation, and are angered when inflation nullifies it. Inflation has not prevented recent rises in the real income of doctors, lawyers, federal workers, and business executives. However, it has reduced the income of teachers, professors, preachers, and welfare recipients because the public is slow to give them raises equal to the inflation rate.

Inflation in itself does not reduce the nation's standard of living. In thinking about money it is difficult to avoid confusing image with reality. Most people think of money as wealth, which for all practical purposes it is. Nevertheless, money is not real wealth; it is a claim on wealth, a medium of exchange. If all of the money in the nation were to self-destruct overnight the wealth of the nation would not thereby be reduced. We could quickly devise another medium of exchange. Goods and services are real wealth and the standard of living is the total production of goods and services divided by the number of people in the country.

Some economists describe inflation as a kind of tax. When the government does not collect enough money through taxes to pay its bills, it creates new money. If it creates new money in an amount equal to 10 percent of the existing money supply it thereby reduces the value of every dollar by 10 percent. The effect is the same as a 10 percent tax on money. Thus inflation is the tax that people pay when they do not pay enough other taxes to cover government spending. It is what happens to them when they demand government services they are unwilling to pay for. On the whole it is not a regressive tax and with some exceptions does not fall more heavily on the poor than on the wealthy.

COMBATING INFLATION

How can inflation be prevented? One way is to either raise taxes or cut spending, or both, and balance the national budget. Apparently this is very difficult. In the twenty years from 1960 to 1980 there were only two years in which the United States government did not have a deficit. In the four budgets 1975 through 1978 the deficit averaged more than $50 billion per year.

Another approach to fighting inflation is to expand the production of goods and services. In a free market the value of money is determined, like the value of goods and services, by the laws of supply and demand. The demand for money is desire plus salable goods and services with which to command money. In general the money supply at any given time is equal in value to the total of goods and services available for purchase. A 10 percent increase in the quantity of goods and services therefore raises the buying power of each dollar by 10 percent and cuts prices 10 percent.

Thus inflation, a rise in prices, is caused by:

1. An increase in the supply of money;
2. A decrease in the supply of goods and services.

Deflation, a drop in prices, is caused by:

1. A decrease in the supply of money;
2. A rise in the supply of goods and services.

Anything that increases the money supply or decreases production is inflationary, while anything that decreases the money supply or raises the supply of goods and services is deflationary.

According to the Council of Economic Advisers any reform that lowers production costs helps to achieve inflationless growth. Much government income is spent wastefully in ways that do little to improve the standard of living, health, or education. Sometimes tax money is spent for unnecessary jobs. Northcote Parkinson wrote, only half in jest, that government bureaus tend to grow 5 percent annually regardless of the amount of work to be done.

Economic production is also retarded to some degree by interference with the market forces that are supposed to keep a free enterprise economy operating efficiently. Oligopolies cut production to avoid cutting prices. Federal farm programs pay farmers to cut production. Import restrictions keep capital and labor inef-

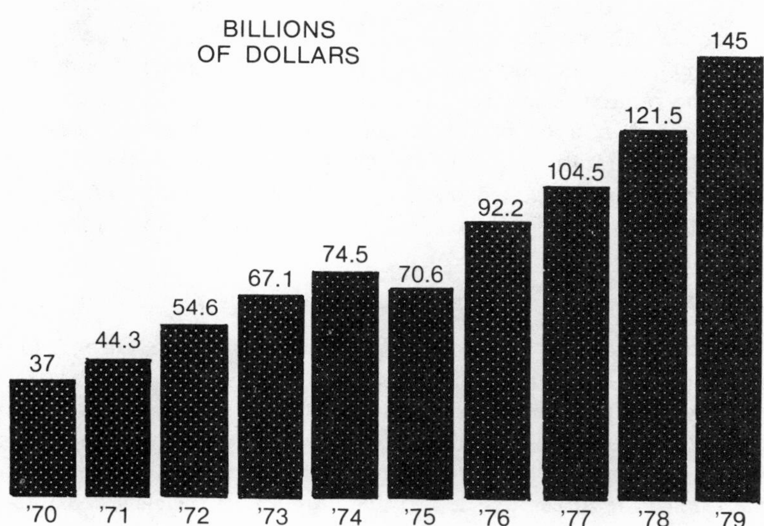

Fig. 5.4. **U.S. Corporate Profits After Taxes.** (U.S. Department of Commerce, 1977; U.S. Statistical Abstract 1979, p. 567; USN & WR 4 August 1980)

ficiently producing some goods at costs higher than they could be obtained through trade. Federal regulatory agencies sometimes reduce competition and raise prices in the industries they regulate.

If the nature of our political system makes inflation a permanent feature of our society how can we adjust to it? One method is *indexing,* providing for automatic money raises to compensate for changes in the value of money. Social Security payments are indexed, and rise automatically in pace with inflation. Many workers have escalator clauses in their wage contracts that provide automatic raises with the rise in prices. About half of Americans benefit from some form of indexing. In Brazil, where inflation of 40 percent or more is common, nearly all salaries are adjusted upward with the rise of the cost of living. Brazilians do not call this a raise, but a currency adjustment.

Recognizing the tendency of politicians to vote for appropriations and against taxes, many states adopted constitutional provisions that require balanced budgets. In 1979 a movement was underway to call a constitutional convention to amend the federal constitution to require balanced budgets. However, unlike state governments, the American people expect the federal government to protect the nation from foreign threats and to protect the economy from depressions and either of these emergencies might require too rapid an increase in spending to be met by raising taxes.

Prolonged inflation produces changes in the mores of a society. Thrift was a traditional American virtue. But with inflation people learn that it is advantageous to spend money quickly before the price of goods rises, and that money put into savings accounts loses value.

MUST WE CHOOSE BETWEEN SLOW GROWTH AND INFLATION?

America has had much experience with inflation. During the period of the Articles of Confederation (1781–1789) some states, under the influence of poor debtors, issued paper money that became so worthless that creditors fled the state to escape being paid with it. The opposition of the propertied classes to such measures was one of the forces that led to the adoption of the new constitution with its prohibition on the creation of money by the states.

America has experienced rapid inflation during all of its wars. In wartime the government runs large deficits and creates much new money. At the same time much of the nation's production is devoted to producing implements of war that do not add to the goods and services available to consumers. Thus, too much money chases too few goods, forcing prices up.

On the other hand, periods of peace in America have usually been periods of deflation. After the Civil War the value of the dollar doubled by 1896. This seriously added to the burden of debt on farmers and many of them lost their farms to bankers. In 1896 the Democratic party called for an expansion of the money supply to halt the fall in prices, but lost the election. During the 1920s a 20 percent deflation occurred. The American dollar in 1941 had almost exactly the value it had in 1800, and a popular expression was "as sound as a dollar."

The experience after World War II is very different. Inflation has been continuous and has tended to become worse. Obviously major changes have occurred in the American economy. Military spending remains high, control of the economy centralizes into fewer hands, and the government does not balance its books.

America has repeatedly achieved high rates of economic growth without inflation. The 1865–1896 period was one of impressive economic growth, and production rose in the 1922–1929 period at an average annual rate of nearly 5 percent. In the early 1960s a period of rapid growth reduced unemployment below 4 percent with very little inflation.

Nevertheless, let us assume for the sake of discussion that the economists who say that we must choose between slow economic growth and high inflation are right. If we cannot have economic growth without inflation which should we choose? Which would have the least undesirable consequences?

As we have seen, inflation in itself does not reduce the nation's production or standard of living. Some economists fear that if inflation becomes excessive it can create conditions that contribute to bringing on a depression, but other economists disagree. In America inflation has usually been accompanied by economic growth. Japan's growth rate of more than 10 percent annually, which doubled her GNP every five years, was accompanied by a much higher inflation than America's, but her real standard of living and national power nevertheless soared.

When some economists warn that rapid inflation will lead to a depression it appears that they do not mean that inflation itself will produce a depression. Rather they mean that high inflation will goad the government into adopting anti-inflation measures that cause a depression. The danger of depression seems to arise less from inflation than from the measures that government uses to combat it.

The standard means of combating inflation are to restrict the money supply and keep unemployment at 5 percent or higher. However, these measures are increasingly less effective. Restricting the money supply raises interest rates, the price of money. Also unemployment has both deflationary and inflationary effects. Holding down wages may be deflationary, but reducing the production of goods and services is inflationary. The postwar series of recessions did not produce deflation, only a slowing of inflation, and even that effect seemed to diminish with each subsequent recession. During the 1975 recession when unemployment soared to 9 percent, inflation slowed only to 4.8 percent. "You get so little deflation from recessions now that it's like burning down your house to bake a loaf of bread," said Arthur Okun.

What are the consequences of combating inflation by deliberately slowing economic growth? It means that large numbers of workers lose their jobs and wages. To the extent that the job loss results from deliberate government policy it can also be regarded as a tax, a high tax that is regressive and discriminatory. Slowing economic growth slows the rise of the nation's standard of living and of its national power. It adds to the severity of social problems such as alienation, crime, suicide, and family disruption. And, in our interdependent world, a slowdown in the American economy has a depressing effect on the economies of most of the nations of the world.

Inflation reduces the burden of debts. While raising prices, inflation also raises wages, salaries, profits, dividends, and government revenues. It does not raise real income, but it reduces the share of current income required to pay debts. Take for example a family whose monthly income is $1,000 and which makes monthly $200 payments, 20 percent of its income, on a home mortgage. If a 50 percent inflation occurs and the family's income rises in pace with inflation, it will be $1,500. Although this represents no more buying power, the $200 mortgage payment now takes only 13.3 percent of income. In the 1946–1971 period inflation wiped out approximately $1.2 trillion of debt in the United States.

This effect of inflation may have been of particular benefit to America in the 1970s. By 1978 total debt, public and private, exceeded $3 trillion, much higher in relation to the GNP than had been reached in 1929. Repayment of debt, not counting mortgages, was taking 20 percent of consumer income. Many economists feared that this much debt seriously retarded economic growth and that if it stopped expanding the economy might enter a major depression.

While inflation does not reduce the standard of living of the population as a whole, it does decrease the real income of some groups while raising the real income of others. Inflation transfers money from some groups to others. Thus the fight over inflation is mainly a fight over the distribution of income. The danger is that groups fighting to enlarge their share of the nation's income will force the government to adopt measures that hurt the prosperity of the nation as a whole.

How Much Economic Growth Is Desirable?

As Americans became more affluent, some sociologists and economists became critical of the "gospel of growth," the high value attached to raising employment and the GNP. They questioned whether increasing production was desirable. Multiplication of automobiles, they said, crowded streets and highways and polluted the environment with noise and fumes. Mining operations ravaged the earth, timber harvesting despoiled natural wildernesses, and power generation contaminated air and water. Growth exhausted irreplaceable natural resources. A much better policy, they said, is to improve the quality of life rather than endlessly to multiply goods and services.

America, with fewer than 6 percent of the world's population, consumes about a third of its oil, steel, and other resources. What would happen to the availability of natural resources, they asked, if the other 94 percent of mankind lifted its rate of consumption to the same level?

Certainly, these questions need to be asked, particularly by countries that produce sufficient goods and services to meet the needs of their people. But much of the world has not yet reached that stage, and the absorbing problem of many underdeveloped countries is still to produce enough food, clothes and houses.

Is America producing enough goods and services? Despite our affluence, an appalling amount of deprivation, even malnutrition, persists among the poor. Perhaps the solution to this problem is not more production but better distribution. Had America's 1978 personal income been divided evenly among America's families, each would have received $22,464, enough to end deprivation and give a comfortable standard of living to every American family.

No one would want to expand the production of some products, such as tobacco, bottles, or even automobiles indefinitely. On the other hand, a trend in the economy is to raising not so much the numbers of products as their attractiveness, convenience, comfort, and beauty. Also the economy has shifted increasingly from producing goods to producing services such as medical care, beauty care, entertainment, and art. Seventy percent of our labor force is now engaged in producing services, many of which do not waste natural resources, pollute the environment, or spoil the quality of life.

Economic growth need not mean producing more for private consumption. Economist John Kenneth Galbraith described America as a land of private wealth and public poverty. What we should produce more of, he implied, was quality roads, parks, schools, hospitals, libraries, museums, and concert halls. Also, the need for further expansion of the economy in the areas of medical care, education, and research is scarcely disputed. Expansion could include reclaiming damaged strip mine areas; purifying air, streams, and lakes; cleaning up seashores, restoring beaches, renovating rural and urban slums; rehabilitating criminals, the mentally retarded, and drug addicts; and research on the causes of heart diseases and war. The issue may be what kind of economic growth is needed, rather than whether growth is needed at all.

CONCLUSION

This brief discussion has, of necessity, oversimplified many complex problems. No general agreement exists among Americans on what government policy best promotes economic growth, or on the relative value of growth and currency stability, or the cause and effect relationships between them. Each economic interest tends to assume that the policy that best serves its own immediate interest is also best for the nation. However, even professional economists disagree widely on some problems.

Obviously, the public needs to be sufficiently well informed so that it can recognize and support wise policies. Fortunately, public understanding of economics seems to have improved in recent years and scholars seem to have narrowed their disagreements on the causes of depressions and the policies needed to avert them. Dips in the economic cycle have been less severe since World War II. This gives us reason to hope that we can find the way to sustain the rate of growth needed to alleviate America's problems.

Questions

1. Give four reasons why maintaining economic growth is important.
2. What is an "economic cycle"? What are its four phases?
3. What causes a recession? How do subsequent developments cause the economy to decline still further?
4. How does America's economic growth rate compare with that of other leading industrial countries?
5. What are the factors that make our economy vulnerable to a depression? What protects our economy from a depression?
6. What measures, or "tools," can the government use to affect the level of economic activity?

7. List factors, other than insufficient demand, that retard economic growth.
8. How do conservatives and liberals differ in the economic policies that they advocate?
9. Is it possible to have economic growth without inflation? If not, which should we accept—a slowing of growth or inflation? Show who would be helped or hurt by either decision.
10. In your opinion, what is the chief obstacle to economic growth?
11. Should a high rate of economic growth remain a national goal? Give arguments for and against.
12. Does economic growth necessarily damage the environment? Explain.
13. Define: recession, inflation, GNP, "built-in stabilizers," Council of Economic Advisers, entrepreneur, monetary policy, fiscal policy, Say's Law, the Phillips Curve.

Suggested Reading

Committee for Economic Development. *High Employment Without Inflation.* New York: Committee for Economic Development, 1972.

Congressional Quarterly: Inflation and Unemployment. Washington, D.C.: U.S. Government Printing Office, 1975.
Discusses the record of inflation over the past ten years, theories of inflation, and the policies of the Nixon and Ford administrations regarding inflation.

Fishman, Betty G., and Leo Fishman. *Employment, Unemployment, and Economic Growth.* New York: Crowell, 1966.

Hayne, Paul T. *Private Keepers of the Public Interest.* New York: McGraw-Hill, 1968.
A critical view of the way businessmen fulfill their social responsibilities.

Keyserling, Leon H. *Full Employment Without Inflation.* Washington, D.C.: Conference on Economic Progress, 1974.
A prescription for economic growth and elimination of poverty by a former chairman of the Council of Economic Advisers in the Truman administration who argues that economic growth reduces inflation.

Lerner, Abba P. *Flation: Not Inflation of Prices, Not Deflation of Jobs*. Rev. ed. Gretna, La.: Pelican Publishings, 1973.
An account of the various attempts to deal with inflation and depression. Analyzes why past remedies have failed to work and the various kinds of resistance to possible solutions.

Malabre, Alfred L., Jr. *Understanding the Economy. For People Who Can't Stand Economics*. New York: Dodd, Mead, 1976.
A columnist for the *Wall Street Journal* gives a basic account for the general reader of such things as the gross national product, consumer price index, index of leading indicators, and international currency exchange.

Okun, Arthur M., Henry H. Fowler, and Milton Gilbert. *Inflation: The Problems It Creates and the Policies It Requires*. New York: New York University Press, 1970.
An argument that inflation is much better than fighting inflation by slowing the economy. Denies that inflation is the "cruelest tax of all," but is a rather progressive tax, while a recession is "wantonly cruel" to the disadvantaged and the young.

Rocks, Lawrence, and Richard P. Runyon. *The Energy Crisis*. New York: Crown, 1973.
Maintains that the energy crisis is real and serious, that rationing of fuel will be required, and that economic depression is a possibility. Outlines the policies that are needed to prevent the crisis from getting worse.

6
Poverty Amid Plenty

What are the causes of poverty?
How adequate are present antipoverty programs?
Can all Americans be lifted out of poverty?

"A measure of the greatness of a powerful nation is the character of the life it creates for those who are powerless to make ends meet."

—President Richard M. Nixon

"The present welfare programs should be scrapped and a totally new system implemented."

—President Jimmy Carter

"Expanding the economy is the essential thing."

—Gunnar Myrdal

The Distribution of Income in America

Unequal incomes are found in all societies. This inequality sometimes results from possession or nonpossession of bodily characteristics such as stamina, large muscles, or resistance to alcohol and disease. Sometimes it results from luck—escaping or not escaping accidents and injuries, insect pests, storms, drought, and war, or finding gold or making the right investment. It can result from personality factors, such as anxiety that impels an individual to keep working after he has met his immediate needs and to postpone gratification in favor of saving for the future.

Once inequalities of income appear they tend to become self-perpetuating. Accumulating a little wealth gives a person superior opportunities to acquire more. In contrast, poverty is hard to escape. Lacking resources to meet such emergencies as sickness or accident, a poor man may be forced to borrow money or sell his land and thereafter pay interest or rent to a wealthier man. When a wealthy man dies he passes wealth and its opportunities to his son, while the poor man bestows poverty and its handicaps on his children.

Different occupations bring different incomes. Occupations that require more skill and training are more highly paid. A brain surgeon may earn hundreds of dollars per hour, while a common laborer is paid only a few dollars per hour. Those who cannot afford the cost of the necessary training are excluded from higher paying occupations.

In most societies, economic inequality is the chief factor in social stratification. More than any other single consideration, a person's social standing is determined by his relative wealth. A lower-class individual who acquires wealth suddenly may not be immediately admitted into the highest social circles, but his sons and grandsons almost always are.

Some sociologists and economists believe that economic inequality is socially desirable. The benefits of high incomes and the penalties of low incomes create incentives, they say, for individuals to work harder, to spend money more wisely, and to invest for the purpose of producing more income—all of which tend to increase society's total wealth. The free enterprise economic system relies on the desire for larger incomes as its chief motive force.

Others maintain that inequalities of income and wealth, especially when they are great, are destructive. Much spending by wealthy people is for nonessentials such as parties, luxury hotels, yachts, racing horses, and social seasons. Economist Thorstein Veblen, in his book *The Theory of the Leisure Class,* called such spending "conspicuous consumption" designed to display publicly that the spenders were wealthy and did not need to work. It consumes resources which might be used to satisfy needs for food, clothing, housing, and medical care.

Some economists believe that great inequalities of wealth tend to retard, rather than promote, the growth of production. Under a free enterprise system, the chief stimulant of businessmen to produce goods and services is the market, defined as people with needs, wants, and enough money to buy goods and services at a price that will give producers a profit. The rich may spend lavishly, but they are relatively few and the amount they can consume is limited. Furthermore, many of them save more of their incomes than do the poor. Consequently, the market is smaller when wealth is highly concentrated than when wealth is broadly distributed.

Inequities of income and wealth in the 1970s were greatest in underdeveloped nations where one could find a few immensely wealthy individuals in a sea of abject poverty. Until well into the twentieth century incomes were more evenly distributed in the United States than in any other large country. More recently, income distribution has become more equal in Sweden, Japan, and communist nations. In 1976 the top 10 percent of U.S. families received an average of 15 times as much income as the lowest 10 percent. In West Germany the same ratio was only 11, in Japan 10, and in Sweden 7.

The distribution of income among American families changed very little between 1950 and 1977.

	1950	1960	1969	1977
Lowest fifth	4.5	4.8	5.6	5.2
Second fifth	11.9	12.2	12.3	11.6
Middle fifth	17.4	17.8	17.7	17.5
Fourth fifth	23.6	24.0	23.7	24.2
Highest fifth	42.7	41.3	40.6	41.5

The increasing generosity of welfare benefits was offset by tax changes that made federal taxes less progressive. The percentage of income received by the lowest fifth rose only 0.7 percent, while the percentage received by the top fifth subsided by only 1.2 percent. After 1969 the slight trend toward broader income distribution was reversed and the trend turned toward less equitable incomes.

Because of the tendency of upper-income groups to save, ownership of wealth is more concentrated than income. Had wealth been evenly distributed in 1976 every adult would have owned approximately $30,000. However, one study concluded that 0.5 percent of the American people owned 25 percent of the nation's privately owned wealth, and the top 20 percent owned 80 percent of the wealth. The bottom 25 percent owned an average of nothing—many of them had debts that exceeded the value of all the property they owned. This degree of inequity in the distribution of material benefits was considered a social problem by many Americans because of its negative economic consequences and its incompatibility with American ideals of individual worth and equal opportunity.

THE POVERTY PROBLEM

America, the richest country in history, on the crest of its greatest economic boom, failed to lift many of its citizens from poverty. Many Americans were unaware of how much poverty persisted in our rich nation because most of it was isolated in rural areas or urban slums. In 1974 12 percent of Americans, a total of 24 million, were classified as poor. Although some of them were fortunate when compared to the poor of other lands (most of them had television sets and half had cars), many others lived in conditions scarcely believable in an advanced country. According to a Citizen's Board of Inquiry, approximately 10 million suffered from chronic hunger and malnutrition. A group of senators found cases of actual starvation among the southern poor.

Despite their low incomes, the poor were exploited in many ways. Studies found that merchants charged them higher prices for inferior goods and higher interest on credit purchases. State and local taxes took a bigger share of their low incomes than of the incomes of the rich. They were seldom consulted, even on the antipoverty programs that most concerned them. They lived, said the Council of Economic Advisers, in a world "where a minor illness is a major tragedy, where pride and privacy must be sacrificed to get help, where honesty can become a luxury and ambition a myth."

The nation also paid a high price for poverty. Private and public welfare costs were high, and the kinds of disease and crime that accompanied poverty also required huge expenditures. "We pay twice for poverty," said the Council of Economic Advisers. "Once for production lost in wasted human potential, again in diverting resources to cope with poverty's social byproducts." In hurting the prestige of our nation and economic system, it added force to the communist challenge that we spent many billions to meet.

WHO ARE THE POOR?

By definition, America's poor are people with incomes below what is required to maintain a decent standard of living. This level, according to Social Security economists, varies with the size and location of families. In 1979, when median family income was $18,500, a nonfarm single person was considered poor if his income was less than $3,400, and a family of four was considered poor if its income was less than $6,700. This amount allowed $4.59 for each person per day for food, clothing, shelter, and all other living expenses.

More than three-fourths of the American poor in 1976 were white, and nearly half of them were children. A third of them lived in urban ghettos; nearly half lived in the South. They were more likely than the general population to be:

Unemployed. The heads of millions of families were unable to work because they were too old, handicapped, or were mothers caring for young children. Others were unable to find jobs.

Members of minority groups. Blacks, Mexican-Americans, Puerto Ricans, and Indians were often the last to be hired and the first to be fired. Their jobless rate was double that for whites. In 1970 almost one-third of non-white families were poor.

Uneducated. In 1975, forty-two percent of poor families were headed by a person with less than a ninth-grade education.

Aged. More than one-fourth of all persons 65 or older were poor in 1974 and they included nearly 13 percent of all poor people. Job opportunities for older people were rare, and Social Security pensions were insufficient to keep many retired persons out of poverty.

Members of families with no adult male breadwinner. In 1975, 43 percent of all poor families were headed by women, and most families headed by women were below the poverty line.

Children of the poor. Malnutrition caused organic brain damage; retarded learning rates; increased vulnerability to disease, and apathy. They were more likely to drop out of school before qualifying themselves to fill available jobs. "The poverty of the fathers is visited upon the children," concluded the Council of Economic Advisers.

Inhabitants of depressed regions. In the 1930s, the South was the "nation's number one economic problem," and although some southern states made rapid progress, Mississippi, Arkansas, and Alabama remained at the bottom of most measurements of prosperity. In the 1940s and 1950s Appalachia, the mountainous region that includes West Virginia and parts of eleven other states, was hard hit by the decline of small farms and the mechanization of mining. In the 1970s the per capita income of this depressed area was little more than half the national average, and its unemployment was far above average. Other concentrations of poverty were found in urban ghettos where one-third of the men were either unemployed or partly employed.

Sick. Illness which limited ability to work or brought large hospital bills reduced some people to poverty. Many were unable to function effectively because of alcoholism, drug addiction, mental illness, or subnormal intelligence.

Members of large families. Such families needed a breadwinner with above average earnings to keep them above the poverty line.

Workers in low-wage jobs. One-third of the poor lived in families whose head worked throughout the year.

MASS UNEMPLOYMENT

Early America had less labor than it needed to utilize its abundant land and resources. As manufacturing grew, industrialists sent agents to Europe and China to hire workers and pay their passage here. When replaced by agricultural machinery, farm workers quickly found jobs in rapidly growing industries.

Industrial workers, however, were not as independent as farmers. The actions of distant business executives or the operation of market forces could deprive them of their incomes. The ability of the population to consume did not grow enough to keep our productive facilities fully employed. Mass unemployment, according to President Kennedy, became "our dominant, relentless domestic problem." A long period of economic expansion reduced unemployment to a fifteen-year low of 3.5 percent in 1968, but it rose irregularly to 9 percent in 1975.

Unemployment can be tragic. To be forced to remain idle and to accept charity can destroy one's self-respect. It excludes one from the material blessings of the American way of life, denies one of the dignified role of chief provider for a family, cheats one of the satisfaction of contributing to society, and makes one feel like an unwanted burden on others. It raises the suicide rate, contributes to many social ills and deprives society of the goods and services that the individual is capable of producing.

One widely held view is that everyone could find a job if he were willing to work, not too particular about the job and wages, and did not prefer to live on government handouts. But this theory fails to explain why unemployment sometimes vanished in the past, and it assumes that Americans are more reluctant to work than Europeans, who have both generous welfare handouts and full employment. Some countries reduced peacetime unemployment to 1 or 2 percent.

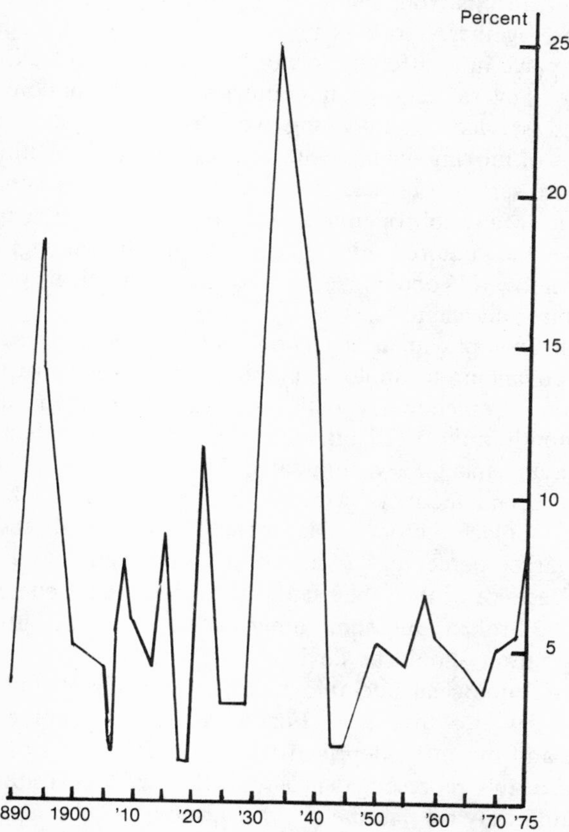

Fig. 6.1. **Unemployment Rate.** Unemployment was worse in the depressions of 1893 and 1929, then set a new high for the post-World War II period in 1975. (U.S. Bureau of the Census, 1967)

Most unemployment seems to be involuntary. The Labor Department counts as "unemployed" only those who are actively seeking jobs and for whom government employment offices are unable to find work. During both world wars, when plenty of jobs were available, more Americans took jobs than had been counted in the labor force. A 1962 survey found that nearly all of the unemployed had looked for jobs by two or more standard methods and were willing to work for less than their former wages.

If men are willing to work, why are they unable to find jobs? There are several kinds of unemployment. One, *frictional unem-*

ployment, results from the difficulty of bringing qualified workers and jobs together. Workers may be unaware of the openings, or they may live in a different part of the country and lack the money to move. Several European countries provide nationwide computerized services of matching workers and jobs, and pay the expenses of moving unemployed workers and their families to jobs.

A more serious obstacle to full employment is *structural unemployment.* Many job openings exist for which the unemployed do not have the required education or technical training. Untrained men cannot fill openings for engineers, medical doctors, accountants, and chemists.

Much unemployment is *technological unemployment.* As a result of advancing technology, manufacturers were able to increase production tremendously with no increase in their labor force. Each month in the 1970s, it was estimated, the introduction of new labor-saving machinery eliminated 35,000 jobs.

Some social theorists doubted that enough new jobs could be found to replace the ones that technology abolished, and predicted that a larger percentage of the population would lose its job income. Because of this, they said, the tie between income and work should be broken, and some other criteria for distribution of purchasing power should be devised.

But technological unemployment, although real and serious, is neither new nor insoluble. For hundreds of years advances in science and invention deprived farmers and workers of jobs. And, of course, this represented progress. If it were desirable to do so, we could easily reverse the trend. Cartoonist Rube Goldberg once drew a plan for a sixty-three-man peanut-cracking machine that cracked only one peanut at a time. Looked at in one way, the mechanization of farming deprived nine out of ten farmers of work. Viewed in another way, it liberated them from farm drudgery and gave them time to produce furniture, automobiles, and television sets, and to become teachers and doctors.

Although advances in technology reduce the number of workers needed to produce a given quantity of goods and services, no economy has ever produced all of the goods and services of all kinds that people wanted. Human wants are practically unlimited, and it is unlikely that any economy can ever produce enough to satisfy everyone. As needs and wants are met new ones develop. How many of your grandparents wanted psychedelic posters, surf boards, stereo sets, psychoanalysis, or heart transplants? Also new public needs and wants develop for better education and cleaner air and streams.

Why, then, could we not keep American workers fully employed? A principal cause of chronic mass unemployment was insufficient buying power, which economists called lack of *effective demand*. Many of the people who wanted goods and services did not have enough money to buy them. If we could raise their buying power to the point that they could buy all the goods and services that our economy is capable of producing, new jobs would open up faster than technology eliminated them. Several European nations and Japan, whose technological advance was as rapid as ours, achieved full employment. Some of them even had such labor shortages that they imported workers.

Traditional Attitudes Concerning Poverty

In early America poverty was considered to be a man's own fault and a just punishment for a life of idleness, sin, and waste. Some wealthy men claimed that common people were naturally inferior and would persist in living like pigs no matter what one tried to do for them. If so, it was best to show them that if they did not work, they would not eat.

In early America this opinion was not entirely unreasonable. The labor shortage made it easy to find some kind of job. Any able-bodied man could escape poverty by thrift and hard work. Few women held paid jobs, but there was such a shortage of women that any woman, if not unbearably ill-tempered, was sure to receive a proposal of marriage. Of course a number of orphans, cripples, and sick people were unable to work and were cared for by churches, private charity, and local governments.

The idea that unemployment resulted from weakness of character long outlived the conditions that produced it. When men moved into cities to work in factories, they held their jobs at the pleasure of others. Depressions or new machinery might deny them the opportunity to work. Even in good times, jobs were fewer than job seekers. Willingness to work alone could no longer guarantee one a job.

In recessions or depressions unemployment rose to disaster proportions. As businesses closed they discharged workers who were anxious to work and who were trained to produce goods and services desperately needed by society. This was called *cyclical unemployment*. In 1933, one-fourth of our labor force was idle.

This was not caused by a mass moral collapse, but by complex economic developments.

GOVERNMENT EFFORTS TO REDUCE UNEMPLOYMENT

Mass unemployment in industrial towns and cities during depressions brought deprivation on a scale beyond the resources of private charity and local governments to meet. State governments came to the rescue. In the Great Depression, for the first time federal funds were used to aid the unemployed.

The cheapest form of welfare is to give money, and the second cheapest is to give food and clothing. But many felt that giving people handouts hurt their character and self-respect, so instead federal funds were used to create jobs for the unemployed. The largest of these programs, the Works Progress Administration (WPA), employed an average of two million men to build roads, dams, athletic fields, sewage systems, and public buildings. The National Youth Administration gave part-time work to students to help them stay in school. Also, a beginning was made toward social security.

SOCIAL SECURITY

The Social Security program enacted in 1935 was designed to protect workers against some of the consequences of involuntary unemployment. It provided workers with a monthly income when they retired or were disabled and, after their death, provided an income to their surviving dependents. At first it protected fewer than half of workers, but it was broadened to cover nine-tenths—all except federal employees, some farm workers, and self-employed persons who had low or irregular incomes.

Normal retirement age is sixty-five, but a worker can retire as early as sixty-two on a reduced pension. If he retired in 1978 at sixty-five, he received a pension of between \$114 and \$460 monthly, depending on the number of years worked and the wage earned. In 1978 the average pension was \$263 per month. Pensions rise automatically with inflation so that they do not lose buying power. One also receives a pension if he is totally disabled before he reaches retirement age. To qualify for maximum old-age and disability benefits can require up to ten years of employment in a job covered by Social Security.

The money to pay retirement and disability pensions is collected by means of a special tax on wages. This tax is paid only on income up to a specified amount, and income above that is not taxed. In 1980 the amount taxed was $25,900 and was scheduled to rise in proportion to the inflation that occurred thereafter. The tax rate on taxed wages was 12.26 percent, half of which was collected from the worker and half from his employer. According to some economists, the half paid by employers was actually taken out of wages. If so, the tax on the worker who earned $25,900 was $3,175.

Together with Medicare, to be discussed later, these programs formed our Social Security system. In 1977, it paid benefits totaling $81 billion to more than 32 million people, one-seventh of the population.

When first proposed, Social Security was bitterly denounced by conservatives as a step toward socialism, and congressional Republicans voted overwhelmingly against it. However, it later won support from conservatives as well as liberals. Unlike other poverty programs, it is paid for by the same people who benefit from it. Its coverage was broadened and its benefits raised in both Democratic and Republican presidential administrations.

Also established by the Social Security law, but usually considered separately, is the unemployment insurance program. It provides weekly payments to laid-off or fired workers to help them support themselves and their families until they are called back or find new jobs. The quantity and duration of payments vary from state to state, but average about a third of the worker's former pay for twenty-six weeks. The money to finance this program is raised through a 3.2 percent tax on wages collected from employers.

Despite its growth, the Social Security system gives a worker only limited security. It does not insure him against the effects of long-term unemployment. Besides, retirement pensions are low—in 1978 they averaged only $3,156 annually, scarcely enough for subsistence. Furthermore, pensions are not related to need. Nearly half of the benefits go to persons above the poverty line. A family that has a large income from investments receives the same pension as a family with no other income. In 1978 if a retired person worked, his pension was reduced fifty cents for every dollar he earned above $4,000 per year.

The Social Security system is also criticized because it is financed by a special tax on wages that is collected even if a worker's income is below subsistence level. Because it is levied only on the first $25,900 it takes a larger percentage of low incomes than of high incomes. Half of the people pay more in Social Security tax than in income tax. Most other industrial countries have relatively more generous social security programs and finance them by less regressive taxes. Some economists recommend that at least a part of our Social Security programs be paid for through the income tax.

PUBLIC ASSISTANCE

In 1976, state or local governments provided some form of welfare contribution to 18 million persons at a cost of $38 billion, of which the federal government contributed more than half. These federal-state programs provided aid to five categories of persons: (1) dependent children, (2) the aged, (3) the blind, (4) the permanently and totally disabled, and (5) those unable to afford an adequate diet. Aid was provided only to those persons who proved to the satisfaction of social workers that they had no other means of meeting their daily needs for food, shelter, clothing, and medical care. The kinds and amounts of aid varied greatly from state to state.

A large number of children were destitute because their parents were unemployed, or because their father was absent and their mother found it difficult to both care for them and hold a job outside the home. Instead of taking these children from their mothers and putting them into institutions, Aid to Families with Dependent Children (AFDC) supported them in their homes. In 1978 more than 11 million persons (children and the adults who tended them) in 3.6 million families were helped by this program at a total cost of $10 billion. Monthly benefits per recipient ranged from $120 in Massachusetts to $15 in Mississippi—the average was $71.

AFDC was accused of encouraging poverty-stricken families to have more children and criticized for giving aid to illegitimate children. Hostile congressmen demanded that unemployed parents take jobs or work training as a condition of obtaining aid. Some sociologists, however, said that forcing mothers who were caring for small children to take job training was not very helpful. Furthermore, they said, it was not reasonable to penalize children because of the alleged misbehavior of their parents.

In 1977 nearly one million needy persons who did not qualify for any federal program were cared for by state and local governments under their *General Assistance* programs at a cost of $1.6

billion annually. Monthly benefits varied from $144 to $12 per person.

In 1974 the program of assistance to the blind, disabled, and aged people was reformed. It is discussed below under "Welfare Reform."

The federal government also gave food to the needy. After 1961 it emphasized a food stamp program which required the poor to pay a part of the food's cost. It sold the poor food stamps which could be used as money in grocery stores to buy certain economical basic foods. A low-income family was eligible for an amount of stamps determined by the Agriculture Department to be sufficient to provide it with a plain but adequate diet, and it paid for them an average 23 percent of its disposable income (the amount left after paying necessary living expenses such as rent and electricity). However, the necessity of making a money payment for them handicapped many, and only about half of the families eligible for them actually received them. In 1977 the requirement to pay for the stamps was dropped in favor of a plan for giving lesser amounts of the stamps free. In 1980 more than twenty million people, 90 percent of whom were below the poverty line, received them at a cost of $8.7 billion.

Federal surplus food was also given to schools for school lunches. In 1975, 15.2 million children, mostly from low-income families, received lunches free or at reduced prices. Most states gave free lunches to children whose family income was up to 125 percent of the poverty level and reduced the price of lunches to those whose family incomes were up to 175 percent of the poverty level.

The War on Poverty

In the Kennedy and Johnson administrations, beginning in 1961, several new antipoverty measures were enacted in what was called the "War on Poverty." Its purpose was to reduce unemployment by helping the poor improve their education, skills, working efficiency, and, in general, equip themselves for success in the modern economy. In an effort to get local people active, local governments or private nonprofit organizations were required to prepare plans, administer them, and pay 10 to 25 percent of their cost.

The *Job Corps* was designed to give impoverished young people, ages sixteen to twenty-two, sufficient education and training to make them self-supporting. It set up camps, called "conservation centers," where youths worked in forestry and conservation in return for room and board, health care, and small monthly payments. In urban "training centers" it trained young people for jobs in television repair, data processing, office work, health care, beauty care, and homemaking. In 1969, 100,000 received training. Some graduated after a few months and others remained in the program for as long as two years. The program's 1977 budget was $417 million.

The *Neighborhood Youth Corps* gave students part-time jobs to help them stay in school, and it employed other youths in full-time jobs in schools, parks, child day care centers, and government offices. Dropouts from school were required to take at least one night school class.

The *College Work-Study Program* gave college students part-time jobs in college offices.

The *Community Action Program* encouraged cities, counties, and states to design new antipoverty programs to meet their particular needs. The law required "maximum feasible participation" by the poor in planning and managing projects. Among the more popular community action projects were *Project Head Start,* a kind of kindergarten for deprived preschool children; *Foster Grandparents,* which paid retired people to care for institutionalized children; and *Upward Bound,* which gave low-income high school students a summer at college.

Other War on Poverty programs offered the poor loans of up to $25,000 to open small businesses such as luncheonettes, service stations, and drug stores. They gave low-income farm families loans of up to $2,500 to buy additional farm land or machinery to make their farms more efficient.

Volunteers in Service to America (VISTA), sometimes called the domestic Peace Corps, sought to enlist idealistic young people to lead the War on Poverty. For a small living allowance they taught in Job Corps centers, assisted Indians on reservations, worked in mental hospitals, and led community action programs. By mid-1967, 7,400 had enrolled.

The War on Poverty also sought to enlarge private industry's job training programs. If industry would train and employ the "hard core" unemployed, those with the least education, skill, and motivation, the federal government would pay for the extra costs incurred. Businessmen formed a National Alliance of Businessmen, headed by Henry Ford, with a goal of finding jobs for 500,000 of the hard core unemployed in three years. At first encouraging gains were made, but they were largely wiped out by the rise in unemployment in 1970.

The 1965 Appalachian Regional Development Act helped that poverty area. More than $1 billion was provided over a six-year period for over two thousand miles of new highways, plus health centers, land erosion control, restoration of strip-mined land, and vocational education.

The *Office of Legal Services* (OLS) provided free legal assistance to poor people. Soon it had twenty-five hundred lawyers, mostly idealistic young people, working out of nine hundred offices in three hundred communities. Most of their cases involved job or housing discrimination, leases, debts, and fraudulent sales practices. They also helped poor people get welfare assistance when they were illegally denied it. Sometimes, in "class action" suits, they sued state governments in behalf of the needy in order to produce welfare policy changes. Conservatives charged that OLS lawyers were antiestablishment and questioned whether the government should employ lawyers to sue itself. On the other hand, the American Bar Association strongly endorsed OLS, the *New York Times* called it "the most successful" War on Poverty program, and President Nixon said that it had breathed "new life into the cherished concept of equal justice for all."

As one would expect, the War on Poverty had detractors. Local political leaders demanded to be consulted on whom to give jobs, and they fought for more political control of its spending. Offended by the "hippie" dress and conduct of some VISTA volunteers, and by their advice to the poor to fight for their rights, some areas expelled them. Critics said that training costs averaged more than $8,000 per graduate, and that nearly half of them failed to find jobs.

Many War on Poverty programs were merely "pilot programs" designed to test methods for possible larger scale use later. Only a fraction of the poor received benefits. Then-Senator Walter Mondale called it "authorizing dreams and appropriating peanuts." Its first head, Sargent Shriver, said that "it was stifled by the war in Vietnam." Its programs were reduced by the Nixon administration.

The War on Poverty's basic assumption was that education and training would enable the unemployed to find jobs. This was true

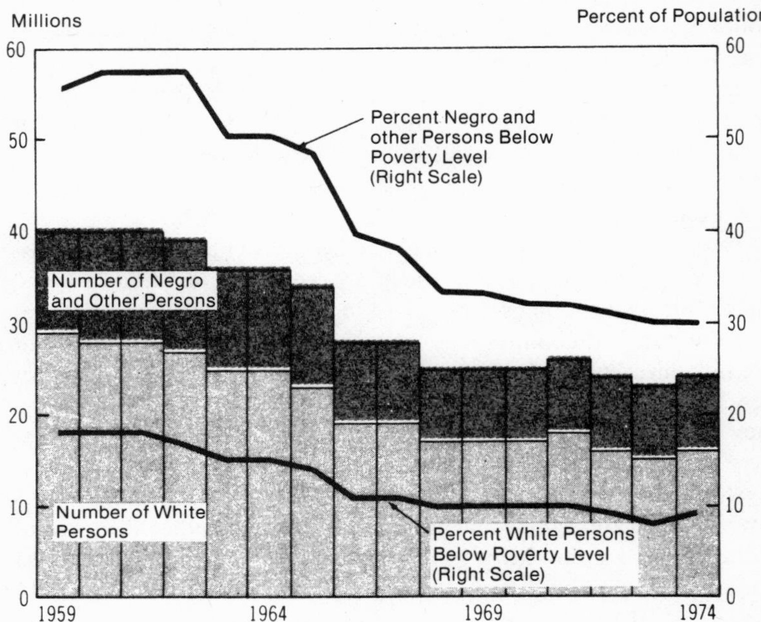

Fig. 6.2. **Persons Below the Poverty Level.** (U.S. Bureau of the Census, 1976)

only to the extent that unemployment was structural in nature. It appeared to be successful when the high economic growth of the 1960s reduced unemployment from 5.5 percent to 3.5 percent and lifted millions out of poverty. But the economic slowdown which began in 1969 and raised the jobless rate to nearly 9 percent caused highly educated engineers and physicists to lose jobs. The percentage of Americans who lived in poverty again rose.

THE INADEQUACIES OF WELFARE PROGRAMS

As one can see, we devised a large variety of programs for combating poverty. Nearly 2,000 federal, state, and local agencies were involved in caring for the poor. In addition, an estimated 200,000 private agencies, including the Red Cross, United Fund, and fraternal, civic, and veterans organizations, plus most of the nation's 300,000 churches, sponsored health and welfare activity.

Nevertheless, fewer than half of the poor received any kind of public assistance and many others received almost none. A 1968 statement by twelve hundred economists said that our poverty programs "excluded" millions who were in need and met inadequately the needs of millions more.

The system was inefficient. Much money was spent to pay the salaries of an army of social workers and administrators. Other billions went to contractors and other businessmen. According to Dr. Milton Friedman, only one dollar in five appropriated for poverty programs ever reached the pockets of the poor.

Even less reached the poorest of the poor. The poverty-stricken states where the poor were concentrated had the most meager poverty programs. Some of them could not even raise the matching money required to take advantage of all federal assistance offered. In 1975, in four states a family of four had to manage on less than $128 per month. In Mississippi the family received $58. Many of the poor were not aware that help was available to them and never applied for it. Some were too poor to buy food stamps or to participate in job training programs.

Moreover, some welfare programs were designed to meet emergencies, not to solve problems. They helped to keep the poor alive, but not to make them self-supporting. Some actually tended to keep people poor. As late as the 1970s many states cut welfare payments by an amount equal to any earnings and thus removed the incentive to take jobs. These features of the system discouraged self-help and encouraged dependency. "This macabre and lunatic welfare system," wrote Joseph Alsop, "virtually outlaws any effort at self-betterment."

America devoted a smaller percentage of its GNP to social welfare than any other Western democracy. One of the difficulties is that America's population is less homogeneous than that of many nations and more divided along lines of race, color, national origin, cultural background, and religion. This makes the achievement of a sense of brotherhood among citizens more difficult and reduces popular support for costly measures to help poor members of minority groups.

In 1971, sociologist Herbert J. Gans of the Massachusetts Institute of Technology pointed out that many groups in our society benefit from the existence of poverty. The poor constitute a "labor pool that is willing—or, rather, unable to be unwilling—to perform dirty work at low cost." They also prolong the economic usefulness of used cars and clothes and run-down buildings. Their presence raises the status of workingmen and provides jobs for social workers, public health workers, sociologists, policemen, and poverty program administrators. Thus, many of the people commissioned to fight poverty profit by its continued existence. No wonder some antipoverty measures tend to perpetuate poverty rather than eliminate it.

With all of its inadequacies, the poverty program is expensive. Between 1950 and 1976 the number of people on welfare (including Medicaid) rose from 6.2 million to 18 million, and the cost of welfare rose from $2.5 billion to $38 billion.

Why did welfare rolls rise sharply when the country was prosperous and the number of people living in poverty was declining? One reason was that the poor were becoming more visible as they moved from isolated rural areas into cities. Rising violence and rioting in ghettos convinced many people of the necessity of doing something to improve opportunities. VISTA workers, poverty lawyers, and the National Welfare Rights Organization made the poor more aware of their rights and how to get welfare payments. The Supreme Court overruled state laws that denied benefits to newcomers. Moreover, the early 1960s was a period of rising idealism and sensitivity to the plight of the poor, and our growing affluence made the continued existence of abject poverty a less defensible blot on the American way of life.

PROPOSALS FOR WELFARE REFORM

Some reformers proposed that the federal government take over and pay the entire cost of all welfare programs, thus *federalizing welfare*. They claimed that this would equalize welfare payments throughout the country, and thus remove financial incentives for the poor to move to northern cities. A 1969 Gallup Poll showed that 77 percent of the people favored equalized welfare payments, and the 1970 National Governor's Conference urged that the federal government assume all welfare costs.

Some sociologists recommended a system of federal *family allowances*. Fifty other nations, including all other industrialized states, have such systems. Because wages do not rise with a family's size every family, rich or poor, receives a monthly government payment for each child in the family. The cost of providing $50 a month for every child in America would be approximately $14 billion annually, from which could be deducted the cost of the existing welfare programs that family allowances would make unnecessary.

Critics of a family allowance system point to its high cost and charge that it would give poor families an incentive to have more children. And because it would not be based on need, more than 70 percent of the money would go to families above the poverty line.

Other reformers seek to *reduce taxation of the poor*. Most state and local taxes take a higher percentage of the income of the poor than of the rich. Federal Social Security taxes also take a large and growing bite out of low incomes. As a result, the Tax Foundation reported, a family with an annual income of only $2,000 paid 28 percent of it, $560, in federal, state, and local taxes. Although a $2,000 annual income can scarcely provide a family with basic necessities, government takes a larger percentage of it than it takes from the extremely wealthy. Taxes could be brought more in line with ability to pay by reducing sales and social security taxes, and collecting more of the needed revenue through income taxes.

Opponents of tax reforms maintain that the poor should be made to pay taxes to make them aware of the costs of government, give them a sense of contributing to their country, and make them better citizens. Reformers reply that taking money from persons who need it for adequate food and medical care teaches lessons of quite a different kind, and contributes to alienation.

The federal government gave the poor some tax relief. By 1977, because of the effects of a minimum standard deduction, temporary tax refunds, and an earned income credit, a single person paid no federal income tax if his earned income was $2,700 or less, and a married person with two dependent children did not pay until income exceeded $6,860.

Guaranteed Employment

Some reformers maintain that the opportunity to work should be considered a basic right of American citizens and that the government should guarantee all citizens who want to work an opportunity to do so. The Full Employment Act of 1946 declared full employment to be a goal of the federal government, and established a three-man Council of Economic Advisers to advise the president on the policies, and level of taxes and spending needed to reach that goal. In 1968 President Johnson said that it was the "nation's commitment to provide a job for every citizen who wants it, and who will work for it." In 1977 President Carter said, "Every family with children and a member able to work should have access to a job."

One proposed plan for full employment is to make the government the *employer of last resort*. Under this plan the government would hire all of those who wanted to work and for whom employment offices could not find jobs, and pay them somewhat less than private business paid for similar work. This, of course, would put an end to unemployment. Its costs might exceed $10 billion per year, minus the welfare payments it would replace. A 1968 Gallup poll found that 78 percent of the people believed that everyone should be "guaranteed enough work to give him a wage of about $60 a week or $3,200 per year."

Of course a socially constructive way to reduce poverty would be to expand private production. During the 1960s, for example, economic growth reduced unemployment from 5.5 to 3.5 percent and cut the number of Americans living in poverty from 22 to 12 percent of the population. Training those on welfare to work would not reduce the number of people on welfare if jobs were not available. Full employment would not end all poverty, but would reduce it dramatically.

GUARANTEED ANNUAL INCOME

Proposals to guarantee every family a minimum income gained increasing support in the 1960s. One of the most widely discussed plans was proposed by conservative economist Milton Friedman as a means of reducing government spending on poverty programs. Friedman suggested that the federal government send every family whose income was below the poverty line a monthly check for an amount sufficient to lift them out of poverty. If they found jobs it should cut payments no more than $1 for each $2 earned.

A guaranteed annual income, its advocates claim, would reach all of the needy, not just the one-half of them currently helped. It would go directly to the needy instead of to bureaucrats and welfare workers. It would meet the basic needs of all without removing incentive to earn more. Furthermore, they argue, its cost would be little, if any, more than the cost of the existing poverty programs that it would replace. In addition, it might indirectly save some of the money required to combat disease, juvenile delinquency, and crime.

Its advocates claim that a guaranteed annual income would stimulate economic growth. Putting money into the hands of the poor, they say, would raise consumer spending, stimulate production, and create new jobs which would take many of the poor off welfare.

An impressive number of economists, businessmen, and political leaders joined reformers in advocating a guaranteed annual income. Among those recommending adoption of some minimum income plan were: the President's Commission on Automation; a panel of twelve business and financial leaders appointed by Governor Nelson Rockefeller of New York; the President's Commission on Civil Disorders; more than twelve hundred economists from one hundred fifty colleges and universities; the United States Conference of Mayors; the President's Commission on Income Maintenance; the AFL-CIO; Americans for Democratic Action; The National Council of Churches; and the Governors' Conference. Between 1968 and 1972 the Office of Economic Opportunity quietly conducted a test of the idea with seven hundred families in five communities in New Jersey and Pennsylvania. The results showed that nearly all of the families with guaranteed incomes worked at least as hard to add to their incomes as other families.

In 1969, in a special poverty message, President Nixon asked Congress to adopt a guaranteed income plan. "Nowhere," he said, had "the failure of government been more tragically apparent than in its efforts to help the poor." Despite the system's soaring costs, he said, it had failed to meet even elementary needs. It was grossly unequal, and it lured people from the countryside into overcrowded ghettos. "Any system," he said, "which makes it more profitable for a man not to work than to work, and which encourages a man to desert his family rather than stay with his family, is wrong and indefensible." He later described the existing welfare system as "a monstrous, consuming outrage—an outrage against the community, against the taxpayer, and particularly against the children it is supposed to help."

President Nixon proposed to replace the Aid to Dependent Children program with direct federal payments of $1,600 annually for a family of four. States could add more if they chose. If a member of the family found a job, he could earn up to $60 a month without any deduction of the federal payment and lose only $1 for every $2 earned above that amount. This program would substantially raise the average income of poverty families in poorer states. It would also reduce the welfare costs of wealthy states. The president estimated that initially it would raise total national welfare costs by $4 billion per year and in the long run would prove less costly than the existing programs it would replace.

Everyone receiving payments, except mothers of preschool children, would be required to work, or to take work training.

The president's proposal was favorably received. Liberals who regarded the payments as too low succeeded in getting a pledge to continue the food stamp program, which would have the effect of raising the income of a family of four from $1,600 to $2,400. Others regretted that it did not apply to unmarried persons or childless couples, but a public opinion poll showed two to one popular approval of the plan. Nevertheless, it encountered heavy opposition in Congress. The U.S. Chamber of Commerce lobbied against it on the grounds that it would increase the number of people receiving welfare. The National Welfare Rights Organization objected to its tightening of eligibility rules, and possible discrimination in favor of the working poor. Of course, it would reduce the need for welfare workers. The plan passed the House of Representatives, but stalled in the Senate.

In 1969 the rules in federal-state welfare programs were changed to reduce the penalties on taking a job. No deduction of welfare payment was made for the first $30 earned above job expenses. And payments were cut only $2 for every additional $3 earned. Although this was an advance, the deduction still had the same incentive-destroying effect as would a 66.6 percent income tax.

In 1974, a new *Supplementary Security Income* (SSI) replaced existing federal-state programs for needy aged, blind, and disabled who did not qualify for adequate Social Security benefits. Application of federal standards of eligibility doubled the number of persons eligible to 6.2 million. The federal government assumed responsibility for guaranteeing persons in these categories a minimum income from all sources. In 1975 that amounted to $158 for a single person and $237 for a couple. This amount was scheduled to rise automatically at the same rate as inflation. Those with no other income received the full payment; those whose Social Security payments were below the guaranteed amount received enough to raise their income to it. States that had been paying more were required to continue to do so. SSI reduced benefits $1 for each $1 of *unearned* income above $20 per month, but only $.50 for every $1 of *earned* income above $85 per month. In effect it is a guaranteed annual income for citizens over age sixty-five and for the blind and disabled of any age. And the federal money to finance it (approximately $5.1 billion the first year) comes from general federal revenues, most of which is produced by the progressive income tax.

Pressure for reform of other government antipoverty programs remained heavy. Many were convinced that much of the welfare system was illogical. The conviction also grew that poverty was not inevitable, that it was a problem that could be solved, and that the cost of solving it was well within the limits of what America could afford. Therefore, the continuing debate focused largely on the question of which of several possible new approaches to take.

Questions

1. How much poverty exists in America? Give evidence to support your answer.
2. In what ways are the poor exploited?
3. What are the costs of poverty to the nation?
4. What groups are more likely to be poor?
5. In what way is the problem of unemployment more serious today than it was in early America?
6. What are the causes of mass unemployment?
7. How did traditional attitudes regarding unemployment delay efforts to help the unemployed?
8. To what extent do the following features of the Social Security system meet the problems of the poor?
   a. Old age pensions
   b. Unemployment compensation
   c. The means of financing Social Security
9. List the criticisms that were made of the Aid to Families with Dependent Children program.
10. Describe the food stamp program.
11. How effective were the War on Poverty programs? Why?
12. In what ways is our welfare system inadequate?
13. List proposed changes in the welfare system and the advantages claimed for each.
14. Describe the guaranteed annual income proposal. Who supported it? Give arguments for and against it.

15. Describe the welfare changes of 1969 and 1974. What recommendations by reformers did they adopt?
16. Give your own ideas on the best way to solve the problem of poverty. Support your opinions with data.
17. Define: "invisible poor," poverty line, effective demand, family allowance, guaranteed annual income, SSI.

Suggested Reading

Aaron, Henry J. *Why is Welfare so Hard to Reform?* Washington, D.C.: Brookings Institution, 1973.
An examination of recent efforts to reform America's welfare system. Discusses how the incentive to work can be maintained.

Citizens' Board of Inquiry into Hunger and Malnutrition in the United States. *Hunger, U.S.A.* Washington, D.C.: Brookings Institution, 1968.
Shows that the popular assumption that something is being done to help the poor is often wrong. Reports that poverty programs often are not carried out due to negligence, indifference, and ignorance. Concludes that an alarming amount of malnutrition exists.

Goodwin, Leonard. *Do the Poor Want Work?* Washington, D.C.: Brookings Institution, 1972.
Based on a survey of more than four thousand people, compares the attitudes of the poor and nonpoor and rejects the view that the poor refuse work because they are lazy.

Harrington, Michael. *The Other America: Poverty in the United States*. New York: Penguin Books, 1963.
A book that created a sensation when it directed public attention to the amount of poverty that existed in the world's richest country.

Lens, Sidney. *Poverty Yesterday and Today*. New York: Crowell, 1974.
Written for high school and college students. An excellent introduction to the history of poverty and social struggles in America, and the background to our present poverty programs and problems.

Levitan, Sar A. *Programs in Aid of the Poor for the 1970's*. Baltimore, Md.: Johns Hopkins University Press, 1969.

An introductory account of government programs to assist the poor.

Wogaman, Philip. *Guaranteed Annual Income: The Moral Issues.* Nashville, Tenn.: Abington Press, 1969.

In nontechnical language, a professor of Christian social ethics describes various plans and gives arguments for and against them.

7
America and the World Economy

How important are America's economic relations with other parts of the world?
What new problems do we face in international trade?
What factors affect the balance of payments?

"For the past 35 years, the United States has steadfastly pursued a policy of freer world trade. As a nation, we have recognized that American trade policies must advance the national interest—which means they must respond to the whole of our interests, and not be a device to favor the narrow interests."

—President Richard M. Nixon

"Farmers will lose more than they gain if the United States returns to protectionist policies. Not only will our farm products be shut out of foreign markets in retaliation, but farm costs will soar if domestic industry and labor are sheltered from competition."

—Charles B. Schuman, President of the American Farm Bureau Federation

"We are opposed to the unregulated flow of American capital to build foreign plants to compete unfairly against United States wages."

—William Bywater, President of District 3 of the International Union of Electrical, Radio and Machine Workers, 1971

Reasons for International Trade

During some periods of our history we have sought to isolate ourselves from Europe's wars, but we have never tried to isolate ourselves economically. We have always sought to enlarge our international trade. We have even fought wars to protect our ships on the seas and to keep doors open to America's trade. Today America conducts more foreign trade, gives more foreign aid, and makes larger investments abroad than any other country. However, we are encountering troublesome problems in adjusting to changes in international trade, and in bringing our spending abroad and income from abroad into balance.

World trade is conducted on a vast scale and is rapidly growing. In 1977 the nations of the world exchanged goods and services valued at $1.2 trillion, of which America's share was nearly $300 billion. About one-sixth of the world's productions of goods was exported.

Nations trade with each other because it is profitable for them to do so. Because nations vary greatly in climate, soil, natural resources, transportation, and technological development, some of them produce particular crops or goods more efficiently than other nations do. All can raise their standards of living by using their available labor, resources, and capital to produce what they make at lowest cost and trading it for what they can produce only at high cost. Such *geographical specialization* makes possible larger world production.

For example, it is possible to grow bananas in the United States. To do so, however, would necessitate building expensive greenhouses and keeping them heated. Consequently, American-grown bananas would cost more than ten cents each to produce. Honduras, on the other hand, can grow bananas for less than one cent each. However, it would cost Hondurans at least $20,000 each to manufacture automobiles, while the United States can produce them for $3,000 each. Thus a Honduran corporation that needed five automobiles could spend $100,000 to build them in Honduras. Or it could buy 3 million Honduran-grown bananas for $30,000, sell them in the United States for $40,000, buy five Ford automobiles for $20,000, pay $20,000 in two-way shipping charges, and thus save $70,000. In the same way, a U.S. corporation could either grow 1 million bananas at a cost of $100,000 or, for $24,000, it could buy eight U.S. automobiles, sell them to Hondurans for $30,000, buy 1 million bananas for $10,000, pay $20,000 in shipping charges, and thereby get a million bananas for $76,000 less than it would cost to grow them in the United States. In this way geographical specialization and the exchange of goods

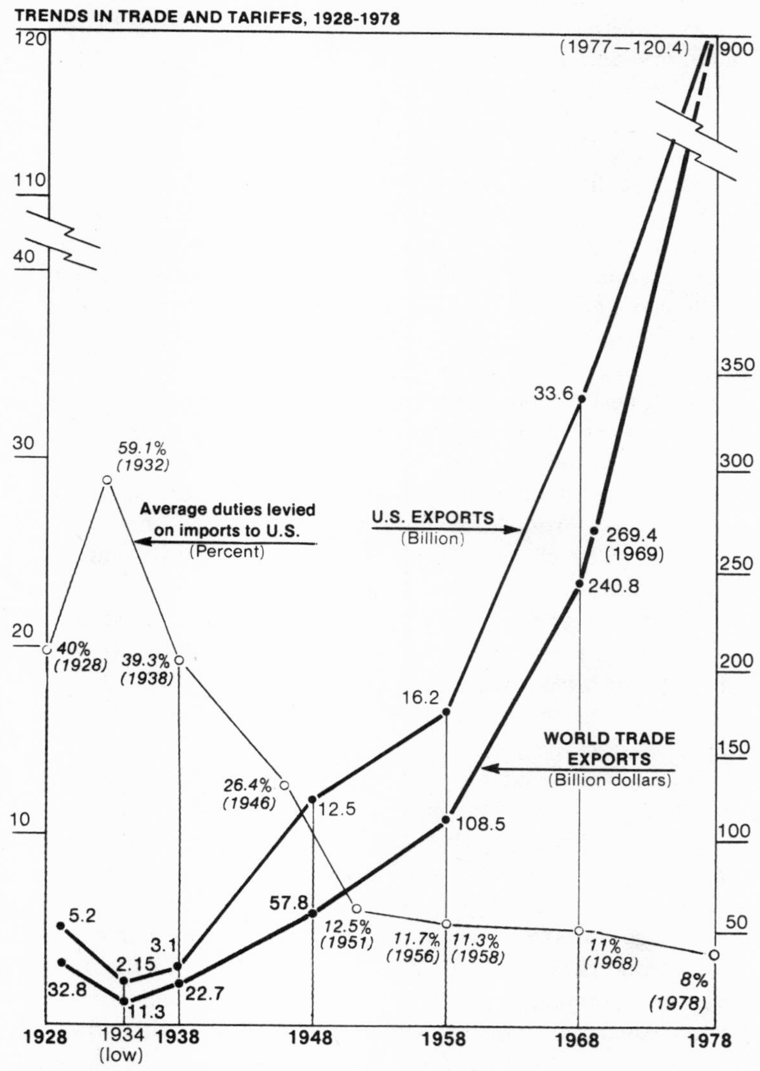

Fig. 7.1. Since 1934 U.S. tariffs have plunged and U.S. exports have soared.

enrich nations. No wonder that wars are fought over international trade opportunities!

In order to reap the profits of increased trade, several groups of nations, the most important of which is the European Economic Community, agreed to abolish all tariffs between them. As they did so their production and standard of living rose.

OBSTACLES TO INTERNATIONAL TRADE

From time to time nations erect barriers to the free flow of trade. Two major types of obstacles are tariffs, or taxes on goods brought into the country, and quotas, or fixed limits on the number of certain goods allowed to enter the country. America originally had a low tariff, later adopted a high tariff, and has in recent years cut tariffs again. But we still maintain many other restrictions on trade. Why?

When America won independence, most Americans were farmers, and we exported farm and forest products in return for manufactured goods, mostly from England. When a long war (1803–1815) between England and France disrupted this trade, we found it necessary to produce manufactured goods in America. Our goods were relatively crude and our new industrialists feared that the end of the war would bring a renewed inflow of high-quality, low-cost British goods and they would lose their customers. To protect our "infant industry" from such competition, Congress doubled the tariff on imported manufactured articles with the intention of raising the price of them above the price of American-made goods.

At first, advocates of a high tariff argued that it was needed only until U.S. industry became sufficiently large and efficient to compete with foreign industry. But, a high tariff enabled manufacturers to charge higher prices and make larger profits and they demanded that it be raised ever higher. Inducing Americans to buy American-made goods, they argued, would help our industry to grow, provide workers with more jobs, and contribute to the nation's wealth and strength. And if not protected by a high tariff, they insisted, American industry could not compete with low-wage foreign industry without cutting American wages to the same low levels.

Denying these arguments, opponents of a protective tariff charged that its chief effect was to enable industry to charge higher prices. They denied that a tariff was necessary to maintain the

American wage level. America's advanced technology, they said, enabled American workers to produce at lower cost than foreign workers. Also, foreign wages rose much more rapidly than American wages, and by 1980 the wages in several countries were higher than in America.

Also, these economists said that high tariffs injured exporting industries. A tariff on steel, for example, raised the cost of steel to American manufacturers, a handicap in competing with foreign automobile manufacturers. If we did not buy goods from other countries, they asked, how could foreigners earn the dollars with which to buy our products? In the 1960s when imports were setting new highs, America achieved almost full employment.

Also, high tariffs caused America to use its capital, resources, and labor inefficiently. If we gave up inefficiently producing bananas at high cost, for example, and put our resources into producing automobiles, airplanes and computers, we could become much richer. By reducing international trade, they said, high tariffs denied America the benefits of geographical specialization.

The arguments of both high and low tariff advocates have some validity. Imports do hurt some American industries. Importing Belgian glass, for example, reduces the sales of West Virginia's handblown glassware. But, because nations use different kinds of money that are legal only in the country of issue, the dollars received by Belgians must sooner or later be spent in America—perhaps for West Virginia coal. Thus in the long run exports equal imports, and when imports subtract a dollar's worth of sales from one industry they eventually add a dollar's worth of sales to another business. While imports depress some individual industries, they give an equivalent boost to others and, therefore, do not reduce total production or jobs. In 1980, producing goods and services for export provided nine million jobs for American workers.

Freeing the channels of international trade does not necessarily depress wages. For every job that imports cost one industry, they add a job in another industry. As exporting industries pay on the average higher wages than do industries that need protection from foreign competition, this shift of jobs raises average wages. Also, admitting low-cost foreign goods increases the buying power of wages and, hence, real wages.

When the managers of more efficient industries realized that they could sell more of their products abroad if we imported more foreign goods, they called for lower tariffs. American aircraft manufacturers, for example, favored buying Japanese cameras in order to provide the Japanese with the dollars they needed to buy our aircraft.

Beginning in 1934, we negotiated a series of reciprocal trade agreements, lowering our tariffs in exchange for agreements by other nations to cut their tariffs on American goods. In thirty years our tariff level fell from an average of 60 percent to 12 percent. In the same period U.S. exports multiplied more than ten times. More tariff cuts followed. We helped organize the General Agreement on Trade and Tariffs (GATT), which eventually brought seventy nations together to negotiate mutual reductions of trade barriers. The 1967 "Kennedy Round" of GATT agreements slashed the average tariffs of members by one-third and brought America's tariffs down in stages to an average of 8 percent.

However, many nontariff trade barriers remained and, in some instances, were increased. Despite the general advantages of lower tariffs, individuals continued to pressure governments to give them special protection from foreign competition. They demanded that limits, or quotas, be set on the number of competing goods admitted to America. Under their pressure, we imposed quotas or pressured other countries into imposing "voluntary" export quotas

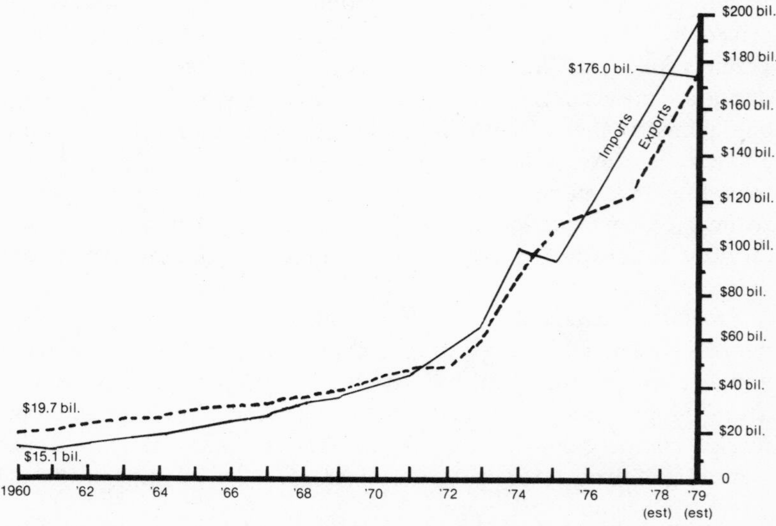

Fig. 7.2. **Exports and Imports of Merchandise, 1960–1979.** (U.S. Bureau of the Census, 1977)

on meat, cotton, oil, steel, textiles, sugar, shoes and other goods. Quotas are more certain in their effects in reducing imports than tariffs. Unlike tariffs, they produce no income for government—all the benefits of the resulting higher prices go to the protected industries. Among other nontariff trade barriers are preferential buying arrangements (for example, a requirement that the U.S. government buy U.S.-made generators unless the price of foreign-made generators is more than 20 percent lower), sanitary, safety, and environmental regulations that unfairly discriminate against foreign products, export subsidies, border taxes, and subsidies for domestic producers.

Actually, foreigners had more trouble competing with us than we had competing with them. For many years after World War II our high technology and efficient large-scale production enabled us to undersell most competitors. We consistently exported more goods than we imported—a difference that totalled $90 billion by 1972. For example, in 1966 we sold $29.5 billion in goods abroad, while importing only $25.6 billion. What explains this exception to the rule that exports equal imports? During this period it was not always necessary for foreigners to sell their goods in America in order to acquire the dollars with which to buy American goods—we gave them many billions of dollars in foreign aid.

However, America's surplus of exports over imports dropped irregularly from $4 billion in 1967 and became a $2 billion deficit in 1971. Contributing to this change were reductions in our foreign aid and high inflation in America which raised the cost of American goods to foreigners. A trade surplus reappeared in 1973 and 1975, but in 1979 we imported nearly $30 billion more than we exported. The deficit, however, mostly represented rising imports of oil; in 1979, our oil imports alone cost us $60 billion. Our exports of farm and manufactured goods exceeded our imports by $30 billion. Nevertheless, the disappearance of our export surplus raised new demands for protection against imports.

In addition to economic reasons, nations impose restrictions on international trade for purposes of defense. Each nation seeks to become as self-sufficient as possible to guard against the possibility of its losing a war because of the lack of vital goods and war materials. Therefore, they levy high tariffs to protect the industries that they consider to be essential to fighting a war. For example, America restricted imports of natural rubber in order to maintain the sales of higher priced synthetic rubber and thereby guarantee a supply of rubber in the event of war. Until they find a way of removing the threat of war as the dominant factor in national decisions, nations will not enjoy the full economic advantages of geographical specialization.

Most discussions of foreign trade treat it from the vantage point of the producer. American manufacturers look upon foreign trade chiefly as a means of increasing their sales, a point of view that is shared by the workers and union leaders in their plants. They seek to export as many of their products as possible and to restrict the importation of competing goods. Sometimes their discussions leave the impression that the ideal policy would be to multiply exports and to import nothing. Of course this would be impossible even if it were desirable. Foreigners would soon be forced to stop buying from America if they could not sell us their products.

All Americans are consumers and benefit from the wider choice of goods at low prices that imports provide. Shipping American goods abroad and refusing to allow foreigners to ship goods into America would, of course, reduce the number of goods available to American consumers. Other things being equal, consumers benefit if we import more and export less. Also, competition between producers, including American and foreign producers, helps to keep prices low and quality high.

CURRENT TRENDS IN AMERICA'S FOREIGN TRADE

In recent years America's foreign trade has shown a remarkable rise. Between 1960 and 1979 our combined imports and exports soared from $35 billion to $574 billion annually. By 1980 one-third of our farm acres and 9 percent of our industrial workers were producing for export.

America's foreign trade is larger than that of any other country. It supplies nearly one-fifth of the basic raw materials used by our industries. We import all gem stones, industrial diamonds, natural rubber; at least 97 percent of manganese, aluminum ore, and cobalt; at least 85 percent of tin, asbestos, chromium; more than half of zinc and nearly half of oil. Tropical areas supply coffee, tea, cocoa, bananas, and sugar. Most of these raw materials and tropical foods are produced by underdeveloped countries in exchange for manufactured goods. Two-thirds of our foreign purchases are raw materials.

America's exports also include large quantities of food and raw materials. We export the products of approximately one-third of our cultivated land. More than half of our wheat and soybeans, and a third of our cotton, rice, corn, and tobacco is sold abroad.

A growing share of America's foreign trade involves manufactured goods. In 1975, 80 percent of our shipments abroad were manufactured goods, and we exported 14 percent of the goods we manufactured.

Most of our trade is with the highly developed nations of Canada, Japan, Great Britain, and the Netherlands, and about 35 percent of our exports goes to developing countries. In 1977 our leading trading partners, in descending order, were Canada ($55.1 billion), EEC ($48.6 billion), Japan (29.1 billion), Saudi Arabia, Mexico, Venezuela, Nigeria, Brazil, and Iran. Exports to Asia, which took more than 25 percent of our exports, were rising more rapidly than to any other area.

Trade between the United States and communist countries developed slowly. Excepting Poland and Yugoslavia, America charged a higher tariff on imports from communist countries and refused to sell them some goods or to extend credit to them. However, the trade of our allies with the communist bloc nearly tripled between 1970 and 1976 to $55 billion. In 1972 we relaxed some restrictions, particularly on China, and made credit available to Russia. China bought jet airliners and Russia bought enormous quantities of wheat. In 1973 President Nixon proposed "most favored nation" status for Russia to put trade with her on the same basis as trade with noncommunist nations. But when Congress amended the treaty to make it conditional on a liberalization of Russia's emigration policy, Russia rejected the treaty. In 1977 the United States exported $2.7 billion in goods, mostly machinery and equipment, to communist countries and imported from them $1.1 billion in goods, mostly raw materials.

America's exports to the European Economic Community (EEC) exceeded our imports from the EEC by $4.4 billion in 1977, and our excess of exports over imports in trade with communist countries was $1.6 billion. This $6 billion surplus of exports largely offset the $8.1 billion excess of imports in our trade with Japan. The larger imbalance in our trade with oil-producing countries caused most of our trade deficit that year.

Major American concerns in the late 1970s were how to persuade the Japanese to remove more nontariff barriers to the sale

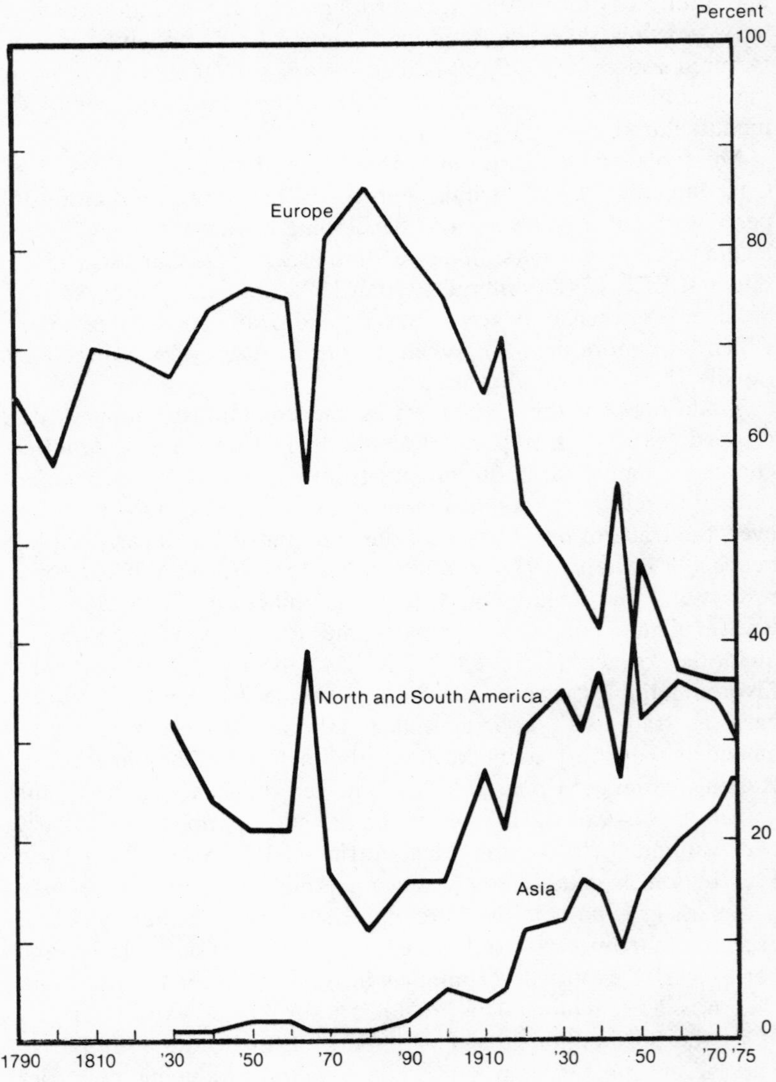

Fig. 7.3. **Destination of U.S. Exports: Percent of Total Goods.** Sales to Asia rose much more rapidly than sales to Europe. (U.S. Bureau of the Census, 1977)

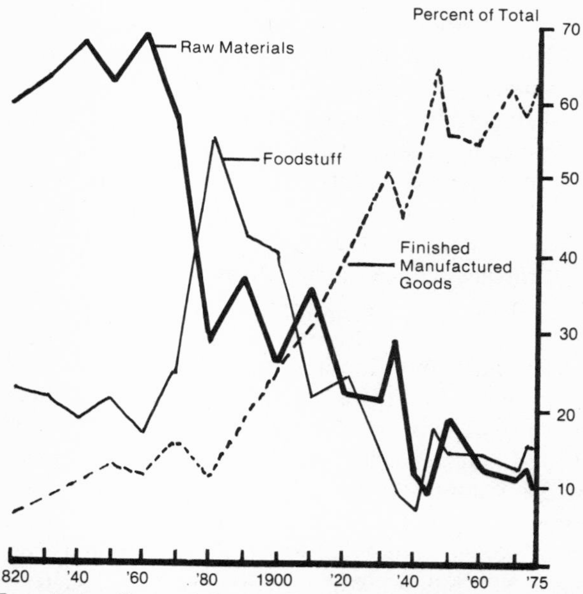

Fig. 7.4. **Exports by Class of Goods, Based on Dollar Value.** Early America's principal export was raw materials, which yielded first place to foodstuffs in the latter part of the nineteenth century. Today, America's chief export is finished manufactured goods. (U.S. Bureau of the Census, 1977)

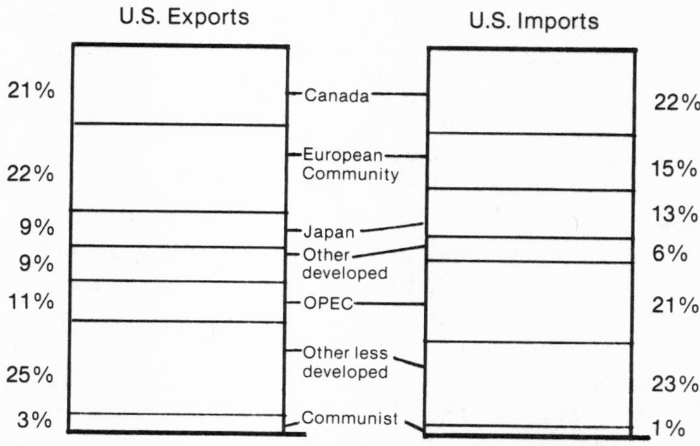

Fig. 7.5. **U.S. Trading Partners, 1976.** (Council on International Economic Policy, 1977)

of American goods in Japan, and how to reduce imports of oil, increase exports to oil-producing nations, or otherwise offset the high cost of oil imports.

In 1972 trading nations began a new effort to reduce "tariffs, nontariff barriers, and other measures which impede or distort international trade." In the Trade Act of 1974 Congress authorized the president to negotiate international agreements to make further large cuts in America's tariffs, and to reduce nontariff trade barriers. International negotiations for that purpose, involving nearly one hundred nations, produced an agreement in 1979, the "Tokyo round," to further reduce barriers to world trade.

AMERICA'S FOREIGN INVESTMENTS

Americans have more money invested abroad than the people of any other country. This is a relatively recent historical development. In our early history, Europeans invested large sums in U.S. railroads and industry which gave them ownership of much of our economy. Not until World War II did America's foreign investments become larger. In 1976 total foreign-owned business investments in America (not counting U.S. government bonds) were estimated at $85 billion, while American-owned assets and investments abroad totalled $182 billion.

The nature of American foreign investments has undergone gradual changes. At first American businessmen were mainly interested in extracting natural resources in underdeveloped nations. Americans bought mineral rights to vast acreages of land, drilled oil wells, and opened tin and copper mines. Later, they built railroads and established banks and agricultural plantations. In more recent years American corporations have bought and built factories abroad. Sometimes they were attracted by the availability there of important raw materials. Sometimes the attraction was low-cost labor—American laws allow citizens to import tax free any goods they manufacture abroad with American raw materials. Another important motive, particularly for building factories in Europe, was that it allowed them to sell their products tariff-free inside the expanding EEC.

The investment of American money in foreign industry was both criticized and praised. The advantages of getting raw materials from abroad, particularly those not produced in America, were indisputable. Labor unions, however, objected to the practice of building factories overseas, particularly when the products of those

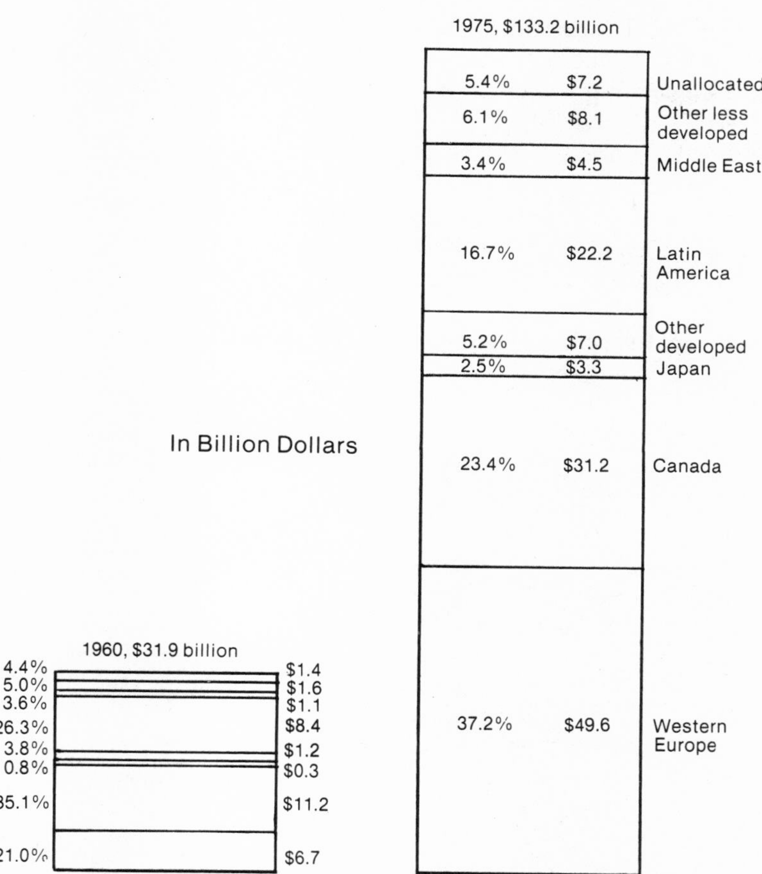

Fig. 7.6. **U.S. Cumulative Direct Investment Abroad in Billions of U.S. Dollars.** The most rapid rise has been in investments in Western Europe. (Council on International Economic Policy, 1977)

factories were brought back to be sold in America. Labor called this "exporting jobs." Others charged that these factories added to the productive capacity of other countries and strengthened their ability to wage war. In reply, defenders of foreign investments pointed out that 90 percent of the goods that American corporations produced abroad were sold abroad. Furthermore, they said, businessmen invested abroad only when they were confident they would earn profits and bring back more money than they exported.

By 1980 income from foreign investments was $16 billion annually.

Our foreign investments were of two general types. "Direct investments" included building or buying factories or buying enough of the stock of a foreign corporation to gain control of it. "Indirect investments" were those that did not give Americans control of foreign enterprises—such as the purchase of less than 10 percent of the stock of foreign corporations. In 1979 $168 billion of our foreign investments were direct investments, as compared to $40 billion of direct investments by foreigners in the United States. Nearly half our direct investment was in manufacturing; another large share was in petroleum. We had $61 billion in direct investments in Europe, $35 billion in Canada, and $41 billion in developing countries.

Direct foreign investments often produced political complications. When Americans invested large sums in other countries, particularly small underdeveloped countries, they thereby acquired potential political influence. Many Americans were pleased by this expansion of American power, but patriots of other lands who wanted freedom from foreign control often resented it. Denouncing our growing role in their societies as "economic imperialism," they demanded that their governments expropriate (seize with compensation) American-owned properties. When our investments were thus endangered, American corporations called on the United States government for help, and often charged that the threatening nationalists were Communists. Sometimes this drew America into quarrels with nationalistic movements she might otherwise have favored and gave her enemies an opportunity to form alliances with them against her. Such quarrels could ultimately cost the U.S. far more than the value of the endangered properties. The Japanese government considered this kind of complication so undesirable that it notified Japanese corporations they could look for protection of their foreign investments only in the courts of the countries in which they invested.

THE ECONOMIC CONSEQUENCES OF FOREIGN AID

America has extended large-scale foreign aid for a generation. The Marshall Plan, inaugurated in 1947, was a program to help war-torn Europe recover economically so it could play a more effective role in stopping communist expansion. It was outstandingly successful and Europe quickly recovered its economic health. For similar reasons we gave aid to nations in Asia, particularly those around the borders of Russia and China, and in Latin America and Africa. By lifting them out of poverty and helping them strengthen their armed forces, we sought to strengthen their resistance to communism.

By 1977 we had provided a total of $221 billion—$145 billion in economic and $76 billion in military aid. Much of the economic aid was really disguised military aid. East Asia received more than any other geographic area—$67 billion. Europe was second with $58 billion, followed by the Middle East and South Asia $42 billion, Latin America $24 billion, and Africa $8 billion. Most aid was a gift, but more than $75 billion of it was in the form of loans that must be repaid with interest. Economic aid was administered by the Agency for International Development (AID), a division of the Department of State.

The individual countries that received the larger amounts were South Vietnam, $24 billion (exclusive of the expenses incurred by the United States in the fighting there); South Korea, $14 billion; Britain, $10 billion; India, $10 billion; France, $10 billion; Israel, $9 billion; Taiwan, $8 billion; Turkey, $8 billion; Italy, $7 billion; Jordan, $6 billion; and Pakistan, $6 billion.

Foreign aid originated largely for the purpose of stopping communism, but it was supported by many Americans for other reasons. Humanitarians were pleased to share some of America's great wealth with poverty-stricken peoples. Some leaders were alarmed by the growing gap between living standards in developed and underdeveloped countries—UN Secretary General U Thant called it the "most explosive issue" of our time. Because nearly 90 percent of foreign aid consisted of American goods transported in American ships U.S. manufacturers, farmers, and shippers favored it as a means of increasing their sales and profits. By introducing American goods to foreigners it opened markets for future sales. To labor unions all of this promised more jobs.

Foreign aid was less costly to America than was popularly supposed. As stated, much of it was in loans that must be repaid. Ninety percent of it was in American goods. Much of it was surplus military equipment or farm products, and most of it was hauled in American ships. Only a small part of it represented an expenditure of gold or foreign money. And it helped make possible America's pre-1971 surplus of exports over imports.

The impact abroad of American aid was not all that had been hoped. It was outstandingly successful in helping Europe to recover, but it was less effective, with some exceptions, in raising production in underdeveloped countries. Sometimes the gift of complicated military equipment to such countries burdened them with heavy maintenance expenses. Sometimes aid seemed more effective in raising the income and power of ruling oligarchs than in improving the lot of the common man. Nor was aid as effective as hoped in winning friends. Furthermore, our experience of being drawn step by step from aid into war in Vietnam caused many to fear that aid might draw the United States into other unwanted wars. The advent of a balance of payments deficit and the loss of gold reserves seemed to make a reduction of aid necessary. Consequently U.S. economic aid dropped from 1 percent of America's GNP in the 1950s to only 0.2 percent in 1977. This was a smaller percentage of GNP than was given in foreign aid by Sweden, the Netherlands, France, Canada, West Germany, and the Soviet Union.

BALANCE OF PAYMENT PROBLEMS

A problem of rising concern to Americans in the 1970s was the persistent deficit in America's international balance of payments. We were spending, lending, giving, and investing more money abroad than we were earning from trade, services, and returns on investments. The result was the decline of U.S. reserves of foreign exchange (foreign money) and gold.

This was a sharp turnabout in America's international financial position. During World War II America's GNP almost doubled while the economy of much of Europe and Asia was terribly damaged. In the postwar period America was almost the only source of the goods that other nations desperately needed and, as they bought enormous quantities of food, raw materials, and war supplies, we accumulated vast reserves of foreign exchange and more than half of the world's gold supply. For years after the war Europeans and Asians continued to buy more from America than they sold to her, giving the United States a surplus of exports above imports of several billion dollars per year. The dollar was the most highly valued of world currencies and the standard by which other currencies and values were measured.

Consequently, many Americans were shocked in 1971 when they discovered how near we had come to international insolvency. Our formerly large reserves of gold and foreign exchange had fallen far—we still had nearly $10 billion in gold, but foreigners held $80 billion in U.S. currency for which we were obligated to exchange gold on request. If all foreign-held dollars were turned in for gold simultaneously we could redeem only one-eighth of them.

How had the United States gotten into this predicament? Basically, it was because over a long period of time we had spent more than we had earned. The excess of our exports over our imports was large, but not large enough to give us sufficient gold and foreign exchange to pay the total costs of our foreign aid, foreign spending by tourists, military forces abroad, and the Korean and Vietnam wars. In 1971, for the first time in seventy-seven years, the value of U.S. exports fell below imports. The gap between our international spending and income widened.

Interestingly, most of the dollars abroad were held by our defeated World War II enemies, Germany and Japan. Not burdened by the expense of maintaining large military forces, both had developed large and efficient industries, and both were rapidly expanding their exports. Their monetary reserves rose as ours dwindled.

In efforts to balance the books, America reduced foreign aid, put restrictions on new investments abroad, and withdrew troops from Vietnam. We demanded that other countries import more American goods. We stopped exchanging gold for foreign-held dollars. But the deficit in our balance of payments continued to grow.

In 1971 we concluded that these circumstances made it necessary to devalue the American dollar, to admit that it was no longer worth as much. By agreement with other countries, we reduced its value relative to other currencies more than 20 percent by 1973. This cut the price foreigners had to pay for American goods, and raised the price Americans had to pay for foreign goods. This was intended to increase exports and discourage imports. It also made foreign travel more expensive for Americans and travel in America cheaper for foreigners.

Unfortunately, some of the effects partly offset the ones desired. By cutting the cost of American raw materials to competing industrial countries like Japan, devaluation cut their manufacturing costs. At the same time it forced American industry to pay more for imported raw materials and raised the cost of U.S. manufactured goods.

Also, devaluation brought some unpleasant shocks to American consumers. The price of many imports—Volkswagens, cameras, shoes—sharply advanced. As devaluation cut the price of American goods to foreigners, they bought more of them and that raised their prices. In 1972 and 1973 foreign purchases of wheat, soybeans, and feed grains raised prices American housewives paid for bread and meat, and similar upsurges of foreign buying raised prices of lumber and scrap iron. Urging foreigners to buy less lumber, President Nixon put temporary export quotas on soybeans and feed grains. Thus devaluation adversely affected the American standard of living.

Furthermore, the fall in the dollar's value made foreign aid more expensive and raised the cost of maintaining American troops abroad and fighting foreign wars. In short, devaluation made it more difficult for America to play as large a role as before in world affairs. It indicated that a part of our great strength had been spent.

THE BREAKDOWN OF THE BRETTON WOODS SYSTEM

In 1971 at the same time that we devalued the dollar, we announced that we would no longer redeem foreign-held dollars in gold. This "closing of the gold window" changed the system of international exchange that had prevailed since World War II.

The period before World War II had been one of extreme uncertainty in international finance and trade. The value of the money used by one nation had no fixed relationship to the value of the money used by others, but constantly fluctuated. As a result it was impossible to predict their relative values very far in advance. This handicapped long-range business planning that involved international trade. The world depression after 1929 brought a period of intensified economic warfare in which nations, fiercely competing for dwindling markets, manipulated the value of their currencies in order to gain temporary advantage, heedless of the effect on other nations or on world trade. Their general approach seemed to be "beggar thy neighbor." World trade dropped.

During World War II leaders of the allied nations decided to create a system of fixed exchange rates to stabilize the value of each nation's currency in relation to other currencies. They agreed to maintain the value of the dollar at $35 per ounce and to fix the value of other currencies in terms of dollars. Each country promised to maintain a large reserve of gold and dollars to prevent its currency from changing in value. For example, by making a standing offer to exchange dollars for francs, or to exchange francs for dollars at the fixed rate, France could prevent the value of the franc from changing. In turn, America committed herself, on request, to exchange gold for dollars at the rate of $35 per ounce. They formalized these plans at the Bretton Woods Conference in 1944 and established an International Monetary Fund to help implement them.

Under this system the dollar was as "good as gold." Because the world's supply of gold is limited, governments increasingly added dollars to their reserves. Private businessmen also used dollars to buy goods from other countries. Thus the dollar became an international money.

Dollars became available to foreign users through U.S. government spending on foreign aid, military bases, and supplies for the Korean and Vietnam wars and by private spending on imports, foreign travel and business properties. At the same time, a smaller number of dollars was brought back to America through the sale of American goods abroad and the exchange of gold for dollars. As long as America had a large supply of gold, Europeans did not worry about having so much of their wealth in the form of dollars.

However, developments in the early 1970s shook confidence in the dollar's value. America's overseas spending soared so much during the Vietnam war that it opened a wide gap between the amount of the dollars spent abroad and the dollars we earned abroad. And in 1971 America's exports of goods fell below our imports of goods. Consequently, the amount of dollars abroad soared and foreigners exchanged more of them for America's gold. Our gold reserves fell.

Exhaustion of our remaining gold reserves was regarded as unacceptable, and to avoid it President Nixon announced in 1971 that we would no longer exchange gold for dollars. This of course knocked the prop from under the prevailing system of international exchange and took the world back to the system that existed before World War II. The value of the dollar in terms of French francs "floated" to be determined by market forces, by whatever purchasers of dollars were willing to pay. Its value might shift from day to day.

Some economists felt that the change to floating exchange rates was not all bad. Fixed rates, they said, failed to allow for changes in different economies and, when long preserved, were apt to give currencies false values. They had caused the dollar to be overvalued, which made it unrealistically cheap for Americans to make foreign purchases and for American tourists to travel abroad. After the dollar was allowed to float, these costs rose, discouraging excessive imports and travel by Americans. The float's disadvantage was the uncertainty it added to long-term business planning. Some economists suggested combining features of both systems—setting official exchange rates but allowing the exchange rate of currencies to float a maximum of 1 or 2 percent up or down per year.

THE OIL CRISIS

The devaluation of the dollar and the closing of the gold window eased America's problems with the balance of trade and payments. The merchandise trade balance, a $6.4 billion deficit in 1972, showed a surplus of $1.7 billion in 1973, while the balance of payments (current accounts and long-term capital) moved from a deficit of $9.8 billion to a surplus of $1.2 billion. But the improvement was temporary. In 1973 the oil-producing countries quadrupled the price of oil. America was importing 34 percent of her oil requirements, and our bill for imported oil soared from $9 billion in 1973 to $23 billion in 1974 and caused a trade deficit of $9.5 billion. In 1975 we restored a $11.5 billion trade surplus, but moved into a $30 billion deficit in 1979 when our oil bill was $60 billion.

GROWING INTERDEPENDENCE

Important as foreign trade is to America, it involves only about 9 percent of our GNP. Thus, changes in foreign trade cannot have as much impact on America's general economic health as what happens in the other 91 percent of the economy. The principal problems affecting the rate of economic growth remain internal ones and solving them would help to reduce the severity of problems in our international trade.

Nevertheless, the long-term trend is for foreign trade to become more important. By 1985, it is expected, we will need to import an estimated half of the oil we use, 55 percent of the iron, 62 percent of the lead, and 72 percent of the zinc. Growing dependence on imports creates a corresponding need to increase exports.

These developments demonstrate the extent to which the different parts of the world have become interdependent. Progressively, nations are losing independent control of their own economies. A striking evidence of the extent of their interdependence is the trend of the economies of the world to keep in step through the phase of economic cycles. The boom of 1973 was a worldwide boom, and the recession of 1974–75 was a worldwide recession. By 1977 the European nations and Japan were urging the United States to take strong anti-inflation measures, and the United States was urging Japan and Germany to take measures to stimulate their growth rates to help the world back to prosperity. Economically we were obviously becoming "one world."

Questions

1. Why is it profitable for nations to engage in international trade?
2. List three types of restrictions that nations placed on foreign trade.
3. How does raising tariffs reduce exports?
4. How can America's high-wage labor produce goods at lower cost than low-wage foreign labor?
5. Can imports reduce the general level of American production? Why or why not?
6. Why did America's export surplus decline?
7. Why do American corporations build factories in other countries? What criticisms have been made of this practice? What has been said in its defense?
8. How can foreign investments embroil America in quarrels?
9. What were our principal reasons for giving foreign aid?
10. Why did we reduce foreign aid?
11. What caused the decline of America's gold reserves?
12. How did the deficit in our balance of payments affect our domestic economy? What changes in our economy could improve our balance of payments?
13. What caused the devaluation of the American dollar? What effect did devaluation have on our foreign trade? On American consumers?
14. How was the international monetary system changed by America's decision to stop redeeming dollars in gold? What were the negative and positive results?
15. How is America becoming less independent economically?
16. Define or identify: geographical specialization, tariff quota, reciprocal trade agreement, GATT, balance of payments.

Suggested Reading

Douglas, Paul H. *America in the Market Place: Trade, Tariffs, and the Balance of Payments.* New York: Holt, Rinehart & Winston, 1966.

A distinguished economist and former U.S. senator discusses the development of trade and tariffs, and the problems of trade with communist and underdeveloped countries.

Pen, Jan. *A Primer on International Trade.* New York: Random House, 1967.

A short and clear explanation of the basic principles of international trade and of the terms such as "balance of payments" that are used in discussing it.

Steinberg, David J. *The U.S.A. in the World Economy.* Published for the Council for Advancement of Secondary Education. New York: McGraw-Hill, 1966.

An examination by a leading economist of America's international trade, foreign investments, foreign aid, and balance of payments problems. Written for high school students.

United States Department of State. *Liberal Trade v. Protectionism: Issues in U.S. Foreign Policy,* No. 6. Washington, D.C.: U.S. Government Printing Office, 1971.

An excellent, well-illustrated description of our foreign trade and balance of payments problems and the arguments for and against lowering trade barriers.

Weil, Gordon L. *Trade Policies in the '70's.* New York: Twentieth Century Fund, 1969.

Zupnick, Elliot. *Understanding the International Monetary System. Headline Series.* New York: Foreign Policy Association, 1967.

An attempt to provide a simplified explanation of a necessarily complex subject.

Part 2
Political Problems

8
Government

What is government and how did it originate?
What functions does government perform?
What questions concerning the proper role and functions of government are being debated?

"Society in every state is a blessing, but government, even in its best state, is but a necessary evil; in its worst state, an intolerable one."

—Thomas Paine

". . . to secure these rights, governments are instituted among men, deriving their just powers from the consent of the governed. . . ."

—Declaration of Independence

"The object of government is the welfare of the people."
—Theodore Roosevelt

The Origins of Government

"If men were angels," said James Madison, "there would be no need for government." Because men are not angels, they find it impossible to live and work cooperatively in close proximity to each other without mutual controls on their conduct. Life in groups requires regulations on the behavior of individuals; they are necessary and unavoidable. Consequently, government is a basic institution and is found in all organized groups, even in the simplest cultures.

Government means formal social controls. It is the complex of political institutions, laws, and customs through which the group holds in check, controls, directs, and compels the behavior of its members. It is the process of settling conflicts within the group, making decisions on actions to be taken by the group, and coercing individuals to conduct themselves in conformity to the group's mores.

Even a small primitive family required social controls. We can imagine, for example, a cave-dwelling family consisting of a father (Dad), mother (Mom), fifteen-year-old son (Jerk), ten-year-old daughter (Ninny), and one-year-old baby (It). Dad, who has returned from the hunt, naps in the nook of the cave that is freest of drafts and smoke. Mom is working hard with a stone knife to remove the hide from a small deer that Dad brought in, while the others are waiting impatiently for dinner. Firewood is almost gone, and she asks Jerk to go outside and gather more. He pretends not to hear, and she gets rather loud. This awakens Dad, who growls and motions with his hand. Jerk goes out.

It's attention is attracted by a crackling twig, and he totters closer to the fire. Mom tells Ninny to stop him, and Ninny pulls him back despite his loud protests.

By the time that Jerk returns, the deer has been cut up. He grabs the nearest long pointed stick to roast a piece of it in the fire. Ninny wails and grabs for the stick until Mom hands Jerk another one.

Later, with the coming of spring, the family will leave the cave for a higher area where more animals, fish, and berries can be found. With some reminders from Mom, Dad will decide when to make the move and he will lead them to a small high meadow where they will build a hut.

In this example, the behavior of each member of the group was regulated in some way by the others. The baby was roughly denied the right to fall into the fire. Jerk was intimidated into going out for wood and manipulated into respecting Ninny's prior right to a cooking stick. Ninny was ordered to police It. Mom performs the hard labor expected of her. Dad allows Mom to manage things and exercises his authority only when it seems to be necessary, and Mom lets him know when that moment arrives. He makes the decisions on when to move, but under the urgings of other members of the group.

A status ranking, or pecking order, is evident. Only It controlled no one. Ninny controlled It but not Jerk. Mom was obeyed by Ninny, but needed assistance to control Jerk. All obeyed Dad when he exerted himself.

What gave some the power to command others? One factor was size—the larger usually commanded. However, Jerk obeyed Dad, whose size and strength may not have been greater. He obeyed because he was accustomed to obeying him. He did not challenge Dad's right to give orders, but accepted his authority to do so. He may have recognized that the survival of the group made it necessary for someone to get wood and for someone to decide which one would be given that task. He may have been influenced by a feeling of affection.

If Dad is not too abusive of Jerk, and enough food can be found, someday Jerk may bring a girl he has found, or who has found him, to the cave. Thus, the simple primary family begins transformation into an enlarged family. Eventually, if the food supply permits a larger concentration of population, it may come to consist of grandparents, parents, children, sons-in-law, daughters-in-law, aunts, and cousins, and thus become a *clan*.

With this growth in the size of the group the problems of social control become more complex. Each father may occupy the top position of authority in his immediate family, but who settles disputes and makes decisions for the whole clan? Dad may hold this authority until he becomes old and feeble. Then he may prefer to stay home and let Jerk lead the hunt. Jerk may then assume the role of the highest authority. Thus, the clan is apt to be headed by a clan leader or chief, and the new chief is likely to be the son of the old one. This kind of government will later develop into monarchy.

By this stage most of the functions of government are present, at least in embryo. There is a recognized organization—a system of status and roles. Group decisions are made, internal order is preserved, and the group presents a united front to outsiders.

The gathering of people into larger groups brings many advantages. It helps satisfy their need for companionship. It helps sons and daughters find mates. It helps them hunt more effectively, particularly for larger animals that have to be cornered or caught in pits. It enables them to build bigger and better shelters. It permits a division of labor with consequent increases in the goods and services available to the group. And, of course, it brings more security. The larger the group the better the protection against outside enemies.

The evidence seems to indicate that elaborate and complex cultures first appeared, not where life was easy, but on flood plains where large-scale group cooperation in building dikes and irrigation ditches was essential to survival.

THE DEVELOPMENT OF GOVERNMENT

Improvements in governmental procedures made it possible for larger numbers to live together. Strangers could gain admittance into the clan by marrying a member or being adopted. It was much more difficult to work out means of enabling different clans to coexist in peace and cooperation, but the incentive to do so was enormous. The elimination of conflict and the growth of cooperation often resulted in dramatic improvement of material well-being and fighting power. When Genghis Khan succeeded in uniting the hostile tribes of Mongols, he made them a great world power, and when Mohammed united the desert tribes of Arabs he made them masters of the Middle East, North Africa, and part of Europe.

The growth of man's ability to live successfully together in larger groups developed along two lines: ethical advance and social engineering.

Agreement on certain mores was essential to group living. Life in groups was impossible unless its members considered killing other members to be wrong. Until this principle became part of their mores, cooperation was limited and guarded. It was also helpful for members to refrain from grabbing food and tools from each other, and to respect exclusive rights to mates. At first, the mores required this behavior only towards members of one's own group. A big advance came when the application of these "in group" mores was first extended to people outside of the immediate family—to cousins and uncles and, later, to people not known to be relatives. This usually meant that men had expanded the size of the group which they considered to be their own "in group." They had enlarged the number of people they meant when they said "we." This could be considered an ethical advance.

The other process, social engineering, was the invention of techniques for settling conflicts between men whose ethics were not very advanced. One early technique was "arbitration," submitting the dispute to an impartial third party for settlement. Some methods utilized the selfishness of men to produce a fair settlement. If two hunters had a dispute on how a deer killed jointly was to be divided, one was allowed to cut it in two and the other to choose the side he wanted. This could produce some very exact justice. Later, as a substitute for civil wars, to determine which of two groups should control the government, men learned to hold elections.

Political advance and economic advance were closely interrelated. Only if the food supply was sufficient could groups larger than primary families live in one place. In turn, larger groups could employ better methods of hunting, provide better care of domesticated animals, better protect crops, and build better dams and irrigation ditches.

Ending hostilities between two or more different clans and bringing them into a cooperative relationship was difficult. Even when it was accomplished by a large clan's conquest of a small one, the problems of adjusting relationships remained. It might seem to be almost automatic for the father of a family or the patriarch of a clan to head the government of one clan, but who was to be the highest authority in a group of clans called a *tribe*? Several different procedures might suggest themselves. If the chief of the strongest clan sought to monopolize the power then the other clans might revolt. The heads of clans could meet in a tribal council and discuss matters until they reached agreements. However, this method was too slow and uncertain to work during a war. Consequently, the power to command was given for the duration of a war to one man, a war chief.

Some war chiefs enjoyed their power and, after a victorious war, succeeded in keeping it by overthrowing or overawing the council and establishing a dictatorship. Dictatorships sometimes turned into hereditary monarchies. The dictator might want to keep his position in his family and have his son fill it after his death. Many members of the group might agree to such inheritance for several reasons. It would avoid a possibly destructive conflict between rivals for the position, and a hereditary monarch might be more inclined than a temporary dictator to think of all of the people as his own people and work for the good of all.

When two or more tribes were combined, the new group was called a *nation*. Cooperation between members of the nation, and a sense of identity with the nation, could be promoted by maintaining (at least as a polite fiction) that all members were descended from a common ancestor, such as Abraham.

As groups living under a single government grew larger, governments became more elaborate and formal. At first in the small family much of the social control could be exercised informally through signs of approval and disapproval including praise and ridicule. As groups grew larger it became necessary to clarify more specifically the kinds of behavior considered right or wrong for the guidance of members of many families. Such clarification provided some safeguards against arbitrary or capricious punishments.

In early societies it seems that individual members were expected to arrange for their own protection and avenge wrongs committed by others against themselves or their families. A kind of unwritten law gave a family the right to take back stolen property and seek out and kill the murderer of a family member. This often resulted in mistakes and in much feuding and bloodshed. Consequently the right to avenge a wrong was taken from individuals and made the exclusive right of the government. The monopoly on the right to use violence is one of the distinguishing features of modern governments.

In early societies the interrelationship between government and religion was strong. Individuals were more likely to honor the mores of a particular culture if they believed that supernatural forces would reward or punish them accordingly. They were taught that certain acts were offensive to supernatural spirits, were taboo or bad luck, and would bring punishments. If they lived in accord with the mores, however, they would be rewarded. Priests often had political influence and sometimes headed the government.

THE STATE

The development of governmental institutions culminated in the formation of the state, which, in modern times, is usually the nation. The state is the largest and most comprehensive social organization. It is characterized by a definite territory, a large population, a common culture, and a common government which has a monopoly on the use of force within the state's borders and is independent of any higher authority. An American state is not a state in this sense because it is subordinate to the federal government. However, the United States is such a state. In 1980 the world contained approximately one hundred sixty states.

The Functions of Government

In modern societies the governments of states perform many functions that tend to grow more numerous and complex with the passage of time. These functions can be classified as follows: (1) Channeling conflicts between individuals and groups into non-destructive channels. This requires a peaceful means of securing justice, and protection of individual rights and freedoms. (2) Formulating, administering, and interpreting the laws which all members of the society are bound to obey. The power to make and change law carries with it the power to make changes in the society. (3) Protecting the society against internal enemies—criminals of various types. For this purpose police forces, courts, and prisons are maintained. (4) Protecting the state against outside enemies. For this purpose armed forces are maintained. This is the most expensive of government functions. (5) Promoting the general welfare of the group, including economic and social. Through its power to tax, the government compels citizens to contribute a more or less fair share of the costs of these functions.

The Different Kinds of Government

One way of classifying governments is on the basis of how widely government power and decision making are shared. *Autocracy* refers to government by one man. There are several different kinds of autocracies. A monarchy is said to exist when the ruler receives his powers through inheritance and passes them on to his son. If it is not hereditary an autocracy may be called a dictatorship. When a monarchy or dictatorship oppresses citizens and violates their rights it is called a tyranny.

Oligarchy means government by a few. An oligarchy in which the few receive power because of merit or inheritance is called an aristocracy. Where the few govern because of the power of their wealth it is called a plutocracy.

Democracy means government by the people or, at least, a majority of the people. Pure democracy has not existed except in small areas with small numbers of people. Nevertheless many modern national governments are somewhat democratic. The people do not rule directly, but they elect officials to represent and rule for them. This kind of government is called a democratic republic. It can be a presidential democracy where the chief of state, as well as congress, is elected by the people. Constitutional monarchies can also be democratic if actual power is exercised by parliaments elected by the people. This is called parliamentary democracy and England is a good example.

Governments may also be classified as either *unitary* or *federal* If the entire country is governed from the national capital it is called unitary. If the nation has local governments which are not appointed by the central government it is federal in form.

States may also be classified as *free* or *totalitarian*. In free states citizens have rights that the state is not authorized to violate, and some spheres of human activity are left uncontrolled by the state. Freedom of speech and business enterprise usually prevail in free societies. Totalitarian states attempt to exercise control over all aspects of society.

GOVERNMENT AND SOCIAL JUSTICE

Men have discussed and written about the problems of government and politics since early times. One of the problems that first concerned such writers was the tendency of the powerful and wealthy to increase their wealth and power at the expense of other members of the society. The ancient Hebrews developed laws to protect women, children, debtors, and the sick from the powerful. The Code of Hammurabi (ca. 1700 B.C.) put an upper limit on interest charges; limited enslavement of defaulting debtors to three years; set maximum fees for doctors, veterinarians, builders, and other professionals; and fixed minimum wages. Under the code, the higher a man's status in the society the more severe his punishment for a crime. Aristotle advocated a government bound by laws to treat all men equally (the rule of law). Warning against selfish class rule he said that "poverty is the parent of revolution and crime," and maintained that an equitable distribution of wealth was essential to peace. The Roman Stoic school of philosophy emphasized the value of and respect due to individuals, including women and slaves.

In the Middle Ages, leaders of the Church sought to impose upon local robber barons ethical and religious restraints such as the concept of a "fair wage," "just price," and "higher law." Without justice, said St. Augustine (354–430) "kingdoms are but great robberies."

WHO SHOULD HOLD THE POWER TO GOVERN?

History has of course seen a vigorous debate among scholars as to what group in a society should exercise the power to govern.

Plato (427–347 B.C.) set forth his ideas on the best form of government in *The Republic*. Preferring the constitution of Sparta over that of Athens, he rejected democracy and advocated rule by the wisest philosophers. His pupil, Aristotle, thought that the people should be the final authority, but he favored a mixed constitution which gave the middle class, rather than the extremely rich or extremely poor, a leading role in the government. Pericles (d. 429 B.C.) was more a practical ruler than a scholar, but he spoke eloquently in support of the basic principles of Athenian democracy.

Few of the earlier writers on government advocated complete democracy. Socrates and Plato thought that the people lacked the information and ability needed to run the state successfully. Others believed that only a strong king or dictator could prevent conflict between different classes and groups from tearing the state apart. They feared that the people might elect fools or scoundrels who appealed to their worst instincts, and that ensuing conflict and incompetency might lead either to breakdown of all government or to seizure of power by a tyrant. Ancient Greeks advocated democracy only for relatively small city-states. When the city-state of Rome, a republic, grew into a large empire, its democracy perished.

In more modern times, Edmund Burke (1729–1797) feared that democracy would lead to damaging excesses. He criticized the French Revolution, which overthrew the monarch in France, as producing more evils than the ones it sought to destroy. The governed, he maintained, do not have the right to decide who governs. He ridiculed democracy as "mere arithmetic." Instead, he maintained, the state should be directed by the aristocracy and the leadership of established institutions such as the church and universities.

John Stuart Mill (1806–1873) defended democracy but cautioned against the tendency of a majority to be tyrannical and violate the rights of minorities. He insisted that the majority must allow "absolute freedom of opinion on all subjects." The majority had no more right to silence a minority, he said, than a minority had to silence the majority.

Montesquieu (1689–1755) studied the influence of such factors as environment and history on government. He concluded that no one form of government was best for all countries in all stages of development. A form of government that worked well for one nation would not necessarily work well for others. He thought that the best way to prevent abuse of power and safeguard rights was to divide governmental power among separate branches of government and to give each checks and balances on the others.

In America, the founding fathers borrowed heavily from John Locke in defending their right to have a revolution and from Montesquieu in establishing a government with separation of powers. Two lines of political thought, liberal and conservative, were led by Thomas Jefferson and Alexander Hamilton. Hamilton feared democracy. He believed that the support of the wealthy was necessary to the success of the new government and advocated government policies which benefitted them, sometimes at the expense of the poor. He thought that government leadership should be exercised by an aristocracy of wealth and ability. "Your people," he once exclaimed, "are a great beast." Thomas Jefferson, on the other hand, ardently believed in democracy and wanted the government to serve the interest of the common man. He had faith that democracy could be made to work successfully if the people were educated.

How Much Power Should the State Have?

Many different forms of government have existed from early times. Aristotle described and compared one hundred fifty different constitutions and political systems known in the ancient world. During much of history the problem was to create a government with sufficient power to prevent civil wars and to preserve peace over large areas.

Clans and tribes lived in villages, some of which expanded into cities. Cities were centers of trade, manufacturing, and wealth, and often city governments extended their control to the surrounding countryside and became city-states. City-states conquered other city-states and became empires, but empires were constantly threatened by the tendency of subjected peoples to rebel.

The ancient Greeks developed their high culture within city-states. But, despite the brilliance of their political thought, they were unable to unite their city-states. Thus weakened, they were conquered by the Romans.

The Romans were more successful at solving political problems than any other people of the ancient world. They excelled at government and administration, and their Stoic school of philosophy emphasized the concepts of human equality and the desirability of uniting men across the boundaries of small city-states. But the practices of the Romans often fell short of their ideals. They ruled the ancient world as an empire in which only a few of the conquered people were given equality, and the rest were exploited for the enrichment of Rome. They practiced large-scale slavery. Weakened by prolonged economic depression and stifling military dictatorship, they were finally overrun by barbarians.

In the Middle Ages following the collapse of the Roman Empire central government disappeared. With trade disrupted by wars, pirates, and robbers, cities lost business and population. Agricultural areas came under the control of semi-independent lords who engaged in frequent wars among themselves. Education and intellectual life, including the study of government, suffered. The principal remaining unifying and intellectual force was the Church, which sought to restore peace and justice.

The leading political development of the modern period of history (since 1500) was the unification of feudal baronies and cities into large national states. This produced a new and larger-scale brotherhood of fellow citizens and superior human cooperation among larger numbers than had ever been achieved before. In giving equal rights to all inhabitants, even those in newly acquired territories, nation-states were far more successful than the Roman Empire in enlisting loyalty and achieving unity. Patriotism grew stronger when citizens felt that they were part owners of the state. As fellow citizens they achieved a broader degree of brotherhood and more extensive cooperation; this made a major contribution to the development of Western civilization. Not surprisingly, the nation-state has become the center of attention for students of politics.

What Is the Proper Balance Between Government Power and Individual Freedom?

As the nation-state grew in unity and power more discussion arose concerning how much power the national government should have and what rights and liberties should be reserved for the people.

Among the leading students of the state was Machiavelli (1469–1527). He favored increasing the power of the state and wrote primarily to describe methods, some of them ruthless, whereby kings could maintain effective control over their kingdoms. He insisted that kings had the right to do things (even murder) which would be wrong if done by private citizens for the maintenance of public order and stability.

Other scholars who sought to increase royal powers argued that kings had a divine right to rule. They had become kings because of the will of God, they said, and therefore they held their authority from God. Thus, to defy them was equivalent to defying the will of God.

Thomas Hobbes (1588–1679) appealed to those unconvinced by the "divine rights" argument. He defended royal authority by saying that kings had received their power as the result of a "social contract." This had occurred when men, in order to achieve peace and order, entered into an agreement (a social contract) to appoint one man as king and give him the power to command them in war and to judge them in peace. This contract, said Hobbes, gave a king all power and, once made, was irrevocable and bound men to obey the king no less than if he had received his kingly authority from God.

John Locke (1632–1704), however, used the social contract theory to argue that the power of kings was limited and that they were obligated to respect and protect the rights and liberties of their subjects. He insisted that the people, in their original contract with the king, had given him only limited power and only on the condition that he respect their natural rights and liberties. The rightful purpose of government, he said, was to administer impartial justice and promote "life, liberty, and property." Because the people were the source of authority they had the right to change their government. Indeed, if the government did not respect the law, it was their duty to change it.

Even if one believes that the people are sovereign, the question remains of how much power the people should give the government to fulfill its functions of preserving law and order and promoting the good life for its citizens. Liberals such as John Locke wanted to restrict the state's authority to preserving order and administering justice. All other spheres of human activity, such as economics, religion, and speech, were to be free and uncontrolled.

Other men believed that law and order could be preserved and progress and happiness maintained only if the state were all-powerful and exercised strict control over all aspects of human activity. The philosopher Hegel (1770–1831) maintained that the state was the fulfillment of the divine plan in history and that the first duty of man was allegiance and obedience to it. Those who advocated complete state control were called *totalitarians*. The totalitarian dictator Benito Mussolini (1883–1945) demanded "everything for the state, nothing outside the state, nothing against the state." The development of interdependent economic systems and electronic communication devices gave the state the means of exerting more control over the lives of more people than before. Totalitarian states exercised tight control over the economy and news media, and outlawed all but the ruling political party.

At the other extreme are the anarchists. They argue that the state was established neither by divine edict nor by social contract. Instead they maintain it was established by force and violence. The strong, they insist, took control because they were able to do so and used their power to enrich themselves at the expense of the weak. If so, government had no ethical justification. Some of these ideas were shared by early Communists. "The state," said Karl Marx, "is nothing more than a committee for the administration of the affairs of the ruling class."

Is the Government an Unnecessary Evil, a Necessary Evil, or a Positive Good?

The point of view of the anarchists was that government was evil, a system for perpetuating injustice, and that it ought to be abolished. Others admitted the need for government to keep order and insure the survival of the group, but considered it a necessary evil to be given only that power absolutely necessary to protect citizens from criminals and foreigners and help them settle their disputes without violence.

Other writers, however, did not take so limited a view of the proper function of government. Aristotle thought that government should not only preserve law and order but promote the good life and the general welfare of its citizens. Abraham Lincoln said that the government should do "what the people needed to have done, but cannot do so well for themselves in their separate and individual capacities." According to President Franklin D. Roosevelt, "as new conditions and problems arise beyond the power of men and women to meet as individuals . . . the government has the definite duty to use all its power and resources to meet new social problems with new social controls. . . ."

Many important services, these men maintained, can be provided by the state more conveniently than by private individuals.

In a highly interdependent society, life and property are sometimes threatened by unemployment and inflation, over which citizens have no private control. The people also need protection against contagious diseases, environmental pollution, or even the ignorance of others. School, postal services, and highways can be operated much more effectively by governments than by private citizens.

Thus, some men thought of government as potentially, at least, a positive good. They advocated what came to be called the welfare state. Partly under their influence, the functions of all modern governments tended to grow. Among others, they sought to secure foreign sources of raw materials and markets, to protect industry against foreign competition, to educate the people and to protect and improve their health, to develop superior methods of producing crops, to protect the environment against pollution, to improve transportation facilities, to maintain a dependable money system, to provide ample water, and to control floods and fires.

Advocates of a welfare state hoped that if the government were kept democratic and under popular control, its growth need not unduly restrict the rights and liberties of the people. The preservation of liberty, however, required an active citizenry. As Aristotle said, "If liberty and equality, as is thought by some, are chiefly to be found in democracy, they will be best attained when all persons alike share in the government to the utmost." President Franklin D. Roosevelt felt that "the only sure bulwark of continuing liberty is a government strong enough to protect the interests of the people, and a people strong enough and well enough informed to maintain its sovereign control over its government."

Some political scientists have suggested that the advance of technology and its effects in bringing all parts of the world closer together is rendering the state as it has thus far been known obsolete. The economies of all nations are becoming more closely related and interdependent. In an age of hydrogen bombs and ballistic missiles, it is no longer possible for the state to perform its traditional role of defending the freedom, lives, and property of its citizens from foreign attack. Therefore, they argue, new and more powerful international institutions must be created to take over many of the powers and functions of the state.

This chapter has highlighted concepts concerning government in general. The next chapter will concentrate on concepts that underlie government in the United States.

Questions

1. Why is government found in all organized groups?
2. How did improvements in government make possible increases in the size of groups?
3. What ethical advance made it possible for man to live in larger groups?
4. What is meant by social engineering?
5. Show the interrelationship between economic and political advance.
6. How did hereditary monarchy appear? What were its advantages?
7. Show the differences between the primary family, clan, tribe, and nation.
8. What are the basic functions of government?
9. In what ways did early governments protect the weak against the strong?
10. Give the arguments advanced for and against democracy.
11. Give the arguments for and against an all-powerful state.
12. Show how Hobbes and Locke used the "social contract" argument to reach different conclusions.
13. What are the current trends in government?
14. Define or identify: Edmund Burke, Montesquieu, autocracy, aristocracy, anarchy, and totalitarianism.

Suggested Reading

Almond, Gabriel A., *Perspectives on Political Development.* Boston: Little, Brown, 1970.
A useful college text.

Aristotle, *The Politics.* New York: Penguin Books, 1969.
Remarkable insights into the political problems that still perplex mankind.

Ebenstein, William, *Great Political Thinkers,* 3d ed. New York: Holt, Rinehart, and Winston, 1963.
Useful short accounts.

Hacker, Andrew, *Political Science Theory and Ideology.* New York: Macmillan, 1961.

Interpretive essays in thirteen great political thinkers from Plato to John Stuart Mill.

Hobbes, Thomas, *Leviathan*. New York: Penguin Books, 1969.
A discussion of the growth of the power of the state.

Locke, John, *Two Treatises on Government*. New York: Cambridge University Press, 1960.
A defense of natural rights and the right of revolution.

Machiavelli, *The Prince*. New York: Penguin Books, 1969.
A handbook of advice, often unscrupulous, to rulers on how to hold people in subjugation and defeat rivals.

Plato, *The Republic*. New York: Penguin Books, 1969.
A modern colloquial translation.

9
The American Form of Government

Why did America's founding fathers choose a democratic republican form of government?
What safeguards did they provide against dictatorship?
How is American government changing?

"To secure these rights, governments are instituted among men, deriving their just powers from the consent of the governed."

—Declaration of Independence

"All, too, will bear in mind this sacred principle, that though the will of the majority is in all cases to prevail, that will to be rightful must be reasonable; that the minority possess their equal rights, which equal law must protect."

—Thomas Jefferson

"We here highly resolve . . . that this nation, under God, shall have a new birth of freedom—and that government of the people, by the people, for the people, shall not perish from the earth."

—Abraham Lincoln

A Democratic Republic

With the achievement of independence, the United States became history's first large-scale republic. At that time the leading form of government throughout the world was monarchy. In most countries kings and nobles held all political power and used it to take most of the wealth for themselves. The common man, they argued, was incapable of self-government. They hoped that the American experiment in self-government would collapse in disorder, discrediting the idea of democracy forever. The American experiment was thus a test, as Abraham Lincoln said later, of whether a government "conceived in liberty and dedicated to the proposition that all men are created equal . . . can long endure."

The word democracy is derived from two Greek words, *demos,* meaning people, and *kratos,* meaning rule. Thus, it means rule by the people. In ancient Athens and in New England town meetings all adult men met periodically to enact laws, vote taxes, and select officials. America, of course, was much too large for this *direct democracy*. The people could rule only by electing men to act as their representatives in making laws and levying taxes. Thus, they established a representative *republic* which, while not a pure democracy, was democratic, especially when compared to other governments of the time.

SOVEREIGNTY OF THE PEOPLE

On what political principles did the leaders of the American Revolution base their new government? The first principle was sovereignty of the people. Monarchists argued that God chose kings to rule men. If this were true, kings ruled by "divine right," and to disobey them was to disobey the will of God. American revolutionaries, on the other hand, believed that government had been established by the people who gave it limited power and who remained themselves the ultimate source of authority. "Governments derive their just powers from the consent of the governed," said the Declaration of Independence. The people were sovereign, the supreme power, and if the government exceeded the authority they had given it, or violated their rights, said the Declaration, the people had the right to "alter or abolish it," and to "institute a new government."

THE PROTECTION OF FREEDOM

A second basic principle on which American revolutionaries based the new government was that the powers exercised by government must be strictly limited. Every citizen, they believed, has *natural rights* which are "inalienable," and which he could not surrender even if he wanted to and, therefore, which no government has authority to violate. Having suffered under a British government that oppressed them, they took care to establish elaborate safeguards against any danger that their own democratic government might violate their rights.

In drafting their first national constitution, the Articles of Confederation (1781–1789), they were overcautious and gave the central government too little power to enable it to defend America's international interests or to preserve order. The new 1789 Constitution of the United States of America gave the government more power, but also set clear limits on its authority. The framers of the Constitution were not trusting of human nature. They believed that men who acquired power were inclined to seek more power and to ignore the rights of others. To guard against any reappearance of dictatorship, they reserved to the people the right to oppose the government or to change it at their will. By setting elections at regular intervals, they provided a regular peaceful procedure by which the people might dismiss their officials and choose new ones.

The Constitution also specifically prohibited a number of practices which had been commonly employed by dictators to crush freedom. In order to prevent the government from using charges of *treason* to suppress opposition, the Constitution specified that nothing short of an "overt act" of levying war against the United States or "adhering to their enemies, giving them aid and comfort," could be considered treason. It forbade the government to suspend the right of *habeas corpus* (the right of an arrested person to consult a lawyer and to have a speedy hearing before a judge) except in time of war. Congress could pass no *ex post facto* law (providing punishment for acts committed before the law was passed), no *bill of attainder* (condemning political rebels by legislative vote instead of by judicial trial), or *corruption of blood* (punishing a guilty man's family). Indeed, the government might not punish a citizen at all unless a jury of impartial fellow citizens concluded that he had broken the law.

Nothing is more basic to democracy than *free speech.* Unless the people have unrestricted access to the facts and arguments bearing on public questions, they cannot acquire the information they need to control the government. In a democracy the people act as a great jury which hears the arguments of opposing sides and then gives its verdict on questions of public policy. Of course, the people can make independent judgments only when they can hear each side present its case in its own way. If any one person is given the power to suppress evidence or arguments, he can control public opinion, and thereby deprive the people of their right to decide for themselves. This is the most dangerous form of dictatorship, for the people may not realize that their opinions are being manipulated. "On the altar of God," said Thomas Jefferson, "I have sworn eternal hostility to every form of tyranny over the mind of man." "Congress," says the First Amendment to the Constitution, "shall make no law . . . abridging the freedom of speech, or of the press."

The founding fathers also took care to protect the right of the people to oppose government policies. The Constitution specified that Congress "shall make no law" abridging "the right of the people peaceably to assemble, and to petition the government for a redress of grievances."

The Constitution also protected citizens against state governments. It forbade states to "pass any bill of attainder, ex post facto law, or law impairing the obligation of contracts," and said that "the citizens of each state shall be entitled to all privileges and immunities" of citizens of other states. Furthermore, the federal government guaranteed "to every state in this union a republican form of government."

The Constitution separated church and state. It prohibited any religious requirement for holding government office and, in the First Amendment, forbade Congress to contribute money to a church or to prohibit the free exercise of religion.

A standard practice of dictators was to employ professional armies to enforce their will on the people. Thomas Jefferson was convinced that "without a standing army no tyranny ever existed, with a standing army no other form of government can exist." Therefore, the framers took great precautions to keep the military under the control of elected representatives. By requiring that money appropriations for the military could be made for "a term of no longer than two years," they sought to keep the armed forces financially dependent on Congress. They stipulated that no war could be waged without a declaration of war by Congress. And, to prevent professional troops from monopolizing weapons, the Bill of Rights specified that "the right of the people to keep and bear arms shall not be infringed."

The Constitution forbade officials to search the homes of citizens unless they first obtained a warrant to do so from a judge on the basis of sworn testimony that illegal activity was being conducted there. When charged with a crime, a man could not be compelled to testify against himself and, when put on trial, he had a right to confront and question witnesses against him, to summon witnesses to testify for him, and to have a lawyer assist in his defense. He was protected also against excessive bail or fines and cruel or unusual punishment.

Later amendments provided that all of the rights of citizenship must be given to former slaves and forbade the states to deprive them of any of their rights, particularly the right to vote.

Thus, the founding fathers apparently feared that efforts might be made in the future, even in a democratic republic, to deprive people of their rights and freedom, and they sought to protect the people against that danger. They knew that those who hold power are tempted to use it to suppress their opposition. As they feared, our government has sometimes deprived Americans of liberties; but Constitutional guarantees have helped to restrict such violations and have always held up to Americans the ideal of freedom.

Separation of Powers

Another precaution that the founding fathers took against possible dictatorship was to divide power among three independent branches of government. According to James Madison, "the accumulation of all powers, legislative, executive, and judiciary, in the same hands . . . may justly be pronounced the very definition of tyranny." Alexander Hamilton called it a "fundamental maxim of free government" that these three "great departments of power . . . shall be essentially distinct and independent, the one of the other." The power to make laws was given to Congress. The power to administer the government according to law was given to the president. The power to interpret the law was given to the Supreme Court.

Furthermore, the Constitution gave each branch of the government certain *checks and balances* on the others to prevent them from acting in a dictatorial manner. It made the president commander-in-chief of the armed forces but specified that he could not fight a war unless Congress declared war. It authorized him to negotiate treaties but provided that they did not take effect unless approved by the Senate. It empowered him to direct the administration but provided that men could not be appointed to high administrative office unless approved of by the Senate. His administrative acts could be declared to be illegal by the Supreme

Court, and, if he violated the law, he could be impeached and removed from office by Congress.

The Constitution empowered Congress to enact the laws but provided that the laws which it passed could be vetoed by the president or ruled unconstitutional by the Supreme Court.

The Constitution empowered the courts to interpret and apply the law but authorized the president to pardon persons the courts convicted. If Congress did not approve of the courts' interpretation of a law, it could change the law or submit a constitutional amendment to the states for that purpose. The president was empowered to nominate judges, and the Senate to confirm them, but once appointed, judges became independent of both because they could not be removed from office unless convicted of a crime by the whole Congress. Thus, if any branch of the government attempted to violate rights of the people, such rights could be protected by other branches.

HOW MUCH DEMOCRACY?

Belief in democracy rests on faith in the common man's ability to govern the nation. The men who established our government were fully aware of the shortcomings of the mostly illiterate people of their day. Nevertheless, they had faith that man was "a rational animal." "The people," said Jefferson, "may safely be trusted to hear everything true and false and to form a correct judgement between them." Furthermore, they believed that the people were improvable through education. "We must educate our masters," said Jefferson. Even with public education, they realized, democracy would work imperfectly. Nevertheless, they felt that if they wanted the government to serve the greatest good of the greatest number, they could entrust power to no one except the people. If they gave power to any one man or any small group of men, they feared, it would be used to exploit the people. As Reinhold Niebuhr said much later, "Man's capacity for justice makes democracy possible, but man's inclination to injustice makes democracy necessary."

Nevertheless, they approached democracy cautiously and slowly. Most states at the time restricted the right to vote to those who owned property, and some states restricted it to church members, so that not more than one-fourth of white adult males could qualify to vote. The authors of the Constitution trusted even these select voters with the power to choose only the lower house of Congress. Senators were chosen by state legislatures. The president was chosen by the Electoral College, the members of which were elected by the people but were supposed to use their own independent judgment in selecting the president.

From the first, however, the trend was strongly toward more democracy. Popular election of the president quickly developed in practice, though not in theory. Differences of opinion on the policies of Washington's first administration led to the formation of two opposing political parties. In 1800 both parties put up lists of their members as candidates for the Electoral College, and the people knew, of course, that Federalist electors would vote for John Adams and that Republican electors would vote for Thomas Jefferson. This, in effect, gave the people the privilege of choosing between these two men for president. Thus, the development of political parties deprived the Electoral College of power and reduced its meetings to a ceremony. The names of the presidential candidates later replaced the names of presidential electors on the ballot.

Furthermore, the right to vote was gradually extended to a larger part of the population. The frontiersmen who carved out farms from the forests of the West considered themselves to be the equal of any man, and the constitutions they adopted for their new states usually allowed all men to vote. Older eastern states also gradually lowered or abolished property and religious requirements for voting. The post–Civil War Fourteenth and Fifteenth Amendments sought to guarantee the right of blacks to vote. The Nineteenth Amendment gave the vote to women, the Twenty-Third Amendment enabled the people of the District of Columbia to vote in presidential elections, and the Twenty-Fourth Amendment forbade the states to deprive anyone of his vote in federal elections because of failure to pay a poll tax.

The method of nominating a political party's presidential candidate grew more democratic. At first, the parties chose their candidates at *caucuses* (closed meetings) of the party's members in both houses of Congress. Later, *national party conventions,* which included governors, mayors, and other party leaders as well as congressmen, were called to nominate candidates. On the state level, instead of leaving the choice of candidates in the hands of conventions of party leaders, many states set up *primary elections* (preliminary elections) which permitted all party members to choose the party's candidates for state offices through intraparty elections.

In 1917 the Seventeenth Amendment transferred the power to elect United States senators from state legislatures to the people. In 1964 the Supreme Court ruled that electoral districts for state legislatures must be equal in population in order to give all voters an equal voice in the selection of members of both lower and upper houses of state legislatures.

The American people were firmly wedded to the principle of political democracy. The growing complexity of the problems of modern civilization made democracy more difficult, and new threats to democratic freedoms arose from time to time, but the long-term movement in America was toward putting the ideal of democratic government into practice.

A FEDERAL REPUBLIC

When American revolutionaries succeeded in throwing off Britain's control, each of the thirteen former colonies claimed to be an independent nation. The first constitution that they adopted, the Articles of Confederation (1781–89), reserved so much power to the states and gave so little power to the general government that it resembled a league of nations more than a union. "Each state retains its sovereignty, freedom, and independence," it specified. Presumably, any state could withdraw from the confederation at any time. It provided no president or chief executive. In its one-house Congress each state could cast one vote. Congress had no taxing power, no control of trade between states, no courts, and no police, and was forced to depend on the states voluntarily to enforce its laws.

This government was too weak to command the respect of foreign nations who, contemptuous of democracy, discriminated against our trade, pirated our ships, and refused to send ambassadors. The thirteen states levied tariffs against each other, fought small boundary wars, and suffered riots and domestic disorder. Such conditions caused George Washington, Alexander Hamilton, and others to launch a movement to form a stronger federal government by adopting a new constitution.

The Constitution adopted in 1789 established a much more powerful government. According to its preamble, it derived its power from the people directly and was not a creature of the states. Instead of relying on state governments to enforce federal laws, it gave the federal government its own system of courts. It also gave the federal government the power to levy and collect taxes, to control foreign and interstate trade and immigration, to coin money, establish post offices, and issue patents and copyrights. It made the federal Constitution and laws the "supreme law of the land . . . anything in the constitution or laws of any state to the contrary notwithstanding."

However, as we have seen, the founding fathers wanted a division of powers, and any powers "not delegated to the United States by the Constitution" were reserved to the states. Among these were the power to conduct local government, to police, conduct elections, regulate marriage and divorce, and to provide for health and education.

The question of how much power should be exercised by the federal government and how much should be reserved to state governments has been a subject of controversy throughout American history. Opposition to enlarging federal powers at the expense of "states' rights" has been led, in turn, by Thomas Jefferson, New England Federalists, southern slaveholders, big business corporations, and southern segregationists. As a rule those who were a minority in the nation and who feared that their minority interests were threatened by the national government wanted to restrict federal powers and enlarge the power of state governments, while a majority that controlled the national government tended to enlarge federal powers at the expense of the states.

Most such disputes, in the end, were settled in favor of Washington. Ruling that the federal government might exercise powers that were merely implied by the Constitution, the Supreme Court, on occasion, declared state laws and the decisions of state courts to be unconstitutional. The Civil War firmly established federal supremacy over the states. The growing complexity of American problems, the increasing economic interdependence of the people, and the rising importance of international affairs tended further to enlarge the role of the federal government.

Contrary to popular impression, the powers of state and local governments are not fading away. Their powers remain substantial and in recent years their activities have grown at a more rapid rate than those of the federal government.

The Enduring Constitution

The United States Constitution was 192 years old in 1981. Only the British and Swiss governments rival its long life. Revolutions have overthrown governments in every other country. What explains the extraordinary stability of our government?

The Constitution was drawn up by men of rare education,

ability, and experience. Of the fifty-five lawyers, merchants, financiers, plantation owners, physicians, college presidents, professors, and ministers of the gospel in the constitutional convention, thirty-one had attended college and all but one were experienced in government. Seven had been governors, and three-fourths had served in the Continental Congress. Among them were two future presidents of the United States, nineteen future senators, and four future cabinet members. Some of them, particularly James Madison, had read deeply in history and political science.

Moreover, for generations political life in America had revolved around constitutional problems. We had quarreled with England over rights and had wrestled with the problem of achieving unity among the colonies. We had formed a Continental Congress to lead the Revolution and had drawn up constitutions for state governments. We had learned from our failures under the inadequate Articles of Confederation. Nowhere else at that time existed a group of men whose education and experience equipped them so well to cope with the problems of drawing up a new constitution.

Secondly, the Constitution was the result of debate, deliberation, and compromise. No group got everything it wanted, but no group was badly defeated; and most groups won protection for their interests. Small states were protected from large ones; those who wanted democracy got the popularly elected House of Representatives; those who feared democracy got the indirect election of the Senate and the president. Fears by the common man that the rich and powerful would use the federal government to hold the poor in subjugation were eased by the protection given to the rights of men in the Constitution and the Bill of Rights. Thus the Constitution had no irreconcilable enemies.

A third reason for the continuing survival of the Constitution was its flexibility. Its framers made it short. They were satisfied to set up the general framework of government and to leave the details of day-to-day operations to be filled in later by laws, court decisions, or customs which easily could be adjusted to changing circumstances. They also provided a practical method for amending the Constitution. Either Congress or the states could propose amendments which became effective if endorsed by a two-thirds vote in each house of Congress, or by a Constitutional Convention, and ratified by three-fourths of the states, through either their legislatures or special constitutional conventions. Thus, the Constitution proved to be broad and flexible enough to serve both a rural agricultural nation of 4 million people and an urban industrial world power of 225 million people.

The Changing Constitution

What kind of changes have been made in the Constitution? One kind was the addition of further guarantees of rights. The first ten amendments, called the Bill of Rights, protected the right of the people to freedom of religion, of speech and of the press, and the right to assemble and petition, to keep and bear arms, to be secure in their homes against the quartering of soldiers and unreasonable searches, and to have a fair trial by jury. The Thirteenth Amendment, which abolished slavery, and the Fourteenth Amendment, which was designed to give former slaves the same rights as other citizens, also belong in this rights-protecting group.

A second type of amendment was intended to correct technical difficulties that developed in the practical operation of the government: the Twelfth Amendment provided for separate voting for president and vice-president, the Twentieth Amendment advanced the date of the inauguration of the newly elected president from March 4 to January 20, and the Twenty-Fifth Amendment specified the procedure to be followed if a president were disabled.

A third kind of amendment was designed to make the government more democratic: The Fifteenth Amendment sought to give blacks the right to vote, the Nineteenth Amendment gave the vote to women, the Seventeenth Amendment gave the people the right to elect United States senators, the Twenty-Second Amendment limited a president to two terms, the Twenty-Third Amendment gave the people of the District of Columbia the right to vote in presidential elections, and the Twenty-Fourth Amendment made it unconstitutional for any state to prevent anyone from voting because of nonpayment of a poll tax.

A fourth type of constitutional amendment empowered the federal government to bring about social reforms: the Sixteenth Amendment legalized use of the income tax, and the Eighteenth Amendment (later repealed by the Twenty-First Amendment) outlawed the consumption and manufacture of alcoholic beverages.

Substantial changes have also been brought about by Supreme Court decisions. The clause that Congress can "make all laws which shall be necessary and proper for carrying into execution the foregoing powers" leaves the question of what is "necessary and proper" to the judgment of the courts. For example, the Supreme Court first ruled that Congress had no authority to regulate manufacturing and agriculture, but decided later that it did. Until 1954 it upheld segregation in public schools, but in that year ruled that it was unconstitutional. Thus, in President Woodrow Wilson's words, the Supreme Court sits as "a kind of continuous constitutional convention," developing, expanding, and changing the meaning of the Constitution.

How Much Freedom in National Emergencies?

The Constitution is highly honored in America, yet some of its provisions are sometimes violated. In wartime, the Bill of Rights notwithstanding, the government usually restricts freedom of speech, assembly, and the press. Even in time of peace these freedoms are not always enjoyed by groups such as Fascists or Communists who challenge the basic features of our political or economic system. The Constitution does not enforce itself. In practice it means what the Congress, the president, and the courts say it means at the time. The degree to which its provisions are observed depends largely on the strength of public devotion to its principles.

Freedom and constitutional government meet their most severe test in times of national emergency. Many people believe that democratic government is not strong or efficient enough to meet great national emergencies, which instead require the suspension of freedom and a temporary resort to dictatorship. During World War I, men and women were given stiff prison sentences for such offenses as saying that they would rather die than kill or predicting that the Germans would win the war. In World War II, 110,000 American citizens were arrested, forced to abandon their homes and businesses, and held in "relocation centers" for up to five years merely because their ancestry was Japanese.

All of this occurred despite the fact that the Constitution itself gives the government only one emergency power—the power to suspend habeas corpus in time of war or invasion. The Supreme Court has sometimes condemned the government's assumption of additional emergency power. "No doctrine involving more pernicious consequences was ever invented by the wit of man," it once protested, "than that any of its provisions can be suspended during any of the great exigencies of government." "Emergency does not create power," the Supreme Court ruled, nor "diminish the restrictions imposed upon power." Nevertheless both the Constitution and the Supreme Court are usually put "on ice" during a war. So far, constitutional government has recovered each time after the emergency was over. But if democracy and freedom are ever abolished, it will probably be on the argument that some great emergency requires a dictatorship in order to save democracy. President Thomas Jefferson anticipated this argument in his first inaugural when he said:

> I know, indeed, that some honest men fear that a republican government cannot be strong, that this government is not strong enough. . . . I believe this, on the contrary, the strongest government on earth. I believe it the only one where every man, at the call of the law, would fly to the standard of the law, and would meet invasions of the public order as his own personal concern.

The Limits of Freedom

Despite the guarantees in the Constitution and the Bill of Rights new threats to freedom constantly appeared. Many citizens who enjoyed the American way of life seemed to forget how difficult it was to achieve freedom. Some seemed to believe that they could themselves enjoy freedom while denying it to others. Several public opinion polls indicated that most Americans objected to the protection that the Bill of Rights gave to unpopular groups.

Despite our constitutional position on toleration in religious matters, problems still arise when religious teachings and practices come into conflict with the laws or customs of the community. Jehovah's Witnesses, for example, believe that the biblical law against worshipping idols forbids them to salute the flag. A series of Supreme Court decisions finally established their right to attend public schools nevertheless. Members of the Society of Friends, or Quakers, believe that it is wrong to take the oath required of witnesses at trials. Again the state yielded and permits them merely to "affirm" the truth of their testimony. Atheists successfully maintained that their freedom of religion was infringed by the reading of the Bible in schools. On the other hand, we do not permit Mormons to practice polygamy, their religious views notwithstanding.

Another serious problem arises in regard to "conscientious objection" by some young men to fighting in wars. They interpret the commandment, "Thou shalt not kill," and the New Testament teaching to "resist not him that is evil" as forbidding them to fight in wars. Most major religious denominations give them the same support that they give church members who fight in wars. And the government has decided to honor their objections. In World War I and World War II, conscientious objectors were allowed to perform other service of national importance, such as serving as attendants in mental hospitals.

But the government honored only *religious* objection to *all* wars. Controversy continued on the questions of whether men who objected to war on nonreligious grounds, or who objected on religious grounds only to a particular war, should be exempted from military service. Objectors to war who refused to register or who burned their draft cards, thus violating the law, were subject to fines and imprisonment.

Another area of disagreement concerned whether the citizen should be protected against electronic eavesdropping and telephone tapping on the part of the government. In 1966, the FCC declared that the use of electronic devices to listen to or record private conversations without the consent of the persons involved was illegal. But a 1968 law permitted the police to eavesdrop on private individuals for up to forty-eight hours without first obtaining an order from a judge—and if they obtained such an order they were allowed to listen indefinitely. Not until 1972 did the Supreme Court rule that wiretaps were illegal unless authorized by a judge.

Particularly heavy pressure from public opinion was applied against the Fifth Amendment's protection of individuals against being compelled to testify against themselves. Popular indignation was aroused when a number of men suspected of being Communists refused to tell Congressional investigating committees if they were, in fact, members of the Communist party. At times it appeared that the indignation might lead to abolition of the constitutional protection of a citizen against being coerced into providing the government with evidence that could be used to convict him.

In the late 1960s the rights of citizens accused of crime came under attack. Many political leaders charged that Supreme Court decisions protecting citizens against being coerced into signing confessions overprotected the rights of the accused, handicapped the police in combatting crime, and thus denied law-abiding citizens adequate protection against crime. Defenders of these Supreme Court decisions agreed that convicted criminals should not enjoy equal rights. However, they argued that America's constitutional principle was that a man was presumed to be innocent until proven guilty and that one could not withdraw such rights from persons suspected of crime without depriving innocent citizens of protection against being coerced into confessions.

Of course, freedom was inseparable from responsibility. All Americans enjoyed liberties, and all Americans had obligations to preserve them. In guaranteeing freedom, the Constitution embodied the faith that American citizens were capable of exercising freedom with responsibility. Anyone who took advantage of liberties to abuse his fellow men added to the difficulties of preserving liberties. Reckless driving by young men, for example, increased pressure for a law to deny driver licenses to anyone below the age of twenty-one, and the use of firearms to kill fellow citizens increased public pressures to disarm the people.

The men who framed the United States Constitution gave Americans a heritage of sane democracy and freedom. Its preservation requires continuing effort. Changing economic, social, and world conditions challenge America to develop governmental responses that are new but still in harmony with our traditions of freedom and democracy. "Eternal vigilance" remains "the price of liberty." The survival of the American form of government depends in the long run on how well the American people understood its basic principles and how alert they are in devotion to those principles.

Other Democracies

The world has many kinds of government. As early as 400 B.C. Aristotle counted one hundred fifty varieties. A brief look at leading characteristics of other forms of government can help to clarify the features of the American government that are most distinctive.

Americans attached much importance to the division of powers between federal and state government, and the separation of federal powers among semi-independent executive, legislative, and judicial branches. We also sought to protect individual rights and freedoms by incorporating them into a written document that constituted the basic constitutional law of the land. Other countries, however, developed democratic governments without all of these safeguards.

When America won independence, England was already well along in developing parliamentary democracy and protection for the "rights of Englishmen." In theory England remained a monarchy, but the royal family, although extravagantly admired and maintained, lost all political power. Government authority, instead, was won by the democratically elected lower house of Parliament, the House of Commons.

The English government is not federal, but unitary. Nor does England separate powers among different branches of government. The House of Commons is the center of all government power. It enacts law and names judges, and its executive committee, a cabinet of ministers, wields the executive power as long as a majority of Parliament so desires. Furthermore, England scarcely has a written constitution in the American sense of a document which cannot be altered by a simple majority vote of Parliament.

Nevertheless, without question England is a democratic country in which democratic rights and freedom are at least as strongly entrenched and highly respected as in America. The English have very strong traditions and deeply ingrained principles whose violation seems to be scarcely thinkable for either the people or political leaders. Someone once said that the British constitution could be summed up in two common expressions: "That wouldn't be cricket," and "That isn't done here."

France's government, also, is a unitary parliamentary democracy. However, it differs in some respects from that of England. It is modified by the presence of a president who is chosen, not by parliament, but by a direct vote of the people and whose powers resemble those of a constitutional monarch. Most other democratic governments can be thought of as variations on the American, British, and French models, with the parliamentary form more widely imitated than the presidential form.

Democracy seems to have found Northwestern Europe, England, and America to be its most fertile soil. To the east conditions seem to have been less favorable. Germany developed democratic society later than Western Europe, and the movement was even slower in Russia. Except in a limited form on a local level, China has not known democracy in modern times.

Nevertheless, in the twentieth century aspirations to democracy rose everywhere, and nearly every government made some claim either to being democratic or to working to create democracy. Adolph Hitler claimed that the huge majorities he got in his rigged elections proved that his government was more representative of the people than the so-called democracies. Communists called the governments which they established after World War II "peoples' democracies." However, in 1981 freedom under democratic government was enjoyed by only a minority of men, and most of mankind lived under some variety of dictatorship.

How Modern Dictatorships Differ from Democracies

What are the distinguishing differences between modern democracies and modern dictatorships? First, let us review some of their common characteristics which do *not* clearly differentiate them. As we have seen, both make professions of devotion to the principles of democracy. Some dictatorships stage elections and even adopt democratic constitutions. Either may have a unitary government without checks and balances. Nor does the presence of a free enterprise economy seem to guarantee a democratic government, nor the presence of socialism guarantee dictatorship. Most European countries are more socialistic than America. Denmark and Sweden, among the more socialistic countries, are also among the more democratic and free. Hitler was helped to power by right-wing capitalists. Thus we have had both left-wing and right-wing dictatorships, and both socialistic and free enterprise democracies.

What features, then, distinguish dictatorships from democracies? One is the degree of tolerance of opposition parties—whether there is a legal way for the people to organize and work to overturn and replace the government and whether the right of the people to do so is respected and protected. In dictatorships, normally there is only one party, and opposition parties are outlawed or suppressed.

A second distinguishing feature is the denial of free speech and a free press. In democracies the press is free, and opposition newspapers are published freely. Dictators suppress opposition newspapers and extend their control over the news media and, usually, over education, and try hard to silence criticism by the church.

A third difference lies in the degree of respect for individual rights. Democracies respect the rights of citizens to fair and public trials and to privacy, and protect them against false or arbitrary arrest or illegal search or seizure. Dictatorships are characterized by secret police who ignore those rights.

Some modern dictators sought complete control over all aspects of national life, and developed systems of ideas and beliefs, called ideologies, to justify such total control. They argued that the power and wealth of the nation were more important than individual rights, and that, when necessary, individual rights must be sacrificed in the interest of national survival. They asserted that rulers had the duty to regulate and control all aspects of the life of the people, economic, social, intellectual, religious, and even recreational, to insure that all worked for the best interest of the nation. Where they acted on this principle with efficiency and vigor, utilizing modern communications as instruments of control, they were called *totalitarian*. The leading examples were the fascist dictatorships of Mussolini in Italy and Hitler in Germany and the Communist dictatorship of Russia. Total control was difficult to achieve in practice, and none of the dictators was quite able to do so.

Political scientists have given much time to the study of the factors which influence nations to adopt democratic or dictatorial government. A democracy requires more moderation and restraint on the part of the people. It works best in lands where it has grown over a long period of history giving the people the time to obtain experience and develop the necessary attitudes. It is not easy, for example, to learn that the government cannot spend more money than it collects in taxes without causing inflation. It is painful to acknowledge that unless one allows one's enemy freedom of speech, one cannot securely enjoy it oneself. It is difficult to resist the temptation to try to annihilate one's enemy when one has the upper hand. Habits of restraint, legality, and fair play come hard.

The presence of peace or war seems to influence the prevailing degree of democracy or dictatorship. In the midst of war some democracies established as complete control over their economies and news media and were almost as intolerant of dissent as were totalitarian dictatorships. Also, they enacted draft laws which seemed to express the philosophy that individual rights were secondary to the needs of the state. Someone defined a totalitarian state as a modern industrialized nation at war.

Thus the degree of security of the nation against foreign invasion seems to affect its development of democratic traditions. In the British Isles, where surrounding seas added to the difficulty of an invasion, democracy flourished to a greater degree than in Central Europe, where nations stood on guard against powerful enemies on all sides. Conditions of war and national emergency seem to be conducive to dictatorship, and conditions of peace and security conducive to democracy.

We will now turn to an examination of the different branches of the American government and how the foregoing principles are applied in practice.

Questions

1. How does a representative republic differ from a direct democracy?
2. How did our interpretation of the origins of government differ from that of European monarchists? Why was this important?
3. Why does the Constitution define treason?
4. Why is free speech basic to democracy?
5. In what ways does the Constitution protect the right of the people to change their government?
6. How does the Constitution guard against military dictatorship?
7. Why were government powers separated among three branches? List the checks exercised on each branch by the others.
8. Why did the founding fathers prefer democracy to other forms of government? How did they limit democracy? Why?
9. In what ways has the government become more democratic since the adoption of the Constitution?
10. What groups usually favor states rights?
11. What accounts for the fact that the Constitution has endured so long?
12. What three types of amendments have been made to the Constitution? Give an example of each.
13. How do Supreme Court decisions modify the Constitution?
14. What provisions of the Constitution are sometimes violated? Why?
15. What are the internal dangers to the American form of government?
16. Why is it difficult to preserve civil liberties? What liberties do many people want to abolish?
17. Define: Divine right, sovereignty of the people, Articles of Confederation, tyranny, habeas corpus, ex post facto, bill of attainder, search warrant, Electoral College, caucus, national convention, Bill of Rights, suffrage.

Suggested Reading

Asch, Sidney H. *Civil Rights and Responsibilities Under the Constitution*. New York: Arco, 1969.

Discusses the provisions of the Constitution and court decisions on censorship of the press, obscenity, and protest demonstrations. A clear and readable account that emphasizes the responsibilities of the citizen.

De Tocqueville, Alexis. *Democracy in America*. Edited and abridged by Richard D. Heffner. New York: Mentor Books, 1956.

The classic description and analysis by a brilliant Frenchman.

Jefferson, Thomas. *Democracy*. Selected and arranged by Saul K. Padover. New York: Appleton-Century-Crofts, 1939.

A short selection from Jefferson's writing.

Meiklejohn, Alexander. *Political Freedom: The Constitutional Powers of the People*. New York: Oxford University Press, 1960.

An eloquent defense of rights and freedom under the Bill of Rights.

Padover, Saul K. *The Meaning of Democracy: An Appraisal of the American Experience*. New York: Praeger, 1963.

An excellent short description of democracy as an idea and form of government, its history, and its weaknesses and strengths.

Schulz, Ernst B. *Democracy*. New York: Barron's Education Series, 1966.

An excellent straightforward description of democracy as an idea and how it is practiced in the world. Describes political parties, the liberties essential to democracy, discusses whether a particular economic system is required for democracy, and gives the arguments for and against democracy. Includes readings.

Summers, Marvin S. *Free Speech and Political Protest*. Lexington, Mass.: D. C. Heath, 1967.

Gives historical background and a review of leading Supreme Court decisions, and includes sections on draft resistance and black demonstrations.

Warren, Earl. *A Republic, If You Can Keep It*. New York: Quadrangle, 1972.

One of our most influential chief justices of the Supreme Court, and leading champion of civil liberties and civil rights, writes a "short, direct, simple, and unpretentious" essay on preserving the integrity of the Constitution and protecting and expanding freedom.

10
Congress, the Courts, and the Presidency

What are the strengths and weaknesses of Congress?
What roles do the president and courts play in lawmaking?
What factors contribute to success or failure in the presidency?

"Because Congress is without leadership and its organization is disintegrated . . . national interests are subordinated to sectional and special interests, and Congress fails to perform adequately its tremendously important function of holding the executive branch accountable."

—The National Committee for
Strengthening the Congress, 1970

"No man is allowed to be a judge in his own cause, because his interest would certainly bias his judgment and, not improbably, corrupt his integrity."

—James Madison

"There can be no mistaking the fact that we have grown more and more inclined from generation to generation to look to the president as the unifying force in our complex system, the leader both of his party and the nation."

—Woodrow Wilson

The Federal Government

The federal government at Washington is "where the action is." Washington is the residence of the best-known people in America outside of show business. It is visited by more heads of government than any other capital. It is the place where more than $600 billion in government funds is spent per year and where hundreds of special interests fight for their conflicting plans of spending it. The great national campaigns that elect its officials are the modern substitute for civil wars, and the federal government resembles an arena to which different sections and interests send their elected champions to do battle for them. It is the government of the world's most powerful nation and makes more decisions affecting more people than any other.

In this chapter we will examine issues relating to the functions of, and relations among Congress, the courts, and the presidency. Political parties and elections, financing government, state and local governments, and foreign policy are treated in separate chapters.

CONGRESS

As the result of a compromise in the constitutional convention between the larger states, who wanted representation based on population, and the smaller states, who wanted each state to have an equal vote, the states have representation in proportion to population in the House of Representatives and equal representation in the Senate. One result is that people are unequally represented in the Senate. In 1970, California's 19,953,000 people had no more voting power there than Alaska's 300,000. The 20 percent of the nation's population in the twenty-five smallest states had as many senators as the other 80 percent of the people.

Another reason for dividing Congress into two houses was to give protection to different economic interests. It was assumed that the House of Representatives, elected by the people, would represent lower income groups while the Senate, selected by state legislatures, would protect the property interests of the wealthy.

As our population grew, the House of Representatives expanded to 435 members. Present policy is to let it grow no larger, which makes it necessary periodically to reapportion it by taking representatives from nongrowing states and giving them to growing ones. This is done every ten years following the census. In 1970, each state had a minimum of one representative (six states had only one) plus another representative for each additional 465,000 people. Representatives serve for two-year terms and the entire membership of the House is up for election every two years.

House members are elected by congressional districts. The state legislature divides the state into as many congressional districts as the state has representatives. Election by districts gives a minority party a better chance to elect a candidate in some district in which it may happen to be strong than it would have if all representatives were elected by the state as a whole. In 1964 the Supreme Court ruled that congressional districts, on the principle of "one man, one vote" must be made as nearly equal in population as practicable.

The one hundred senators, two from each state, serve six-year terms, and one-third of them are elected every two years. The 1913 Seventeenth Amendment took the power to name senators from state legislatures and required them to be elected by popular vote.

There is some division of responsibilities between the two houses. Money bills, involving taxes or spending, must originate in the House, the body that is presumably closest to the people. The Senate, on the other hand, has powers that the House does not share. The president must obtain its approval, by a two-thirds vote, of his appointments to high positions in the executive departments, the military and the courts, and of the treaties which he negotiates.

Each house is self-governing and makes its own rules for the conduct of its business. The Senate is by far the more informal body. Normally, it puts no time limit on a senator's right to debate any measure. Only rarely does the Senate vote to impose a one-hour limit on each senator's speaking time on a particular bill, a measure which is called cloture and which requires a two-thirds vote. The presiding officer, the vice-president or the elected president pro tempore, follows a policy of permissiveness.

It is much more difficult for the House of Representatives, with more than four times as many members, to debate matters as thoroughly. In order to get its work done, it must be controlled by its leaders. Its most powerful official is its speaker. Elected by the members, he is usually a leading member of the majority party. As presiding officer he determines who may speak and to which committee to refer bills, decisions which can greatly affect the chances of bills to be passed. Another center of power is the *Rules Committee*, which makes rules for the conduct of business and controls the *calendar* (the program) of the House. This committee decides which of the hundreds of bills reported out of committees will be brought before the House for debate and voting.

Each political party has its own organization in each house.

Party members meet in a *caucus* (closed meeting) to decide which bills to support and to choose a steering committee to carry out their decisions. The chairman of this committee is called the majority (or minority) *floor leader*. He is assisted by *party whips,* officials who round up party members for important votes. Party control however is not strong and most congressmen show considerable independence because they feel that their re-election depends more on pleasing the voters in their districts than on pleasing the national party organization.

The Constitution gives Congress the power to levy taxes, regulate foreign and interstate trade, coin money, establish post offices, issue copyrights and patents, declare war, and provide for "the common defense and general welfare of the United States." Furthermore, in a so-called *elastic clause,* the Constitution empowers it to "make all laws which shall be necessary and proper for carrying into execution" the aforementioned powers. The Constitution also forbids Congress to discriminate between geographic sections in taxation or commerce, to suspend the right of habeas corpus in time of peace, to pass any bill of attainder or ex post facto law, to grant any title of nobility, to tax exports, or to violate individual rights. Congressmen cannot be sued for libel or slander for anything they say on the floor of Congress. They cannot be arrested for a civil matter (but may be arrested for a crime) while going to, attending, or leaving a session. Their salaries are $60,663 per year plus liberal expense allowances and retirement pensions.

In 1975, 52 percent of all congressmen were lawyers, 27 percent were businessmen and bankers, 15 percent were educators, 8 percent were farmers, and 5 percent were journalists. Three-fourths of them were college graduates. In age they ranged from twenty-five to eighty-two; most of them were between fifty and sixty. Eighteen were women, and eighteen were black.

Congresses are numbered by each election of the House—the 97th was elected in November 1980, to serve in 1981 and 1982. Regular sessions begin annually on January 3 and have no fixed length, but sometimes extend through the summer. The president may also call special sessions.

CONGRESSIONAL COMMITTEES

A visitor to a session of the Senate or the House is apt to be disappointed by appearances. Except on unusual occasions, he will find few congressmen present. Most of those present will be reading, writing, conversing, or walking around, and few seem to pay any attention to the one who is making a speech. Occasionally, a bell rings and congressmen hurry in from the halls, offices, and lunchrooms to answer a roll call, and then stroll out again. Such an appearance hardly conforms to the visitor's idea of the power and importance of Congress.

One reason for this is that most of the work of Congress is done in committees. When introduced, each bill is referred to a committee for study with a recommendation that it either be enacted or rejected. The Senate has sixteen and the House has twenty standing (permanent) committees. Among the most important are the committees on taxation and appropriations (called "finance" in the Senate, and "ways and means" in the House) and those that deal with foreign relations. Each party holds seats on a committee in approximately the proportion in which it is represented in Congress. Membership on important committees is eagerly sought and assignments are made by the party leadership in each house.

How a Bill Goes Through Congress

The route of a bill through Congress basically is quite simple. *Introduction,* the "first reading," requires a motion in the Senate, but in the House the bill is simply dropped into a box on the clerk's desk, called the "hopper." Secondly, the bill is given a number and referred to a *committee*. Committees sometimes change or combine bills, or draw up new ones, and hold public hearings at which interested persons may present information and arguments for or against them. If the committee opposes the bill it pigeonholes or tables it (puts it away and forgets it). Most bills "die in committee." If the committee favors the bill it reports it to the House with the recommendation that it be passed. Thirdly, the bill is added to the calendar (the list of bills to be considered). When its turn comes, it is read a second time (usually only its title is read because printed copies have been distributed), debated and possibly amended, and then read a third time and *voted* upon. If passed, it is sent to the other house to go through the same process.

If the second house amends the bill in a way to which the first house objects, or if the other house has passed a different bill on the same subject, a special *conference committee,* composed of members of both houses, is appointed to iron out the differences, perhaps compromise them, and recommend an amended bill. Then the bill in its new form is voted upon once more by each house.

Conference committees exercise what many critics consider to be excessive power. The typical conference committee consists of fewer than fifteen members who are selected by the chairman of the committee in each house to which the bills were originally referred. A powerful committee chairman can pack his delegation to the conference with men who favor his point of view. They work in secrecy and do not allow even their own members to take notes on the proceedings. Seldom does the news media carry any report on their deliberations or votes. Usually the representatives of each house argue for the provisions passed by their own house, but not always. They are not supposed to put new matters into the bill, but sometimes they do. After they put the bill in final form it cannot be amended by either house but must be accepted or rejected as written. Conference committees have proved useful in eliminating frivolous or damaging amendments which may have been added in either house, but they also provide an opportunity for special interest groups to exert influence unobserved and get provisions added or deleted from the law. The late Senator George Norris called these committees "the third branch of Congress," and former Senator Albert Gore said that their powers were "dictatorial-like." They perform a necessary function, but under existing procedures they are one of the least democratic aspects of Congress.

If passed, the bill is sent to the president for his *signature,* whereupon it becomes law. If the president objects to the law he may veto it, in which case the bill is dead unless both houses repass it by two-thirds majorities, which is called *overriding the veto.* The president also has other options. If he chooses not to sign a bill, it becomes law at the end of ten days if Congress is still in session. If Congress has adjourned when the tenth day elapses, the bill dies without the necessity of a veto message—killing a bill in this manner is called a "pocket veto."

SHOULD COMMITTEE CHAIRMEN BE CHOSEN ON THE BASIS OF SENIORITY?

In a recent session more than fourteen thousand bills were introduced, far too many to be acted upon. Most of them were never reported out of committee. Because committee chairmen decide which bills get serious attention, the post is a most important one. How is it filled?

When Thomas Jefferson was president he successfully insisted, as head of his party, on choosing committee chairmen. Later, however, the custom developed of giving chairmen their positions on the basis of *seniority*. The member of the majority party who had served longest on the committee automatically became its chairman.

In defense of this system it is argued that a chairman needs the thorough knowledge of federal laws which only years of experience could bring. Furthermore, the member who has been reelected more times has more proof that he has the confidence of the people. He is apt to be older, more cautious, and less likely to approve of ill-considered changes in the laws.

Critics of the seniority system (some of them call it the "senility system") argue that the fact that a man has been a member longer does not necessarily mean that he is better qualified for leadership. Nor does it necessarily mean that he has greater popular support. It might mean merely that he comes from a state where the opposition party is so weak that he faced no real challenge and was therefore automatically re-elected, again and again.

In practice, when the Democrats controlled Congress the chairmanships of most committees were held by southern congressmen who were usually more conservative than Democratic presidents and, therefore, frequently opposed presidential programs. When the Republicans were in control, the chairmen were likely to be from the more conservative Republican states. In 1970, fifteen of the thirty-two committees in the House and Senate were headed by members in their 70s and 80s. Committee chairmen sometimes frustrated the will of the majority by blocking action on programs endorsed by the people in nationwide elections. In 1968, for example, Chairman Wilbur Mills (Dem.-Ark.) of the House Ways and Means Committee delayed a congressional vote on President Johnson's request for a tax raise for eighteen months.

The seniority system came under increasing attack. In 1974 the Democrats changed the rules to require a secret ballot in the Democratic caucus on the selection of committee chairmen, which made it easier to challenge the automatic elevation of the most senior members. In 1975 two important chairmen—of the Ways and Means Committee and the Senate Banking Committee—were removed and two less senior men given their positions. The actual removals were important. Of equal importance was the knowledge that they could be removed. This exerted pressure on other chairmen to be more responsive to the will of their party's majority.

THE PRESIDENT AS LEGISLATIVE LEADER

In theory, the legislative and the executive are separate branches of the government. In reality, the president became the leader of the legislative branch. So accustomed did the American people become to his leadership that they expected him to formulate a program of legislation and to push it through Congress.

The framers of the Constitution did not expect him to assume such a dominant role, but they did give the president important legislative duties. The Constitution requires him to "give to the Congress information on the state of the Union," and to recommend "such measures as he shall judge necessary and expedient." At the opening of each regular session he delivers a "State of the Union" address to Congress outlining the nation's problems and the measures he considers necessary to meet them. His recommendations usually become the principal business of the session. He can also call Congress into special session, in which case his message calling for special measures commands particular attention.

If Congress passes a bill to which the president objects, he may return it with a veto message, and his friends in Congress usually can prevent its backers from mustering the two-thirds majority needed to override his veto. (President Eisenhower vetoed 201 bills, of which only three were passed over his veto despite the fact that the opposition party controlled Congress.) Normally a vetoed bill either dies or is revised to meet his objections.

In practice, the president's legislative power goes beyond these constitutional provisions. He has the assistance of large executive departments in preparing programs and in drawing up bills. Congressmen also have research and legal assistance, but their sources of information do not match those available to the president. Consequently, the president and his assistants draw up most of the important bills considered by Congress.

The prestige of his office also gives the president great powers of persuasion. A congressman seldom declines an invitation to the White House to discuss the president's program. The president is the only official (except for the vice-president) who is elected by the nation as a whole to represent the interest of the entire nation, not just one state or district. Popular interest focuses on him, and his unrivaled access to press, television, and other media of com-

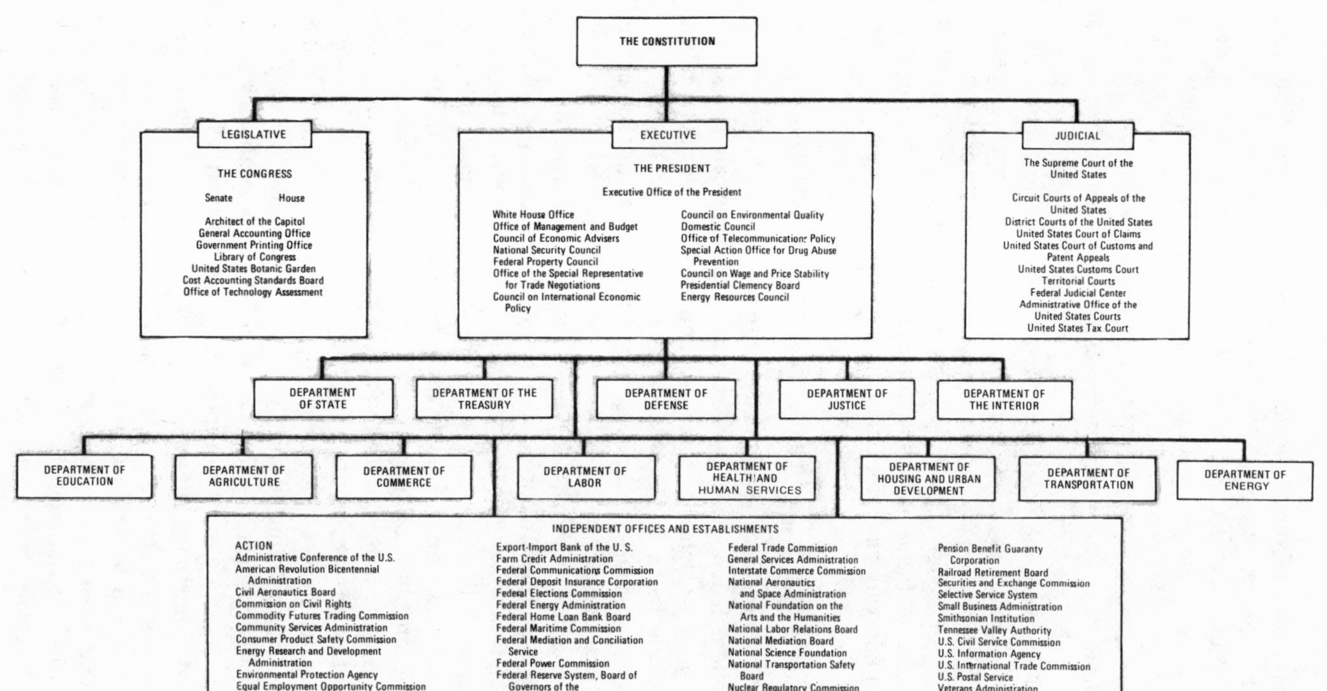

Fig. 10.1. **The Government of the United States.** (U.S. General Services Administration)

munication enables him to muster wide popular support. He is also the head of his party, and the party needs a record of success to help it win the next election. Many congressmen seek to be known as supporters of the administration and to ride to reelection on a popular president's coattails.

As chief executive, the president also hires thousands of government employees. Congressmen are expected to get their political supporters federal jobs, and they cannot do so unless they stay in the good graces of the president. Giving jobs in return for political support is known as *patronage*. The president's power to decide whether supporters of particular congressmen get federal jobs and which congressional districts get new roads, dams, or post offices enables him to influence many congressional votes. All of which helps explain why he is not only chief executive but chief legislator as well.

THE ROLE OF THE COURTS IN LAWMAKING

Federal courts have jurisdiction over all cases concerning the Constitution, federal laws and treaties, trials between states, citizens of different states, or foreign countries. They decide what the laws actually mean and how they apply to specific cases.

The federal court system has eighty-six federal district courts, at least one in every state. In these *courts of original jurisdiction,* where cases are first tried, a single judge presides, trials are by jury, and a complete record is kept of all proceedings. If convicted, a defendant has the right to appeal to a court of appeals to change the decision. The system has ten courts of appeals, each composed of three to nine judges. Usually their decisions are final, but cases involving constitutional questions may be reviewed by the Supreme Court. The nine judges of the Supreme Court are the nation's highest authority on constitutional and legal questions.

The courts early assumed the power to overrule a law if they found that it contradicted the Constitution, although the Constitution did not specifically give them that power. Most appeals to the Supreme Court are for the purpose of testing whether a law is constitutional. Sometimes laws are not fully enforced until the courts complete this last step in the lawmaking process.

Critics of the Supreme Court attacked it from opposite sides. The judges were men of high ability and integrity, but they frequently disagreed among themselves. Some important cases were decided by five to four votes. Critics charged that the judges' interpretations of the law were influenced by their political philosophies. In the nineteenth century, when most judges were conservative, the Supreme Court ruled that the income tax was unconstitutional, usually decided against labor unions, and protected the great corporations against regulation. At that time liberals called the Court a barrier to progress. But in the post–World War II period, when most judges were appointed by liberal presidents, the Supreme Court protected civil liberties, upheld equal rights for blacks, required electoral districts to be made equal in population, and upheld government's right to regulate the economy in the interest of social justice. In consequence, the Supreme Court was bitterly denounced by right-wing groups. Naturally, both sides sought to get men who shared their political philosophy appointed to the courts.

Lobbying

Congressmen receive hundreds of letters and telegrams every day from constituents urging them to vote for or against various bills. Labor, farm, business, and veterans organizations keep them informed of their wishes. Many special interest groups maintain permanent agents in Washington for the purpose of influencing congressmen. Such agents are called lobbyists.

Most of the activities of lobbyists are legitimate. They appear before congressional committees to present facts and figures that support their point of view. They prepare bills for congressmen. They notify organizations back home when to send letters, telegrams, and petitions to influence congressmen. However, some lobbyists engage in improper activities. These include bribery, sometimes disguised as opportunities for profitable investments, jobs for relatives, campaign contributions, or entertainment.

The 1946 Regulation of Lobbying Act required lobbyists to register and to list their employers, how much they were paid, the bills they supported or opposed, and a detailed account of their expenditures. This act did not reduce lobbying but brought it more into the open. In a recent year more than two thousand registered lobbyists in Washington reported expenditures of over $10 million for the year.

As lobbying illustrates, the chief pressures on a congressman come from watchful special interest groups. If he votes against their wishes, he incurs their opposition; if he votes for them, he may be rewarded with personal and business favors and campaign contributions. The general public on the other hand often appears to be indifferent, and if he defies special interests to vote for the general welfare there may be no sign of appreciation from his constituents. Consequently, powerful self-interest groups often get generous government favors at the expense of the people. All of which, of course, illustrates the need for a better-informed and more concerned electorate to give representatives more incentive to vote for the greatest good of the greatest number.

The Demands on a Congressman's Time

So many complex bills come before each session that few congressmen have adequate time to study all the laws upon which they vote, and less time for the thought and research necessary to prepare new legislation. Consequently, most of the bills are drawn up by the executive departments or by industry, labor, veteran, and other special interest groups. Comparatively little legislation originates in Congress.

Routine duties absorb much of an average congressman's attention. Some of the procedures in Congress waste his time. A roll call vote, for example, consumes fifteen minutes in the Senate and forty-five minutes in the House, although it could be recorded in a minute by the use of electrical voting devices. The public also expects many time-consuming errands from congressmen. One representative complained that he was expected to be a "messenger boy, employment agency, getter-out of the Army, law explainer, gladhand extender, veterans' affairs adjuster, recoverer of lost baggage, adjuster for traffic violations, good samaritan, contributor to good causes, public building dedicator, and ship christener." Senator J. William Fulbright said that the multitude of requests for personal services "comes close to destroying the personal effectiveness of a great many capable representatives," leaving them with no time "for the intelligent study and reflection that sound legislation requires." As a result, "the legislator often becomes superficial and unable to do constructive thinking on any subject."

This problem is particularly serious for members of the House of Representatives. Because they face re-election every two years, much of their time must be spent in their home states campaigning for the next election. Sometimes they must feel as if lawmaking is the least of the duties expected of them. It has been suggested that a representative's plight might be eased somewhat by having him elected for four-year terms instead of two-year terms. It would be even more helpful if their constituents made congressmen feel that they were appreciated and re-elected not because of personal and political favors but because of their work on national and international problems.

Investigating Committees

An investigating committee is one especially formed to inquire into some particular subject and is empowered to subpoena witnesses (issue official orders for them to be present), compel testimony under oath, and require that documents be produced. Investigations are an ancient function of popular assemblies. In recent years notable investigations have been conducted by the Nye Committee into the prewar activities of munitions makers, by the Truman Committee into the conduct of World War II, by the Kefauver Committee into the connection between politicians and crime; by the House Un-American Activities Committee into subversive activities, and the Senate "Watergate" Committee into illegal campaign activities.

The stated reason for such investigations is to discover whether problems exist that could be corrected by new laws. Actually most investigations are designed to influence public opinion and government policy. They seek to focus the public's attention on the existence of evils, to force the executive department to change its policies, or to expose the mistakes of a president of the opposition party. Investigations have called public attention to government corruption, harmful business practices, unauthorized commitments to defend foreign nations, and illegal activities by the White House staff. Some investigations attract much publicity and boost the political careers of their leaders.

Most investigations serve constructive purposes, but sometimes public hearings amount almost to public trials. Denied constitutional rights of defense against charges of crime, some witnesses are bullied, defamed, and exposed to punishment by public censure. By "taking the Fifth Amendment," a witness can refuse to give answers damaging to himself, but such refusal to testify is regarded by much of the public as equivalent to a confession of guilt. A refusal to answer on any other grounds subjects him to fine or imprisonment for contempt of Congress.

The longest-lived congressional investigating committee was the House Un-American Activities Committee. Concern aroused by the rise of antidemocratic regimes in Europe and the appearance in America of small groups which sought to establish similar systems led to its establishment in the 1930s. At first it investigated fascist groups, and then concentrated on Communists. Its investigations received sensational publicity, especially after the Soviet Union became America's chief rival. Suspicion put foreign policy officials under pressure to prove their loyalty by advocating tougher policies against Communists. Some labor unions and liberals suffered by being falsely associated in the public mind with communism.

Critics of the committee argued that it was not needed, that existing laws against revolutionary violence were adequate and that revolutionaries could be controlled by the police, courts, FBI, and armed forces. Furthermore, they charged, the committee violated constitutional rights of free speech and association. President Truman called it the "most un-American thing in America." In reply, the defenders of the committee said that a society must defend itself against those who sought to destroy it. It faded in importance in the 1960s, its name changed to the Internal Security Committee, and in 1975 it was abolished.

The most sensational congressional investigation of the early 1970s was that conducted by a select Senate committee, under the chairmanship of Senator Sam Ervin (D.-N.C.) of the presidential campaign of 1972. Because its investigation centered on a burglary of the Democratic National Committee's headquarters in the Watergate apartment building, it was popularly called the "Watergate Committee." It questioned top officials in the Committee to Re-Elect the President, the president's cabinet, and the White House; and its hearings were carried on television by national networks. As a result of disclosures by this committee, and by a number of grand juries, two cabinet members, and the president's two top White House assistants, as well as a number of lesser officials, were imprisoned, and President Nixon was forced to resign.

ARE CONGRESSIONAL REFORMS NEEDED?

The Senate rules that permit almost unlimited debate make *filibusters* possible. This means attempts to kill bills by debating them endlessly until their backers give up their attempts to get them passed. The filibuster was employed most often by Southern senators to block the passage of civil rights legislation, but it was also used on occasion by liberal senators. The Senate can end a filibuster by passing a *cloture* resolution limiting each senator's speaking time on the bill to one hour. But the Senate is reluctant to limit its freedom of debate, and it is very difficult to get the votes that cloture requires. However, some political scientists feel that there are some advantages in having a peaceable means by which a determined minority can keep itself from being overruled on matters on which it feels deeply.

Another problem concerns the ethics of congressmen. Some observers feel that congressmen are too susceptible to the influence of special interests. Sometimes it is difficult to determine whether or not a bribe is being offered or accepted. A lobby can give a congressman an opportunity to make a business profit or it can pay high legal fees to his law firm. Some congressmen own newspapers and radio stations to which special interests can pay advertising fees.

Congress established an ethics committee which recommended that congressmen observe high ethical standards but did little to insure that its recommendations were followed. Some congressmen proposed that all congressmen be required to reveal the sources of all of their income. A New York Bar Association committee recommended that congressmen give up their private law practices and refrain from soliciting business for their former law partners. The only results, however, were a Senate requirement that senators disclose the payments they received for speeches and writing, and a House requirement that members disclose their business connections.

Most of the faults of congressmen probably reflect faults of the electorate. Some citizens vote for congressmen who get federal buildings for their districts or who do personal favors for them regardless of their views on important national or international issues. Many also vote for men who share their prejudices and hostilities toward foreign countries in preference to men who are knowledgeable about international relations. Others do not know how their congressmen vote on important issues. When the general public is indifferent, the strongest pressures on congressmen are exerted by alert and active self-interest groups. In a democracy the people get the quality of government that they deserve, and Congress cannot be improved very much without first improving the education, concern, and participation of the people who elect it.

The law-making process in America is slow, inefficient, and cumbersome. Some foreigners wonder how America ever gets governed at all. On the whole, however, the system has served the needs of the nation well. Doubtlessly, it could be made less wasteful, and more responsible to the majority. Because the general public is sometimes indifferent and uninformed, special interest groups are allowed to exert too much influence, often at the expense of the public. This defect of democracy might be remedied by more democracy, by making the people more politically effective through education and experience.

THE EXECUTIVE POWERS OF THE PRESIDENT

The American president is the most powerful official in the Western world. He heads its most powerful nation and leads vast alliances of nations. Selecting him wisely is the major political problem of our democracy.

The Constitution specifies that the president must be born in the United States, at least thirty-five years old, and resident within the United States for at least fourteen years. He receives $200,000 annually, plus expense allowances and, after he leaves office, $60,000 annually in retirement pay. He may serve no longer than two four-year terms. If he dies, his office is assumed by the vice-president who, in turn, would be succeeded by the speaker of the House, the president pro tem of the Senate, the secretary of state, and other heads of departments in the order in which the departments were created.

As the nation's chief executive, it is the president's duty to see "that the laws be faithfully executed." With the consent of the Senate he commissions military officers and appoints high administrative officials. And he directs the largest administrative organization in the Western world with more than 2.8 million civilian and 3 million military employees.

An idea of the extent and variety of the president's executive powers can be derived from a listing of the executive departments and agencies that he commands. Through them he conducts our foreign relations; commands our defense forces; collects taxes; coins money; distributes the mail; supervises hydroelectric dams, national parks, public lands, atomic energy, flood control, and the prison system; operates the weather service, veterans hospitals, and the FBI; administers the immigration service, Indian affairs, farm programs, Social Security, wages, hours and employment security programs, public health services, and health programs; clears slums; controls navigation; insures bank deposits; regulates interstate commerce, corporations, telephone, telegraph, and television transmission, the stock market, and banking; and subsidizes the merchant marine and air transportation. Of course it is an enormous job to keep abreast of all of these departments, agencies, corporations, and commissions, and to plan and direct their activities. Furthermore, in time of war he is given large additional powers over the nation's manpower, resources, and industry. It is no wonder that the presidency is considered to be the world's most demanding job.

What happens when the man with these tremendous responsibilities is disabled? When they were shot, Presidents Garfield and McKinley remained unconscious for days before they died, and when President Wilson suffered a stroke he was almost completely disabled for more than a month. During these periods the vice-president had no authority to assume the powers of the office. Ratification of the Twenty-Fifth Amendment in 1967 provided safeguards against another period of leaderlessness. It specified that the vice-president should assume the powers of the presidency if either the president or a majority of the Cabinet informed Congress that he was unable to perform his duties. The president would resume his powers whenever he informed Congress that he was able to exercise them, unless a majority of the Cabinet, supported by a two-thirds vote in Congress, ruled that he was still incapacitated.

In 1973, Vice-President Spiro Agnew, facing charges of corruption, was allowed to resign to escape indictment. President Nixon, with the consent of the Senate, appointed Gerald Ford to be his successor. Then, in 1974, President Nixon also resigned to avert impeachment for illegal activities, and Ford assumed the presidency. He then, with the consent of the Senate, appointed Nelson Rockefeller to the vice-presidency. Thus the United States had both a president and vice-president neither of whom had been elected. Some political scientists thought it would be better to have a special election if an elected vice-president were not available to fill the office.

Management of the Executive Branch

Much of the president's vast administrative machinery grew up haphazardly as new functions arose, with the result that the system became disjointed and hard to coordinate. In theory, the purpose of this vast administrative organization was to assist the president in performing his duties and in carrying out his policies. But sometimes government bureaus were headed by career men who held their positions far longer than any president and who had policies of their own. They might supply the president with information that supported their own policies and withhold contrary information. Thus, the president was in danger of falling under the control of his own bureaucracy unless he developed other sources of information. Sometimes officials were slow in carrying out presidential orders—President Kennedy said that fighting bureaucratic obstruction was like "wrestling a featherbed."

On the other hand these same factors tend to give the government stability and continuity through changing administrations. Sometimes the resistance of the bureaucracy has saved the country from the damaging effects of unwise policies. Often their advice has contributed to the enlightenment of the president.

Unfortunately bureaucracies have shown capacity for just as much persistence in policies that have proved to be in error. Their directors become personally identified with such policies and are unable to admit that they are wrong without losing status within their department. In such circumstances those who support their bureau chiefs and their erroneous policies may be promoted while those who are right may be penalized.

Extremely important to a president's success is the quality of the advice he receives. President George Washington began the practice of calling the heads of departments together to consult on policies. Such meetings are called *cabinet* meetings. The cabinet has grown too large, however, for efficient consultation, and the president now relies more on meetings with two or three cabinet members or his White House staff for recommendations on major decisions.

There is a tendency for presidents to fail to receive advice that is contradictory to their policies. Every administrator is inclined to choose his devoted followers, whose loyalty to him and his policies is unquestioned, to fill the top jobs in his administration. These men may agree with him completely. Others seeking to get into his good graces may give him only advice they know he wants to hear. Thus, a president may fail to receive the advice that could save him from mistakes. Every president runs the risk of becoming isolated and unaware of disagreeable failures of his policies. "A president's hardest task," said President Lyndon Johnson, "is not to do what is right, but to know what is right." The best presidents have been those who attracted strong and independent men to their service and sought advice from men with different points of view.

For help in administering and controlling the complex executive branch, the president greatly expanded his White House executive office. Its subdivisions included the National Security Council, the Central Intelligence Agency, the Office of Emergency Planning, the National Aeronautics and Space Council, the Office of Science and Technology, the Council of Economic Advisers, and the Bureau of the Budget. To help him supervise them and the regular departments, the president employed nine special White House assistants, a special counsel, a press secretary, and a military adviser.

The president has vast powers, but some authorities maintain that they are not equal to his responsibilities. He can prepare new programs to meet the nation's problems but they can be defeated or amended beyond recognition in Congress. He can give orders, but sometimes the federal bureaucracy or state officials fail to carry them out in the way intended. He has more power at the beginning of his term, when many seek his favor, than toward the end when attention shifts to the choice of his successor.

The power of the presidency also varies greatly with the personality of the man in the White House. Historians classify presidents as strong or weak, according to the degree to which they exercised effective leadership of the bureaucracy and Congress. Theodore Roosevelt, for example, was a strong president, but he was followed by the weak William Howard Taft, who was followed by the strong Woodrow Wilson who, in turn, was followed by the weak Warren G. Harding.

In the last analysis much of the president's power arises from his moral influence. He cannot always command; he must persuade. The country looks to him for moral leadership. No one else can attract such a wide audience for a speech or press conference; no one else is so able to dominate the headlines. Theodore Roosevelt thought that the presidency was the world's best pulpit. The president has a greater chance than anyone to influence political action and theory.

Life magazine observed that the president was most effective when he appealed to the best nature of Americans:

> Moral authority in politics is an appeal to the best, not the worst, in people. It assumes there are still enough conscience-consulting citizens around to make the whole experiment in free self-government worth carrying on. The assumption was never

a certainty, but when presidents act on it, Americans have always responded and found a new unity in shared hope.

PRESIDENTIAL VERSUS CONGRESSIONAL POWER

The struggle for power between the president and Congress is a continuing theme in American history. It has been a seesaw battle. Congress's most complete supremacy came immediately after the Civil War when, by a series of two-thirds votes overriding vetoes, it stripped President Andrew Johnson of power and governed the country for the remainder of his term.

In the twentieth century, the trend seemed to be the growth of presidential power. Sometimes, however, the pendulum swung back the other way just as presidential power seemed to be most overshadowing—notably after the landslide electoral victories of President Franklin D. Roosevelt in 1936 and of President Lyndon Johnson in 1964. Again, after President Richard Nixon's smashing victory in the election of 1972 he seemed to raise the power of the presidency to a new high. His White House staff dominated the bureaucracy, he fought a war in Cambodia without Congressional consent, he refused to spend funds appropriated by Congress, and his nominees controlled the Supreme Court. In little more than a year, however, he had fallen from this summit of power and resigned his office. On the other hand, his appointed successor, Gerald Ford, checked congressional policy initiatives with a series of successful vetos.

The debate on the proper distribution of power between president and Congress continues. Many social scientists believe that Congress is not designed to provide the kind of dynamic leadership necessitated by the growing complexity of modern industrial society. It is too large and cumbersome, they say; its members represent, not the nation as a whole, but merely local interests and it is, therefore, more suitable for responding to proposals than originating them. In foreign affairs, particularly, they felt a strong executive was essential to a great power with world-wide commitments. They argued that Congress tended to be negative or isolationist in foreign affairs, and that only a powerful president could conduct a dynamic foreign policy and long-range strategy with the skill and secrecy required. The power of the presidency in foreign affairs was seldom challenged. The president was the commander of a vast military and intelligence establishment about which most congressmen knew little. On occasion the president even made war without congressional consent. Some political scientists thought that the United States had a near dictatorship in foreign policy.

When presidential foreign policies encountered increasing difficulties, particularly in Southeast Asia, many Americans had second thoughts about leaving the direction of foreign affairs so exclusively to the president. According to Senator Jacob Javits (Rep., N.Y.):

> It was almost embarrassing to recognize that in an era in which the United States has struggled against brutal totalitarianisms we have lodged of our own free will more power in a single individual than does any other system of government that functions today.

The result, he said, had been to produce "an almost grotesque imbalance of power between Congress and the presidency."

In the mid 1970s, for a time at least, Congress regained some power. This resulted partly from increasing opposition to presidential foreign policies and partly from the disgrace and resignation of President Nixon and the imprisonment of members of his Cabinet and White House staff for abuse of power. Partly it was caused by the widening gap between president and Congress on liberal-conservative issues. In any case, Congress put new restrictions on the president's power to make foreign commitments or to order America's armed forces to fight in other countries. It restricted the extraordinary powers he acquired when he proclaimed a national emergency. It increased congressional participation in spending decisions and required that future direction of the Office of Management and Budget be confirmed by the Senate. It benefited from a 1975 Supreme Court decision that the president must spend funds appropriated by Congress. It took steps to combat the bureaucracy's tendency to restrict access to information. At the same time, Congress made some progress toward introducing more democracy and responsibility into its own procedures. And the Ninety-fourth Congress showed new initiative in preparing programs rather than merely waiting to respond to presidential initiatives.

The contest for power between the legislative and executive branches is a built-in feature of the American plan of government, and the precise balance between them can be expected to continue to fluctuate. But, it seems clear that, while a strong presidency is needed, the country also needs responsible congressional exercise of its constitutional checks and balances on both foreign and domestic policies to help save the country from the kind of errors toward which their structures seemed to incline the presidency and the bureaucracy.

WHAT PERSONAL QUALITIES CONTRIBUTE TO SUCCESS IN THE PRESIDENCY?

What kind of man is most successful in the presidency?

First, we must say that presidents display a wide variety in personality, character, appearance, and mental traits. They have included men of the reserved dignity of George Washington, the sour silence of Calvin Coolidge, the homespun informality of Lincoln, the professorial air of Wilson, the stubborn integrity of Cleveland, and the unpretentiousness of Truman. They won their ways to the top in various occupations, none proved to be incompetent, and none, with the possible exception of General Grant, was a real failure. When viewed as a group, their record of performance is an impressive argument for the essential soundness of democracy.

However, some presidents have been more successful than others. A poll of seventy-five leading historians ranked Washington, Jefferson, Lincoln, Wilson, and Franklin D. Roosevelt as great presidents, and John Adams, Jackson, Polk, Cleveland, Theodore Roosevelt, and Truman as near great. On the other hand, they rated Taylor, Tyler, Fillmore, Pierce, Buchanan, and Coolidge as below average, and Grant and Harding as failures. What common qualities were shared by the unusually successful presidents, on the one hand, and by the unsuccessful presidents, on the other?

Of the great and near great presidents only half had college degrees, fewer than half were lawyers, and an equal number were farmers. Only one was a general, and he was primarily a farmer who accepted military leadership in emergencies. Half were aristocratic in origin. They were evenly divided in home areas between North and South and between East and West. Almost the only common characteristic of these eleven superior presidents was that they were all experienced politicians when they became president. All but two had been members of legislative bodies, four had been members of Congress, five had been governors of states, and three had served in the national administration. Of the eight below average presidents, three were military men and three had no previous political experience. Only one had been a governor of a state. Apparently the president's job requires the skills of a politician, and no man has been an outstanding success in the White House unless he had superior previous political training and experience.

The office of president is becoming more demanding. As our economy has become more complex and interdependent, it has become more important that the president understand economic problems and processes. As our involvement in world affairs has deepened, it has become essential that the president have an understanding of international affairs, for a single miscalculation in foreign policy can destroy the results of many years of effective work.

Except for the first president, all of them have been put in the White House by political parties. Let us now turn to an examination of the American political party system and how it operates.

Questions

1. What are the differences between the House and the Senate?
2. What is a party caucus? What functions does it perform?
3. What are the functions of congressional committees? How are the chairmen chosen? What are the arguments for and against this method of choosing them?
4. What legislative powers did the Constitution give to the president? List additional ways in which he can influence the voting of Congressmen.
5. What criticisms from opposite points of view have been made of the Supreme Court?
6. List the legitimate and illegitimate activities of lobbyists. What controls have been placed on their activities?
7. What are the purposes of investigating committees? List some of their accomplishments. What criticisms have been made of their methods?
8. What problems arise in the president's relations with the bureaucracy and his advisers?
9. What changes have occurred in the relative powers of the president and Congress?
10. What qualities seem to contribute to success in the presidency?
11. Define: reapportionment, congressional district, rules com-

mittee, majority leader, party whip, hopper, conference committee, filibuster, "taking the Fifth Amendment."

Suggested Reading

Bundy, McGeorge. *The Strength of Government.* Cambridge, Mass.: Harvard University Press, 1968.

A former White House assistant argues that the federal government and, particularly, the presidency does not have sufficient power to handle the problems with which it is confronted.

Congressional Quarterly: The Supreme Court, Justice and the Law. Washington, D.C.: U.S. Government Printing Office, 1974.

Covers the history of the Supreme Court, its current judges, recent decisions, and proposals for court reform.

Fincher, Earnest B. *The Government of the United States.* Englewood Cliffs, N.J.: Prentice-Hall, 1967.

A brief, well organized, and interesting account written as an introduction for the college freshman level.

Green, Mark J. et al. *Who Runs Congress?: Ralph Nader Congress Project.* New York: Bantam Books, 1972.

A critical examination of Congress which covers its undemocratic features, the influence of special interests, who rules Congress, the illegal activities of congressmen, and conflicts with the executive branch.

Market, Lester. *What You Don't Know Can Hurt You.* Washington, D.C.: Public Affairs Press, 1973.

A clear discussion of public opinion and how government responds to pressures. Maintains that because public opinion controls the country and the media largely controls public opinion, the improvement of the country depends on improving the media.

Schlesinger, Arthur M., Jr. *The Imperial Presidency.* New York: Houghton-Mifflin, 1973.

A review of presidential power by a distinguished historian who concludes that the Cold War and the vast expansion of America's international commitments caused the excessive buildup of presidential power first over foreign and then over domestic affairs.

11

Political Parties and Elections

Why did political parties originate?
What are the differences between Democrats and Republicans?
What are the functions of parties in the American political system?

". . . every boy and every gal that's born into the world alive/ Is either a little Liberal/ Or else a little Conservative!"
—Gilbert and Sullivan, *Iolanthe*

"I belong to no organized political party. I am a Democrat."
—Will Rogers

"Politics is the practical exercise of the art of self-government, and somebody must attend to it if we are to have self-government. . . . The principal ground for reproach against any American citizen should be that he is not *a politician."*
—Elihu Root

The Origin of Political Parties

Those who support or oppose the policies of a government, or who seek to gain control of it, tend to band together into organizations designed to achieve these purposes. Political parties arise from factions into which people divide themselves because they disagree on public questions. In this sense parties are very old, at least as old as ancient Greece and Rome. They exist in nearly every country, but only in democracies do they compete openly to secure control of the government by electing candidates to office. Only in free societies are opposition parties protected by law and, in turn, function as law-abiding and loyal oppositions.

The issues that divide men into opposing parties are similar in all ages and countries. In every country the interests of different social and economic groups conflict. For example, farmers want high prices for their crops, while city dwellers want food prices to be low; workingmen want high wages, while employers want to pay low wages; businessmen want to tax farmers and workers, while farmers and workers prefer to tax businessmen.

Parties are usually divided on economic lines. Sometimes they represent different geographical sections of the country when the dominant economic interests of different sections conflict. Sometimes they appear to represent religious differences, but only where religious differences coincide with differences in economic status as in northern Ireland and Canada. In countries where only two major parties exist, the division is usually between a wealthy aristocracy on the one hand and poor farmers and workingmen on the other.

Many countries, unlike America, have more than two major parties. In Denmark, for example, small farmers, large farmers, urban businessmen, and industrial workers each have separate political parties. France has one party for small businessmen, one for big businessmen, another for revolutionary workingmen, and another for middle-class reformers.

HOW AMERICA'S PARTIES DIFFER

One reason why America has a two-party instead of a multi-party system is our "winner take all" method of holding elections. France, Italy, and other countries use a system of "proportional representation" in which a party that loses an election nevertheless is given representation in the national legislative body in proportion to the share it gets of the total votes cast. For example, a party that gets 20 percent of the vote is awarded 20 percent of the seats in the Chamber of Deputies. In America it is much harder for a minority party to elect congressmen because they run in one-member congressional districts and a party must get more votes than any other party in a particular district to get a seat in Congress. A party that gets 49 percent of the votes in a two-party race gets zero representation in Congress. This creates an incentive for minority groups to combine into coalitions before an election. The ones who build the largest coalition take all of the marbles.

Thus America normally has only two major parties. Third parties exist, but usually do not attract enough votes to elect many congressmen. One of their handicaps is the tendency for one of the two major parties to steal their platform planks as soon as they have attracted much popular support. However, it is possible for a third party to displace a major party as happened on the eve of the Civil War when Republicans replaced Whigs.

The leaders who organized the movement to secure ratification of America's 1789 Constitution and establish the new federal government were called Federalists. One of their leading spirits was the brilliant young Alexander Hamilton, who became secretary of the Treasury in President George Washington's cabinet. Hamilton was a man of lowly origins but aristocratic views. He induced the federal government to assume responsibility for repaying the large sums which states had borrowed from the wealthy during the Revolution, and to raise the necessary funds by taxes which fell heavily on the poor.

These policies were opposed by Secretary of State Thomas Jefferson. He was a Virginia aristocrat, but his sympathies were with the small farmers whose interests he thought Hamilton was sacrificing to enrich the wealthy. To oppose Hamilton's policies, he organized the Republican party (which later changed its name to Democratic party), which was supported by farmers of the South and the West and by small businessmen and workingmen of northern cities. By the end of Washington's second administration, America had two political parties, the Federalists, led by Alexander Hamilton and John Adams, and the Republicans, led by Thomas Jefferson and James Madison.

The Federalists elected John Adams as president, but four years later Jefferson won the presidency in an election that he called the "Revolution of 1800." The Federalists never came close to winning a presidential election again. New immigrants and new western states voted Republican and, after Federalists threatened disunion during the War of 1812, the party disappeared.

This left the Republican party (read Democratic party) in unchallenged control. However, it soon split into two factions. One faction, which held principles similar to those of the Federalists, was called National Republican and later became the Whig party.

The faction more favorable to the common man was called Democratic party. In 1831 De Tocqueville wrote that the split was between aristocracy and democracy, between one party tied to the more privileged and another party tied to the less privileged.

The emergence of slavery as a political issue disrupted the Whig party. In 1854, a new party, the Republican party, was organized to oppose slavery. It attracted antislavery northern and western farmers, workingmen, merchants, and industrialists. The South and some northeastern cities remained Democratic. Strengthened by the Civil War, the Republicans became the party of the rising business and industrial groups. Between 1861 and 1933 Republicans held the presidency for fourteen terms while the Democrats held it for only four terms.

Republicans, however, received the blame for the Great Depression of 1929, which brought a major realignment of voters. A heavy shift in party registration among northern and western farmers, intellectuals, blacks, and workers made the Democrats the majority party. Between 1933 and 1980 the Democrats held the presidency for eight terms compared to four terms for the Republicans.

Recently party affiliation has declined sharply. A 1980 poll of voting age persons revealed that 45 percent identified themselves as Democrats, 33 percent as independents, and 22 percent as Republicans.

The use of the terms *left* and *right* to describe political programs arose from a custom in the French Chamber of Deputies for men who advocated certain political programs to sit on the left side of the house, and for men who opposed those programs to sit on the right. Thus they were called parties of the left or of the right.

As used in democracies, different degrees of leftness and rightness are indicated by the terms liberal, conservative, radical, and reactionary. A *liberal* is slightly to the left of center, and a *conservative* is slightly to the right. One who stands far to the left is called a *radical,* while an extreme rightist is called a *reactionary*.

What are the differences between the left and the right? One difference is in attitude toward change; the left favors change and the right opposes it. A conservative is satisfied with the existing political and economic system and fears that change would make things worse. He seeks to "conserve" existing values. A liberal believes that reforms are needed and wants moderate changes, moderate in degree and in speed. To the left of the liberal, the radical wants to make greater changes and to make them more rapidly. A reactionary not only opposes change but feels that there have already been too many changes and wants to return to conditions as they were in the past.

This explanation is incomplete. It defines the respective attitudes of these groups toward change, but does not specify what kind of change they favor or oppose. And, of course, this is the most important difference.

To attempt to answer this question exclusively in terms of specific issues can cause confusion. On some issues the left and the right have switched positions. In Alexander Hamilton's day, for example, conservatives wanted a strong federal government, while liberals defended states' rights, but today the reverse is true. This issue is really one of tactics—determining which level of government best serves one's purposes. In their fundamental aims liberals and conservatives are more constant.

Who would one expect to be more satisfied with the existing order of things, the poor or the wealthy? Of course, the wealthy are more likely to be satisfied, and the poor are more likely to want change. What kind of change would one expect the poor to favor? Of course, change that they believe would benefit them. Thus in general the left favors changes that it believes to be beneficial to the poor, possibly at the expense of the wealthy, while the right opposes such changes.

Where do America's leading political parties stand on a left-right scale? The answer is not simple, for both parties are coalitions of many groups who differ widely in their views. Nevertheless, it is clear that most Democrats advocate policies that are somewhat to the left of the policies advocated by most Republicans. While there are many exceptions, most Democrats are liberal, while most Republicans are conservative. America's political parties and organizations can be placed on a chart somewhat as follows:

Left		Right	
Radical	Liberal	Conservative	Reactionary
D	e mocra	t s	
	R	epubli c a	n s
Socialists Communists Anarchists			Birch Society

A majority of the Democratic party is liberal, but it has a conservative wing, mostly in the South. The Civil War and Reconstruction made the Republican party so unpopular in the South that for years no one who confessed to being a Republican had any chance of winning an election there. Therefore, in order to get elected, southern politicians who agreed with the policies of the Republican party had to call themselves Democrats. Consequently nearly all southern congressmen ran as Democrats, but once elected many of them voted in Congress with Republicans on the issues in Congress. A smaller number of Republican congressmen from northern states were liberal and on most issues voted with the Democrats.

To the left of the Democrats are the Socialists who favor eventual government ownership of the means of production but are willing to work toward that goal through gradual democratic reforms. To the left of the Socialists are the Communists, who want more complete government ownership and who want to make the change quickly. To the left of the Communists are the Anarchists who want to abolish not only private property, but government as well. No nationwide party exists to the right of the Republicans, but extreme rightists have formed organizations such as the John Birch Society. Groups at the extreme left or right are quite small in America, and most citizens support one of the two major parties.

THE POSITIONS OF THE MAJOR PARTIES ON CURRENT ISSUES

The tariff was once a major political issue. Advocating a high tariff, the Republican party argued that it was needed to protect American workers and that it would cause American industry to grow, strengthening the country. Democrats argued that a high tariff hurt international trade and took money from consumers to enrich industrialists. Perhaps because of a growing realization by powerful exporting industries that the more we import the more we can export, many Republicans stopped demanding high tariffs, and the issue ceased to play an important role in national elections.

The parties advocate different monetary policies. Deflation, the rise in the value of money that is reflected in falling prices, benefits those who own money or property of a fixed money value such as life insurance, bonds, mortgages, or pensions. It hurts those who owe money. On the other hand, inflation, the decline of the value of money that is reflected by rising prices, injures those who own money or property of a fixed money value. However, it helps those, including many low-income people, who are in debt. Both parties oppose inflation, but Democrats are less inclined than Republicans to fight inflation with measures that reduce production and raise unemployment.

The parties usually take opposite positions on tax laws. Republicans resist taxes on upper-income groups. Such taxes, they maintain, prevent the wealthy from accumulating the amounts of capital needed to build new factories and reduce the incentive for the wealthy to take the risk of investing in new businesses. Democrats, on the other hand, prefer higher taxes on the wealthy than on the poor, taxes based on "ability to pay." Such taxes cause less hardship, they maintain, and furthermore, taxes on low incomes take money that otherwise would be spent for consumer goods, and thereby depress sales, production, and profits.

A third issue concerns the relative power of federal and state governments. On this issue liberals and conservatives have reversed their positions. When Jefferson organized his party only one-fourth of the adult men could vote for representatives, state legislatures picked senators, the Electoral College named the president and the federal government favored the rich. In these circumstances, Jefferson considered the more democratic state governments to be more reliable protectors of the common man. During the nineteenth century, however, giant corporations became much too powerful for states to control and threatened the common man with overcharging and underpayment. At the same time, the federal government became more democratic and responsive to the needs of the poor. Consequently, liberals began looking to the federal government to control corporations and to help the underprivileged. Big corporations, on the other hand, now saw federal power as the chief threat to the maximization of their size and income. Consequently, conservatives denounced the growth of federal power and proposed measures, such as reducing the federal budget and sharing federal revenues with local governments, designed to roll back that power.

The clash over federal spending is particularly sharp regarding welfare spending, a fourth significant difference between the parties. Republicans do not object to spending for defense, which both parties support, but they fight hard to reduce the budgets of such Democratic party sponsored programs as food stamps, public service jobs, and aid to dependent children, education and health.

In a fifth area of difference, the Democratic party advocates measures designed to raise the income of farmers and workers, including minimum wage and maximum hour laws, protection of labor unions, and farm price supports. Republicans oppose most of these measures and, instead, advocate policies that more directly raise business profits.

For a long time the positions of the two parties on civil rights for blacks did not fit the pattern of their stands on other issues. The Republican party originated as an antislavery party and gave blacks political rights during Reconstruction. For many years most blacks were Republicans, but they found themselves in a quandary because one party was the civil rights party and the other was the poor man's party. When hard hit by the Great Depression in 1929, most blacks put economic interests first and voted Democratic, but later shifted back to support Eisenhower. In the 1960s, however, Democrats increasingly supported equal rights legislation, while Republicans adopted a "Southern strategy" of wooing white Southern votes, a "go slow" policy on school desegregation, and a "get tough" policy on black violence. Thus the Democrats became the champions of civil rights for blacks, and they shifted en masse to the Democratic party.

CONFUSION ON PARTY DIFFERENCES

If the above description is correct, the two major parties seek to move the country in opposite directions on matters of great importance to every citizen. Yet public opinion polls show that a surprisingly large number of Americans have no clear idea of the difference between the two parties. Why?

1. The two parties have many basic similarities. Both are moderate in their approach to the nation's problems, and endorse the same beliefs and values. Both uphold the basic principles of the American way of life which they define as democracy, freedom, and free enterprise. Both are broad-based coalitions of groups from all geographic areas of the country; both court all categories of voters—even if this involves them in self-contradiction. Thus, the differences between them are not as sharp and clear as those between parties in Europe.

2. Neither party makes its stand on the issues crystal clear. Both know that many of their members belong to the party because their parents did and not necessarily because they agree with its principles. Such members will continue to support the party out of

emotional loyalty as long as it does not make its opposition to their views unmistakably clear. Each party tries to give such members the excuse they want to vote for it. Furthermore, party platforms are often the result of compromises between opposing points of view and therefore employ language that can be interpreted in different ways in attempts to "paper over" splits within the party.

3. Another cause of confusion is that both parties are broad coalitions which embrace a wide range of divergent groups and include men who hold widely different views on some public issues. The Democratic party, as we have seen, contains a few reactionaries, and the Republican party a few liberals. This confuses many people who do not ask who are the exceptions and who are typical of the majority in their respective parties.

4. Because high income groups are a minority, the party that represents their interests would normally lose if elections were decided exclusively on economic issues. It can win only if it wins the votes of large numbers of low income people. Consequently it often seeks to divert public debate from economic to noneconomic issues that appeal to low income voters. For years after the Civil War conservative Southern Democrats won the votes of poor whites by exploiting their racism. In 1952 a Republican slogan was "Communism, Corruption, and Korea." In 1972 Republicans emphasized opposition to "crime in the streets," bussing to achieve integration, abortion, amnesty, and student radicals. The injection of such exciting and distracting issues tends to blur public perception of basic party differences.

5. Each party tends to nominate presidential candidates whose views are middle-of-the-road. Assuming that they will receive the support of most liberals, Democrats concentrate on winning votes from center and conservative groups. To do this they usually nominate a candidate who is more conservative than most Democrats. Republicans, on the other hand, feel sure of receiving the conservative vote, and try to add votes from middle-of-the-roaders and liberals. To do so they usually nominate a candidate who is more liberal than most Republicans. Thus, the personal views of the two candidates are often quite close. H. L. Mencken once described an American election as a "deafening, nerve-wracking battle to the death between Tweedledum and Tweedledee."

Nevertheless, it does make a difference which party wins. The positions of the two opposing candidates may be similar, but behind them are armies of supporters who are pulling them in opposite directions. Thus, the election decides in which of the two opposite directions the federal government will move—whether it will take a step or two to the right, or a step or two to the left.

WHO BELONGS TO EACH PARTY?

Historically, particular groups have become identified as supporters of one of the parties. With exceptions, it has been found that the majority of the members of each of the following groups normally votes for the party under which it is listed:

Mostly Democratic	*Mostly Republican*
Southern farmers	Midwestern farmers
Union labor	Businessmen
Cities	Suburbs and small towns
Low income groups	High income groups
High school graduates	College graduates
Intellectuals	Newspaper publishers
Young people	Older people
Minorities	Old American stock

Of course, exceptions and shifts occur. Midwestern farmers shifted their votes to the Democrats in several recent elections, while southern states shifted to the Republicans. The majority of college graduates are Republican, perhaps because most of them are from well-to-do families, but most of the people in the so-called intellectual professions, such as writing, teaching, and law, are Democrats. Another interesting exception is that many of the leaders of the Republican party have been self-made men who rose from poverty, such as Presidents Hoover, Eisenhower, and Nixon, while many Democratic leaders have been born into wealthy aristocratic families, for example Presidents Jefferson, Franklin Roosevelt, and Kennedy.

THE FINANCING OF POLITICAL PARTIES AND ELECTIONS

In 1956 spending in national, state, and local political campaigns totalled $155 million. By 1972 campaign spending had risen to more than $400 million, and the two presidential candidates spent more than $90 million collected from private sources. In most cases money seemed to be decisive. In 1974, for example, the biggest spenders won in thirty-two of the thirty-four Senate races.

The need to collect large sums from private sources to finance

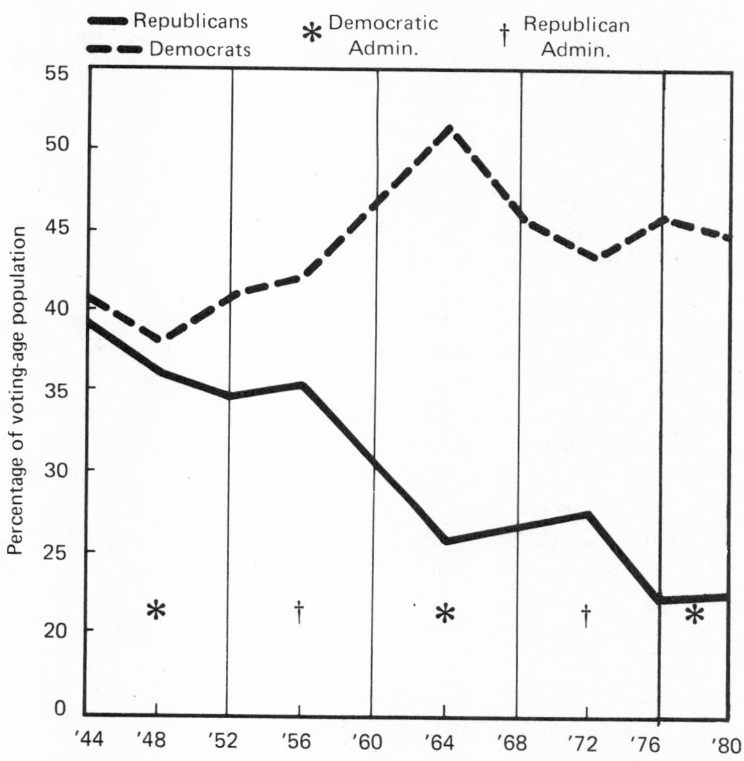

Fig. 11.1. **Changing Party Affiliations, According to Gallup Polls.**

political campaigns endangers democracy. It makes races between poor and wealthy candidates unequal contests. In effect, a candidate must first be elected by moneyed men before he can seek election by the people. It subjects him to great pressures to become corrupt. One veteran political observer said that it was impossible to get elected to a major office "unless you're independently rich or you sell your soul."

If a political party cannot campaign without huge sums, then it is dependent on the sources of the money. If the money is furnished by a few wealthy men, they thereby acquire great influence on the party and the government. According to a former Common Cause chairman, John Gardner, the campaign gift is the modern equivalent of the old-fashioned bribe.

Of course small contributions from the rank and file of the party would reduce party dependence on big contributors. However, the average citizen usually is unwilling to contribute to political campaigns. In 1964, Republicans mailed fund-raising letters to 10 million persons and collected $4 million, but the cost of the effort (postage and stationery alone cost $700,000) made it scarcely worthwhile. Senator George McGovern had more success with mail solicitation in 1972, but under special circumstances that might not recur.

A traditional tactic of political bosses was to require party members who held government jobs to make regular contributions. This gave them some independence of big contributors, but it was criticized by reformers on the grounds that it gave incumbents an unfair advantage and enabled corrupt political machines to keep themselves in power. Compelling office holders to contribute part of their salaries to the party reduced, in effect, their take-home pay and added to the difficulty of attracting better qualified persons to government service. It amounted to an unauthorized transfer of public funds to a political party.

Another common method of raising funds is to solicit "voluntary contributions" from businessmen who sell goods or services to the government. Sometimes they are told that a certain amount is their "fair share" with the implication that they must contribute if they expect continued sales. The necessity of making such contributions causes them to raise their prices to the government. Thus collecting political contributions from them is, in effect, an indirect transfer of government funds to a political party.

In 1962 a bipartisan commission appointed by President Kennedy recommended that the government pay most campaign costs. This proposal was endorsed by former Presidents Truman and Eisenhower. In 1967, President Johnson told Congress that "our ultimate goal should be to finance the total expense for this vital function of our democracy with public funds and to prohibit the use or acceptance of money from private sources."

The 1973 Watergate investigation and its revelations of widespread corruption in the financing of the 1972 presidential campaign provided new insights into the seriousness of the problem. It was discovered, for example, that shortly after the milk producers' association contributed more than $400,000 to President Nixon's campaign fund, they got higher price supports; that after a big financier contributed $200,000, SEC charges against him were reduced; and after ITT contributed $200,000, it got permission to absorb the Hartford Life Insurance Company. Nine corporations, including three oil and two airline companies, confessed to making illegal campaign contributions from corporation funds.

Federal Campaign Spending Laws

Attempts were made in the Hatch Acts of 1939 and 1940 to set upper limits on political spending and contributions, but so many loopholes were found that these laws were ineffective. A new series of laws enacted in 1971–75 promised a significant change in campaign financing.

Their first step was provision of an acceptable means of donating federal funds to political parties for campaign purposes. Many reformers felt that direct Congressional appropriations for such purposes would be improper. They arranged, instead, to allow each taxpayer to indicate on his income tax form if he wanted $1 of his tax payment put into a nonpartisan political fund to be used to pay the campaign expenses of both parties. This cost the taxpayer nothing and resulted in the accumulation of a substantial fund.

Money from the fund is allotted to candidates and political parties as follows:

Money is provided to match private contributions on a fifty-fifty basis to pay the expenses of candidates in presidential preference primaries. Nearly all presidential hopefuls enter primary elections held in a number of states before the parties' national conventions. These elections enable rank and file members of the party to express their preference for the party's nomination. To become eligible for government funds, a candidate must first prove that he is a serious contender by collecting from private sources, in contributions no larger than $250 each, a sum of $5,000 in each of twenty states. If he succeeds, he is given one dollar of federal money for each dollar he receives in private contributions up to $5 million. He is forbidden to spend in excess of the resulting $10 million campaign fund except for $2 million for money-raising expenses.

The federal government provides the major parties $2 million each to pay for their national conventions.

In the general election, the campaigns of the nominees of the two major parties are financed mostly from government funds. Each party receives $20 million, adjusted for the cost of living, and is allowed to spend only $2.9 million additional from private donations. Thus, the upper limit on total spending by both parties in the presidential contest is approximately $46 million—compared to the $96 million spent by one candidate in 1972. In 1977 the Federal Elections Commission recommended raising government grants to allow candidates to wage more vigorous campaigns.

Congressional candidates receive no government campaign funds. However, a limit is placed on the amount of private money they can spend. For candidates to the Senate the limit in primary campaigns is $100,000 or eight cents per eligible voter, whichever is larger, and in the general election it is $150,000 or twelve cents per voter. For House candidates the limit in either a primary or general election is $70,000. Both are allowed an additional 20 percent to pay the cost of soliciting contributions.

The laws also put upper limits on contributions. No individual is allowed to contribute more than $1,000 to any one candidate in a single election—in effect $3,000 if the candidate takes part in a primary, a runoff election, and the general election. No individual is permitted to contribute more than $25,000 to all candidates in one year. Organizations can contribute no more than $5,000 to individual candidates per election. The law also attempted to put an upper limit on the amount a wealthy candidate could spend of his own money in his campaign, but the Supreme Court ruled that this provision was an unconstitutional limitation on free speech.

To enforce these provisions, the laws created a Federal Elections Commission to receive reports of all contributions and expenditures. Each candidate must designate one principal campaign committee to be responsible for reporting the collections and contributions of all other committees working in his behalf. Contributions larger than $100 must be made by check.

These laws were a major step toward democratizing campaign financing. They did not remove, but substantially diluted the power of big money in politics. They did not satisfy those who, like President Johnson, thought that government should be the exclusive financier of elections. And loopholes in the laws remained. For example, in the 1976 election for the House of Representatives, one candidate reported campaign spending of $637,000 ($491,000 of which was his personal money), and another reported spending $555,000 ($507,000 of which he furnished personally). In 1978 a candidate for the Senate spent nearly $3 million on his campaign, and total spending on congressional campaigns exceeded $150 million. The special interests that found it more difficult to contribute to presidential campaigns seemed to be shifting their money to congressional races.

The Structure of Political Parties

Political parties are not mentioned in the Constitution. They began as private organizations and were scarcely regulated by law until the twentieth century. At the bottom of their organizational pyramids are local *precinct workers* (a precinct is a small area, the citizens of which vote at one polling place) and *ward chairmen* (a ward is the smallest administrative subdivision of a city and usually includes several precincts) whose task it is to enlist support for candidates, remind all party members to vote, and furnish babysitters and transportation to the polls. Most cities and townships have party *executive committees,* which are selected by ward or precinct meetings. Above them is the *county executive committee,* whose members are usually elected in party primaries. The county executive committee elects the county chairman, the most important local party official, and assists him in raising funds, mobilizing audiences for visiting campaigners, and getting out the vote. The county chairman normally controls most party funds and appointments to government jobs within the county. *State executive committees* and *state chairmen* perform similar functions on the state level. The party's *national committee* is made up of two committeemen (one man and one woman) from each state. It supervises national fund-raising and campaigning, and chooses the *national chairman,* who manages the campaign of the party's presidential candidate.

County and state committees are usually chosen directly by the party's voters and are only loosely connected with each other and with the national party organization. Party organizations are strongest at the county and state levels, and only every four years do they join in a nationwide campaign. No direct lines of authority run from top to bottom and orders cannot be handed down. But local politicians are anxious to have their friends appointed to government jobs, awarded contracts, and given lucrative legal assignments and are, therefore, more than eager to cooperate with party leaders.

In addition to the regular organization, each party has many special organizations and committees, permanent and temporary. Among these are a Senate campaign committee and a House campaign committee and several affiliated organizations such as the Young Democrats, Young Republicans, Citizens for Johnson and Humphrey, or Independents for Nixon.

NATIONAL CONVENTIONS

The climactic events in the lives of political parties are their national conventions which meet every four years in the summers preceding presidential elections. Most of the important leaders of the party attend: governors, senators, representatives, cabinet officers, and political managers. Their chief functions are to nominate candidates for president and vice-president, adopt statements of the party's programs called platforms, and to whip up enthusiasm for the coming campaign.

The number of delegates sent by each state is based on formulas that take into account its population and whether it voted for the party's candidates in the last election. In 37 states (1980) delegates are elected in presidential *primaries* in which the party's voters indicate their choice of candidate for their party's nomination. Each state's primary differs somewhat from others. Some states require their delegates to vote for the presidential candidate who wins the primary, but some do not. Delegates may vote on the first ballot for their primary winner but desert him on the second ballot for another candidate. Rarely could a candidate win enough votes in the primaries to be nominated.

In some cases, however, presidential primaries have proven to be decisive. For example, the victory of John Kennedy over Hubert Humphrey in the West Virginia primary in 1960 showed that a Catholic could win in a Protestant state, and this enabled him to get the nomination. Also the increase in the number of states holding primaries from seventeen in 1968 to 37 in 1980 made them more decisive. In 1972 and 1976 Democratic candidates who initially had little support among party leaders were able, through victories in the primaries, to capture the Democratic presidential nominations. In 1976 and 1980 the primaries also decided the contest between the leading contenders for the presidential nominations.

In states where delegates are not elected, they are chosen by state conventions, district conventions, state executive committees, or by a combination of these. This usually means that they are chosen by the politicians who control the party. Such delegates are not free to make their own decisions, but follow the instructions of their delegation leaders. Because of his influence with party leaders, a president usually controls his party's national convention.

In the conventions, delegates are seated on the main floor while spectators are admitted to the galleries. Those who watch a convention are apt to be shocked. Amid great confusion, long-winded speakers shout platitudes over public address systems, while the delegates mill about in the aisles, talk, and pay little attention to the speaker. Occasionally the delegates "demonstrate" support for a candidate or proposition by marching through the aisles carrying state banners, shouting, applauding, blowing horns, and singing while the chairman pounds the gavel and pleads for order. Former President Dwight Eisenhower wrote that the "confusion, noise, impossible deportment, and indifference to what is being discussed on the platform" were horrifying.

A convention, however, is not as mindless as it appears. It is mostly marking time and letting prominent politicians get free nationwide television exposure while important work is being completed in committee meetings, in conferences on the floor, and in various headquarters and hotel rooms.

One of the most important convention committees is the *credentials committee*. Sometimes two or more factions of a state party send different delegations to the national convention. The credentials committee must decide which of these groups of delegates is entitled to represent the state. Because the rival delegations often favor different candidates, the committee's decisions can determine the outcome of the convention.

A large *resolutions committee,* composed of two delegates from each state, usually begins work on the party *platform* before the convention meets. The platform is a series of statements (called planks) setting forth the party's position on the questions of the day, such as labor, agriculture, banking, or education. Sharp fights on controversial planks frequently keep the committee in round-the-clock session. Sometimes, a faction that is defeated in the committee will make a minority report urging the convention to adopt its plank instead of that of the majority. Exciting debates sometimes follow.

The selection of the party's presidential candidate involves the highest drama. For years, strong and attractive personalities have been maneuvering for this moment, making speeches, writing articles, seeking leadership of great national causes, and making alliances with the bosses who control state delegations. They campaign in some primaries to show their vote-getting ability or to defeat some dangerous rival. Some, however, enter no primaries, but concentrate, instead, on winning the support of the political leaders who control state delegations. At the convention, rival candidates compete furiously for the favor of uncommitted delegates.

Each contender is put before the convention in a nominating speech emphasizing his admirable qualities, his party service, and his chances of winning the election. His followers then attempt to create an impression of overwhelming enthusiasm for his nomination by applauding, shouting, singing, and parading through the aisles. Seconding speeches follow. The convention must also listen to speeches nominating "favorite sons," men who do not have enough support to make them serious candidates, but whom their states wish to compliment and advertise.

Eventually the chairman begins to call the roll of the states. As each state is called its delegation chairman announces its vote. Sometimes no candidate receives a majority and several ballots must be taken while favorite sons drop out and bargains are made. Finally one candidate emerges triumphant. Now the whole convention goes wild in a tremendous demonstration and the successful candidate appears at the rostrum to acknowledge the applause. When order is restored he makes his acceptance speech, thoughtfully written in advance.

The choice of a vice-presidential candidate is an anticlimax. The convention usually endorses the man picked by the presidential candidate. Normally he seeks to "balance the ticket" by naming a liberal if he is a conservative, or a westerner if he is from the East. Sometimes more attention is given to such political factors than to his qualifications for the presidency.

The wisdom of choosing party candidates in national conventions has been questioned. When conventions originated in the 1830s they were more democratic than previous methods of choosing candidates. Recently a demand has arisen to make the process of choosing party candidates even more democratic and give ordinary citizens more voice in their selection. Some want a nationwide primary to give all party members an opportunity to elect one out of two or three candidates nominated by conventions. A majority of the people favor this reform. However, it would be too expensive unless the election were paid for by the federal government.

Complaints arising from the conduct of the 1968 convention led the Democratic party to appoint a commission to investigate the processes by which delegates were selected. It found that 30 percent of them were chosen before 1968 and in one case a state governor had personally appointed his state's entire delegation. Only 30 percent of the delegates were elected by rank and file party members. Women, young people, and blacks were underrepresented and small states were overrepresented. In its call for the 1972 national convention, the Democratic National Committee said that all delegates must be selected after January of an election year and that candidates for delegate must state their choice for president. It assigned more delegates to large states to bring their representation in line with their population. It successfully demanded more representation for young people, women, and blacks. More than 60 percent of the delegates to the 1972 Democratic convention were elected by the party's rank and file. Similar reforms were adopted by the Republican party.

Presidential Elections

Election day falls on the Tuesday after the first Monday in November, and presidential campaigns begin in July or August. The candidates travel about the country making speeches in the large cities and numerous shorter talks along the way. They feel it necessary to mix with the people and shake as many hands as possible, despite the danger revealed by the shooting of Robert Kennedy in 1968 and George Wallace in 1972. (It would be safer to rely more on television.) They set forth their views and seek to convince the public that they are knowledgeable, effective, friendly, and likeable—wholly fit to be the nation's leader.

Meanwhile hordes of other speakers, including members of the cabinet, governors, and prominent congressmen, reinforce the campaign. Moving pictures, television, radio, and newspaper advertising, billboards, recordings, campaign songs, picnics, coffees, and formal dinners—every device is used to win votes. Particularly intense efforts are made in large states that are closely divided between the parties.

Nevertheless all of this excitement does not succeed in shaking a large part of the American electorate out of its apathy. Scarcely two-thirds of the qualified voters go to the polls even in presidential election years. Unwilling to make the effort necessary to acquaint themselves with the candidates and issues, many voters shirk their responsibility to democracy.

Failure to vote is not always the citizen's fault. Despite our democratic principles, many citizens are not allowed to vote. The Constitution and federal laws forbid states to deny anyone the vote in federal elections on the grounds of race, sex, or failure to pay a poll tax, and in 1970 Congress reduced the age requirement for voting in federal elections to eighteen. But states can put other restrictions on voting. For example, most states bar idiots, prisoners, people on welfare, and those who have not been residents of the state for a required period of time. State, county, and precinct residency requirements of up to two years prevented an estimated six million people, including four out of ten persons between the ages of twenty-one and thirty, from voting in the 1970 election. In 1970 Congress reduced to thirty days the length of residency required to qualify for voting in a federal election.

Forty-eight of the fifty states also require a voter to register in advance of the election. He must provide officials with data on his age, place of birth, length of residence, and place of employment so that they can determine if he is legally entitled to vote. Many citizens neglect to register, particularly when they move to a new place. Consequently, only three-fourths of the nation's potential voters are registered, and half of the 29 million who are not registered (1969) are under thirty years of age. President Carter proposed that the law be changed to allow citizens to vote without advance registration.

A smaller percentage of eligible voters cast their ballots in national elections in America than in any other major democracy. In the presidential election of 1972 only 54.2 percent of voting-age citizens (only 44 percent of those aged twenty-five or less) actually voted. In the congressional elections of 1978 only 36 percent voted.

Who are the nonvoters? The differences between voters and nonvoters are much the same in all industrialized democracies.

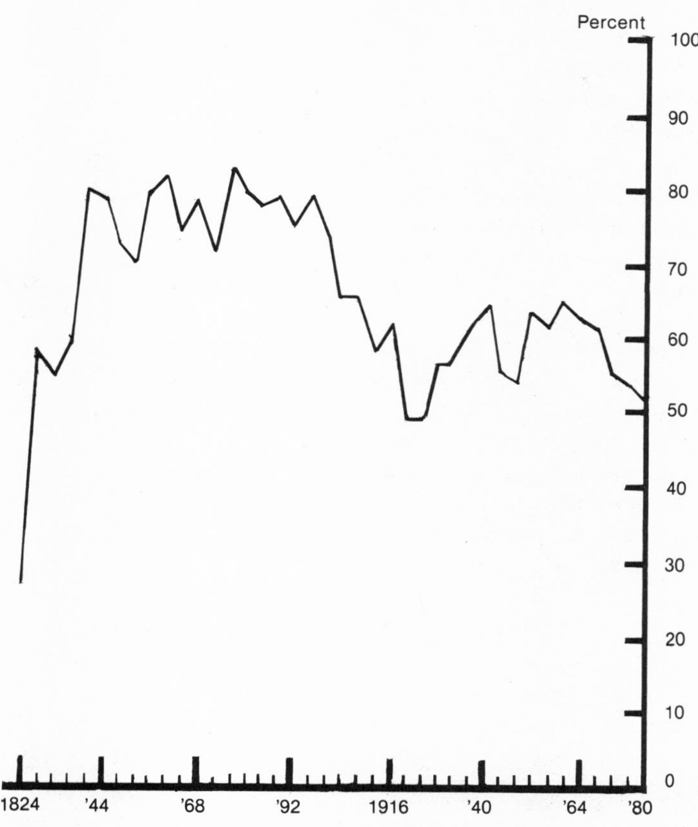

Fig. 11.2. **Voters Participating in Presidential Elections: Percent of Voting-Age Population.** (U.S. Bureau of the Census, 1977)

Most likely to vote are those who are in the upper-income bracket, college-educated, married, well informed, highly partisan, organization members, male, and between the ages of thirty-five and fifty-five. Least likely are those who are in a low-income bracket, less educated, unmarried, apathetic, younger than thirty-five, older than fifty-five, and female. In America, whites, northerners, Republicans, and city dwellers vote more than southerners, Democrats, blacks, and rural residents. Consequently, establishment types are overrepresented among voters, and minority groups and young people are underrepresented.

Does nonvoting indicate alienation from the system? Perhaps that explains some of it, but other nonvoters may feel that either party rule is acceptable to them. In some countries, periods of mass discontent are marked by unusually high levels of voting.

Reform groups urge citizens to vote, and some reformers have proposed that voting be made compulsory. However, a vote by an uninformed or apathetic citizen probably does the country little service. The need, perhaps, is not merely for more voters, but for more well-informed voters.

As described earlier, the framers of the Constitution did not intend to permit the people to elect the president. They allowed them to choose electors whom they expected would exercise their own judgment on whom to name president and vice-president. The development of political parties overrode this arrangement almost immediately, but the Electoral College remained and its continuing existence worries many democratic reformers.

Each state elects a number of electors equal to the number of its senators and representatives in Congress. This means that small states have more votes in relation to population than large states. The system also makes it possible for a candidate to be elected president with fewer popular votes than received by his defeated rival. Furthermore, electors are not legally bound to vote for the same candidate as the people of their state, and a few electors have refused to do so. Many political scientists want to abolish the Electoral College altogether and elect presidents by direct popular vote. According to the Gallup Poll a majority of the people have favored this reform for years.

THE VALUE OF POLITICAL PARTIES

One enormous service of political parties is the role they play in securing compromise and agreement among people on programs of government action. The nation contains many special interest groups: economic, geographic, and cultural. Each might organize a separate political party, but in our political system a single-interest party has not won an election. Therefore, a number of different interest groups form alliances, or coalitions, in attempts to combine into parties large enough to win a majority of voters. In the process, each must agree to forgo some part of its program and to support items favored by others. Party leaders try to formulate programs which the largest possible number of people can support.

Thus, by arranging compromises on many conflicts, political parties help our system to work more harmoniously.

Second, the necessity of winning a majority of votes raises to leadership men of moderate views who unite the country rather than divide it. An extremist cannot win an election and usually cannot win a party nomination. Instead of advocating radical or reactionary causes, ambitious party leaders seek to position themselves near the center of the road. This helps to reduce the sharpness and bitterness of partisan conflicts.

Third, political parties assist voters in making choices. They present the voters with a manageable number of candidates and alternative policies, and give them an informative debate on the issues of the day. The average voter does not have enough time and information to make mature judgments on the relative personal merits of all candidates for political office. He is more likely to be familiar, in a general way, with the political parties and their positions on the public issues, and can make his choice on the basis of the candidates' party affiliations.

Fourth, political parties protect minority groups. If the two major parties are evenly balanced in strength, the shift of a small group from one to the other can tilt the balance between them. Therefore they seek to avoid offending minorities, particularly those located in strategic cities.

Of course our party system also has faults. It frequently puts men of average, rather than superior, abilities in office. Also, members of the defeated party continue to attack and oppose the measures of the party in power. Sometimes it appears that they seek to prevent it from achieving any success that would add to its prestige and popularity. Hence American government is conducted amid constant public controversy, and practically every measure of the government is condemned by one party. Excessive partisanship sometimes has an irrational influence on important national decisions.

On the other hand, the knowledge that its every measure will be subjected to a drumfire of attack makes the party in power more responsive, careful, honest, and aware of the necessity of explaining its policies to the people. It seeks to avoid unpopular acts or scandals that could be used to defeat it in the next election. This adds to the responsibility of American government.

The American system of political parties and regular elections has been imitated by many countries but has worked well in few of them. In less developed countries there is a tendency for partisan controversy to be unrestrained and bitter, for debate to become irrational and emotional, for elections to be conducted unfairly, and for those in power to suppress free speech and the rights of opponents. Consequently, those defeated in elections are sometimes unwilling to accept the results, and, with little hope that the next election will be honest, they may resort to violence.

The success of democracy in America rests largely on political maturity. Building on lessons learned from Europe, we tolerate political opposition, give it freedom of speech and organization, and conduct honest elections. In so doing we provide a means whereby diverse social, economic, cultural, and racial groups can fight for power and possibly win without violence. American society is becoming more complex, but our gains in political maturity and education may enable us to keep the avenues of peaceful change open, and thereby to continue enjoying a large measure of freedom and self-government.

Questions

1. Why are political parties formed and on what issues do they usually take opposite stands?
2. Why does America have a two-party instead of a multiparty system?
3. How do the political left and right differ in their attitudes toward change and in the kinds of change that they favor or oppose?
4. Which party is mostly liberal? Which is mostly conservative? List measures that are favored by liberals and opposed by conservatives.
5. Why do many people find it difficult to understand the differences between the Democratic and Republican parties?
6. What groups have usually voted Democratic? What groups have usually voted Republican?
7. How do radicals and reactionaries differ? In what respect are they similar?
8. What is the basic aim of the left? Of the right? In what way

have both changed their tactics since the nineteenth century?

9. How expensive are elections? Where do parties get the money to pay these expenses?
10. What changes were made in campaign financing by the 1971–74 federal election laws?
11. How does the two-party system help to moderate conflicts between groups? How does it help to protect minority rights?
12. How has the nomination of presidential candidates been made more democratic?
13. Why is political maturity essential to the functioning of a democracy?
14. How do political parties affect the functioning of the American political system?
15. Define or identify the following: Federalists, welfare spending, Hatch Acts, national committee, state central committee, primary, platform, Electoral College.

Suggested Reading

Bagby, Wesley M. *The Road to Normalcy: The Presidential Campaign and Election of 1920*. Baltimore, Md.: Johns Hopkins University Press, 1968.
A short history and analysis that emphasizes the inner workings of national conventions and party campaign committees.

Congressional Quarterly: Dollar Politics. Vol. 2. Washington, D.C.: U.S. Government Printing Office, n.d.
Discusses the Watergate scandals, interest group spending, campaign financing in Europe, and the new campaign spending laws.

Dunn, Delmer D. *Financing Presidential Campaigns*. Washington, D.C.: Brookings Institution, 1972.
Traces the rise of campaign spending and evaluates reform proposals.

Green, Mark J., et al. *Who Runs Congress: Ralph Nader Congress Project*. New York: Bantam Books, 1972.
A critical examination of the shortcomings of Congress, its undemocratic features, its catering to special-interest groups, and its failures.

Hess, Stephen. *The Presidential Campaign: The Leadership Selection Process after Watergate*. Washington, D.C.: Brookings Institution, 1974.

A critical examination of the means by which America selects its presidents and proposals for reform.

Rossiter, Clinton. *Parties and Politics in America*. New York: Signet Books, 1960.

Describes the Democratic and Republican parties, how they are organized, who belongs to each, why the two-party system persists, and the importance of the contest.

Tugwell, Rexford G. *How They Became President: Thirty-Five Ways to the White House*. New York: Simon and Schuster, 1965.

Describes how each of our presidents rose to the top of our political system.

White, Theodore H. *The Making of the President, 1968*. New York: Pocket Books, 1969.

A noted reporter with access to inside information discusses leading issues, events, and figures in a lively style, from a pro-Johnson point of view.

12
Problems in Federal Financing

What are the chief sources of the federal government's income and what does it spend its money for?
What kind of taxation is least objectionable?
Is federal spending excessive?

"Taxes are the price we pay for civilized society."
—Justice Oliver Wendell Holmes

"The power to tax is the one great power on which the whole national fabric is based. . . . It is not only the power to destroy but the power to keep alive."
—United States Supreme Court
in McCulloch v. Maryland

"Reform of our federal tax system is long overdue. Special preferences in the law permit far too many Americans to pay less than their fair share of taxes. Too many other Americans bear too much of the tax burden."
—President Richard M. Nixon

The Taxing Problem

Politics has been called the "art of who gets what." From whom shall money be taken, and to whom shall money be given are the two most basic issues in politics. A nation's taxing and spending policies express its values and priorities. They affect not only the size and vigor of government, but the distribution of wealth among individuals and the relative emphasis the nation gives to public services as opposed to private consumption. How much tax to collect, what kind of taxes to collect, how much to spend and for what purpose are among government's most important decisions.

In England, through a century of struggle, the people forced kings to accept the principle that Englishmen could be forced to pay only the taxes to which they gave their consent through their elected representatives. Britain's attempt to tax Americans without their consent was a major cause of the American Revolution. Our first constitution, the Articles of Confederation, gave the central government no power to tax, which left it too weak to meet the nation's problems. In the 1789 Constitution, Congress was given the power to "lay and collect taxes, duties, imposts, and excises."

The functions, size, and expenditures of the federal government grew slowly for most of our history. In 1933, federal spending was only $4.6 billion and the national debt only $23 billion. Then came a major expansion which, in historical perspective, was breathtaking in its speed and magnitude. By fiscal 1981 federal spending climbed above $530 billion annually and the national debt exceeded $900 billion. Even when one makes allowance for inflation, this was a spectacular explosion of government. Federal spending rose from 8 percent of the GNP in 1933 to 22 percent of the GNP in 1979.

Is such a high rate of spending necessary? Does much of it represent waste and inefficiency? The answer to both questions may be yes. The services and functions that the people demanded, many of them made essential by the growing interdependence and complexity of modern society, required enormous amounts of money. A huge increase in government occurred in all industrialized nations. And, regrettably, certain tendencies in government organizations made them less efficient than private corporations and made waste difficult to avoid.

One wasteful characteristic of government is the tendency to overstaff. The elected congressmen who establish and finance government agencies are under pressure to find jobs for their constituents. Bureau heads also seek to increase the number of people serving under them in order to magnify their power and importance. Once established, agencies seek more money for themselves regardless of need for their services. They spend all the money appropriated to them to avoid giving the impression that they could get by on less. If ordered to reduce manpower, they often choose to cut back their most essential functions first to bring pressure to get funds restored. Sometimes their procedures, involving multitudinous forms and mountains of red tape, seem to be designed to make work for idle employees. Government bureaus are extravagant. Purchasing agents tend to pay high prices for the goods and services that they buy from corporations which, in turn, make a practice of giving jobs to former purchasing agents.

Another form of waste occurs because many government agencies originated, not as a part of an overall plan, but to meet specific problems, with the consequence that their functions sometimes overlap, duplicate, or compete with other ones. The federal bureaucracy is so huge and complicated that no one man can grasp the entire picture of its operations. Special commissions, the most famous of which was headed by former President Herbert Hoover, recommended reorganization and consolidation; and the adoption of many of their recommendations saved billions of dollars per year. But the government has expanded so rapidly that the need for re-examination is continuous.

It should be emphasized that the basic cause of the spectacular rise in the size and cost of the federal government is the demand by people for more services. The largest appropriations are for national defense. Rapid expansion also occurred in Social Security programs, highway building, and education. The increase has continued under both political parties no matter how loudly the presidents had denounced excessive spending before their elections.

What Is a Good Tax?

A tax is a compulsory payment made for the support of public services. One of the more important aspects of a tax is what economists call its *incidence,* by which they mean upon whom does the tax ultimately fall. The person from whom the government collects the tax is not always the one who actually pays it in the end. In the case of a consumer sales tax this is quite clear. The state tax department collects this tax from the managers of retail stores. But, the stores do not pay the consumer sales tax; they add it as a separate charge to their customers' bills. Because the tax appears on the sales ticket, everyone understands that it is ultimately paid by the consumer, and that the store acts as a tax collector for the state.

In the case of another form of sales tax, a gross sales tax, the state collects a tax from retail stores equal to a percentage, perhaps

3 percent, of their total sales. This tax does not appear on sales slips but, of course the store must charge enough for its merchandise to cover all of its costs, including taxes, plus a profit. Therefore, it adds the gross sales tax to the prices it charges its customers. Because the amount is not stated as a separate item on the sales slip, consumers are often unaware that they pay this *hidden* or *indirect* tax in the form of higher prices.

How can we be sure that no part of the gross sales tax is paid by the retailer? If the tax were repealed could not he go on charging the same prices and thus make a higher profit? The answer is that prices charged by retailers are influenced by the prices that competing stores charge. Normally, stores charge as much as they can without losing their customers to the competing retailers who are trying to lure them away with claims that they charge lower prices. Abolishing the gross sales tax would enable a merchant's competitors to cut prices 3 percent with no loss of profit, and force him to do likewise. If neither he nor his competition cut prices, their resulting higher profits would entice other businessmen to enter their business until increased competition forced prices down. As a rule, any tax that falls equally on all business competitors is passed on to be paid by consumers. This includes property taxes on business property, business and occupational taxes, and professional license fees.

Prominent among taxes which cannot be passed on to be paid by someone else are the personal income tax and the corporate net income tax.

Taxes also may be classified according to their comparative impact on low and high incomes. A tax that takes the same percentage of the incomes of a poor and a rich man is called a *proportional* tax. A tax that takes a larger percentage of the income of a poor man than of a rich man is called a *regressive* tax. A tax that takes a larger percentage of the income of a rich man than of a poor man is called a *progressive* tax.

Political scientists and economists agree that it is desirable for a tax to meet several criteria:

1. It should be easy to collect. It should be easy for the people to understand, difficult to avoid paying, and collecting it should cost only a small fraction of the revenue it produces.
2. It should fall equally on persons in equal circumstances.
3. It should take account of ability to pay and not inflict undue hardship on those unable to pay.

4. It should impair economic incentives and opportunities as little as possible and do the least possible harm to the economy.

5. It should produce a predictable amount of revenue.

6. It should help to moderate the up and down swings of the economic cycle by taking more money in periods of boom, and less in periods of recession.

7. It should not discourage socially desirable activities nor reward socially undesirable ones.

It is difficult to find taxes that meet all of these standards, or even most of them. However, some forms of taxation are more objectionable than others. The principal federal taxes are personal income taxes, corporate income taxes, excise taxes, and tariffs. We will analyze these taxes in reverse order to their contemporary importance.

The Tariff

The first tax levied by Congress was a 5 percent tariff (a tax on goods brought into the country from abroad). The government collects the tariff from the businessmen who import foreign goods, but importers add the tax to their selling price. Thus its incidence is on consumers. The tariff was the chief source of federal income until World War I.

American manufacturers favored tariffs because tariffs raised the price of foreign-made goods and allowed American industrialists to charge higher prices for the goods they produced. At their insistence, the tariff was raised repeatedly. Eventually, it reached an average level of more than 60 percent.

In 1934 President Franklin D. Roosevelt began reducing tariffs through a program of negotiating treaties with other countries for mutual tariff reductions. Stronger American industries supported these "reciprocal trade agreements" as a means of increasing their sales abroad, and the reductions eventually won backing from both political parties. By 1979 the average tax on all goods imported for consumption was down to 6 percent, which produced approximately $7.4 billion or 1.5 percent of federal revenues.

Excise Taxes

A second type of tax is the excise tax; a tax on the manufacture or sale of goods, or on the practice of occupations. The most familiar of these is the consumer sales tax. Similar taxes of several cents were put on every package of cigarettes and every gallon of gasoline. Most excise taxes are state taxes, but some are federal.

The excise tax is such a quick and dependable source of revenue that it is much used in wartime. During World War II and the Korean War, excise taxes, usually 10 percent, were placed on nearly all purchases, including telephone calls, telegrams, admission tickets, jewelry, and cosmetics. Some war taxes were repealed, but in 1979 remaining excise taxes produced $18.7 billion or about 4 percent of federal revenue.

The principal remaining federal excise taxes serve as user's charges on government services which are of special benefit to particular groups. Highway users pay for highway construction and maintenance through taxes on gasoline, tires, and trucks. A 5 percent tax on air transportation pays part of the cost of federal air safety programs. A 10 percent tax on fishing tackle and firearms pays for conserving wildlife. A tax on motorboat fuel pays the cost of maintaining inland waterways.

Federal excise taxes on tobacco, alcoholic beverages, and gambling devices are favored by groups who wish to discourage use of these items for moral or health reasons. In 1979, taxes on alcoholic beverages brought in $5.6 billion and taxes on tobacco produced $2.5 billion.

Although they were collected from manufacturers, merchants, or professional men, excise taxes are passed on to be paid by consumers as a hidden or indirect tax in the form of higher prices. Except those on luxury goods, excise taxes take a higher percentage of low incomes than of high incomes. (For example, a rich man and a poor man eat about the same amount of bread and thus pay the same amount of sales tax on bread.)

THE CORPORATE INCOME TAX

A larger source of federal revenue is the *corporate net income tax,* a tax on corporation profits. In 1979 it produced $66 billion, 14 percent of all federal income. The rate is 17 percent on corporation profits up to $25,000 and rises in stages to 46 percent on profits above $100,000. However, corporations are permitted to deduct business expenses such as depreciation (wear and obsolescence of machinery) from their taxable incomes. The corporate net income tax is the most difficult business tax to pass on, and at least a part of it is paid by the corporations themselves out of their profits.

During both world wars we levied an extra corporation income tax called a war profits tax. It took a percentage of the amount that wartime profits exceeded average peacetime profits. Additional revenue was needed to help pay the cost of the war, and it was believed that higher taxes would help control wartime inflation. Many also favored the war profits tax as a step toward taking the profits out of war. It was not imposed during the undeclared Vietnam War.

Few corporations pay the full 46 percent rate. A number of special provisions in the tax laws reduce their tax liability. For example, they can deduct taxes paid to state, local, and foreign governments, losses from previous years and get special tax credits for new investments.

A special *depletion allowance* is given to the companies engaged in extracting natural resources. Owners of oil and gas wells were allowed to deduct 27.5 percent of their gross receipts from their profits before they calculated their taxes. This deduction was justified on the basis that taking oil or gas out of the ground left less oil and gas in the ground and reduced the value of the well. On the average they took depletion allowances totalling nineteen times the original cost of the wells. This tax loophole cost the government $3 billion in 1974. Because of it and other deductions, oil companies in recent years paid an average of less than 8 percent of their profits in taxes. In one recent year an operator with an income of $29 million and another with $4 million paid no income tax at all. American oil producers are reputedly the world's richest men.

A study by the Joint Congressional Committee on Internal Revenue Taxation found that in 1973 ten of the nation's largest companies had profits totalling $1 billion on which they paid no federal taxes at all. The average tax paid by the nation's one hundred largest corporations was 27.1 percent. Exxon, the world's largest industrial corporation, paid 11.2 percent on earnings of nearly $3 billion, and Texaco paid 2.3 percent on earnings of $1.3 billion.

In 1974, Congress voted to remove part of this tax subsidy from the larger oil companies, but not from smaller producers. The first year's revenue gain from this change amounted to nearly $2 billion.

The Social Security Tax

In 1979 the Social Security tax produced $142 billion, which was 30 percent of federal revenue. It is a kind of income tax, but only on wages and salaries and not on income from capital gains, rents, profits, or other sources. It is also levied only on the lower portion of salaries and wages (in 1980 up to $25,900). It is a highly regressive tax that takes a much larger percentage of the income of the poor than of the income of the wealthy. In 1980 the maximum tax levied on wages up to $25,900 was $3,117 (half of which was collected from employees). For many low-income Americans it is a heavier tax than the income tax. No exemptions or deductions are allowed—it must be paid by a man who earns only one dollar a year—and thus is paid by many families below the poverty line.

In the late 1960s and early 1970s, Social Security taxes rose more rapidly than any other federal taxes. In 1965 they produced 19 percent of all federal revenue; by 1979 they produced 30 percent of federal revenue. The growth of this regressive tax made the federal tax structure steadily less progressive.

The Personal Income Tax

Because the Constitution required direct taxes to be apportioned among the states on the basis of population, a constitutional amendment, ratified in 1913, was necessary to legalize the personal income tax. Quickly replacing the tariffs as the largest source of revenue, it produced $218 billion, 47 percent of federal income, in 1979.

As of 1976, single persons with an annual income of at least $2,450 and married couples with incomes of $3,200 or more had to submit full reports of all of their income to the government. A taxpayer could deduct, and thus pay no tax on, the first $1000, which was called his personal deduction. Also, he could deduct $1000 for each member of his family supported by him. The very poor could deduct a "low minimum standard deduction, and special tax refunds income credit," with the effect that an individual did not have to pay income taxes until his income exceeded $2,700, and a family of four was not taxed until its income exceeded $6,860.

Each taxpayer could deduct business and professional expenses, interest paid on borrowed money, losses from uncollectable debts and accidents, contributions to religious and charitable organizations, and excessive medical expenses from the part of his income subject to tax. If a taxpayer did not wish to submit an itemized list of such deductions he could deduct instead a standard 16 percent of his taxable income up to a minimum of $2,400. The tax rate of his remaining, or taxable, income began at fourteen cents per dollar. On taxable income in excess of $1,000 an extra tax (surtax) of one cent was added. Additional surtaxes which took effect as income rose brought the maximum tax rate to seventy cents on each dollar of unearned income and fifty cents on earned income (wages and salary) over $100,000 annually.

Income taxes on wages and salaries were collected on a "pay as you go" basis. Employers deducted 14 percent from their employees' wage and salary checks and turned it over to the government. Businessmen and self-employed persons mail in quarterly tax payments on the basis of the income they expect to earn for the year. Any remaining balance had to be paid, or any refund claimed, when income tax forms were submitted no later than April of the following year.

How Progressive Is the Income Tax?

Originally, the income tax was sharply progressive. In 1929, two-thirds of income taxes were collected from the fifteen thousand Americans whose annual incomes were more than $100,000. As late as 1939 fewer than 4 million Americans paid income tax. However, during World War II the income tax was imposed on middle- and lower-income groups as well.

At first glance the income tax's 14 to 70 percent rates appear to be steeply progressive. In practice, however, deductions and exemptions make it much less progressive than it appears. Families whose incomes are close to the poverty line actually pay income tax at rates almost as high as those paid by middle-income families. Furthermore, special provisions in the tax laws enable upper-income persons to avoid paying the specified high rates. A U.S. Treasury study found that those whose incomes were between $500,000 and $1 million paid an average of 30 percent, and that those with incomes above $1 million paid 28 percent.

Ideally, taxpayers whose incomes and numbers of dependents are equal should pay equal taxes. However, special provisions in the tax laws reduce taxes on particular types of income, with the result that some individuals pay far less than others. Reformers call these special provisions "loopholes." Because their effect is equivalent to government appropriations, a 1974 law required them to be listed as "tax expenditures" in the federal budget. According to the Bureau of the Budget, they cost the government $125 billion in 1980.

Income tax loopholes were much criticized. Some of them were originally put in the tax laws to subsidize some activity that was considered socially desirable, such as home ownership. Others represented victories by powerful and determined special interests over the public interest. They have been called the most wasteful and unfair type of government spending.

Not all tax expenditures, however, benefit the wealthy. The exemption of Social Security, unemployment, and welfare benefits from the income tax causes a $14 billion revenue loss. Most of the benefits of exempting interest paid on home mortgages and state and local property taxes, $16 billion annually, go to middle-income groups. Nevertheless, most of the loopholes benefit the wealthy. In 1972 the average individual in the $3,000 to $5,000 income range received $10 in benefits from loopholes, while one in the $100,000 to $500,000 range got $25,264 and one above $1 million got $725,000. The richest 1.2 percent of taxpayers got 23 percent ($13.4 billion) of the benefits.

Perhaps the largest single loophole is the special tax treatment given to capital gains, the profits resulting from the rise in value of property. Such income is taxed at less than half of the tax on wages and salaries. If a person buys a plot of land, an apartment house, or a share of stock, and holds it eight months or more before selling it, only 40 percent of the resulting profit is taxable, and that cannot be taxed at a rate higher than 25 percent. This tax loophole saves people who make capital gains an estimated $17 billion in taxes annually. In 1974, 66 percent of its benefits went to the 1.3 percent of taxpayers who had incomes of more than $50,000 per year. The exemption of capital gains from the inheritance tax is worth an additional $5 billion annually to mostly wealthy individuals.

Interest on state and local government bonds is exempt from federal taxation, and the resulting tax loss is estimated at $7 billion annually. Defenders of this loophole argue that it is needed to help state and local governments borrow money at low interest rates. It is thus intended to be a subsidy to state and local governments. However, it is wasteful because the federal government loses at least four dollars in taxes for every three dollars that state and local governments save on interest.

Other loopholes are found in certain uses of tax-exempt foundations, entertainment expense accounts, real estate depreciation allowances, and stock dividend exemptions.

Whenever some groups are excused from paying taxes, their share is shifted to other taxpayers. Lower taxes on capital gains and interest mean higher taxes on wages and salaries. Charging that the tax system was "rigged against income from work and in favor of unearned income," President George Meany of the AFL-CIO said that capital gains should be taxed at the same rate as wages. In 1975 presidential candidate Jimmy Carter charged that "carefully contrived loopholes let the total tax burden shift more and more toward the average wage earner."

Much additional income escapes taxation because it simply is not reported to the government. Concealing income is a criminal offense and, if convicted, the guilty person faces punishment. However, it is difficult for the government to obtain records of income from capital gains, gambling, bribes, kickbacks, or even some professional services. In 1967 the chairman of the Senate Finance Committee estimated that $100 billion annually was not reported on income tax forms, and others estimated that as high as 40 percent of all personal income was unreported.

In 1980 the individual income tax collected by the federal government amounted to approximately 10 percent of the total personal income of the American people. Thus, a 10 percent tax on all income, without exemptions or deductions, would have produced as much money as the existing tax with its rates as high as 70 percent.

The tax law of 1969 put a new minimum tax on part of the income that escaped taxation through loopholes. Thirty thousand dollars of tax-free income, plus income from tax-exempt bonds, and any income spent to bore gas wells remained exempt, but other tax-free income was made subject to a special 10 percent tax. This had the effect in 1971 of putting an average 4 percent tax on $4 billion in income that had previously escaped income taxes. Nevertheless, in 1972, 303 persons with adjusted gross incomes (after deducting interest on tax-exempt bonds, half of capital gains, depletion allowances, etc.) of more than $100,000 each paid not one cent of income tax. The minimum tax was raised slightly in 1976.

As a move to reduce the incentive to divert talents from earning money to speculating for capital gains, the 1969 law reduced the maximum tax on earned income to 50 percent. This reduced but did not remove the premium, because the maximum tax on capital gains remained at only 12.5 percent. Reformers scored a small victory when they incorporated in the 1974 Budget Reform Act a requirement that "tax expenditures" and their amounts be listed as a part of the federal budget. However, they were so listed only in a separate booklet and not included in the regular budget.

The government could keep a better check on income and collect taxes on income not being reported if it extended the withholding tax, already levied on wages and salaries, to all income from whatever source.

Politically, it has been extremely difficult to remove special tax preferences. The special interests that benefit from them fight fiercely to retain them. Their ability to make large campaign contributions usually helps them block action in the House.

SHOULD TAXES BE PROGRESSIVE?

Whether or not taxes should be progressive has been debated in American politics for more than a century. Opponents question the justice and morality of taking a larger share of high incomes than of low incomes. Progressive taxes, they maintain, penalize success and reduce the incentive to excel. Furthermore the wealthy must be allowed high incomes to enable them to accumulate the large sums needed to provide the capital to expand the economy. In addition, taxing the profits of businessmen reduces the incentive for them to invest in risky new enterprises, they argue, and thus tends to slow economic growth. Some conservatives proposed a Constitutional amendment to prohibit income taxes in excess of 25 percent.

Advocates of progressive taxation maintain that it is both fair and right to consider ability to pay in levying taxes. The wealthy, it is said, benefit more from such government services as police and fire protection. Furthermore, they can afford to pay taxes without hardships. On the other hand, when the government taxes people whose incomes are already too low, it deprives those people of money they need for adequate clothing, housing, education, and medical care. Often this eventually costs the government more than it gets—in welfare support, hospitalization, and crime prevention. Moreover, progressive taxation helps reduce the extremes of wealth and poverty which cause social tensions, often endanger democracy, and provoke violent revolutions in other lands. And, equally important, they believe, progressive taxation helps to promote economic growth by raising the buying power of low-income groups and enlarging the market.

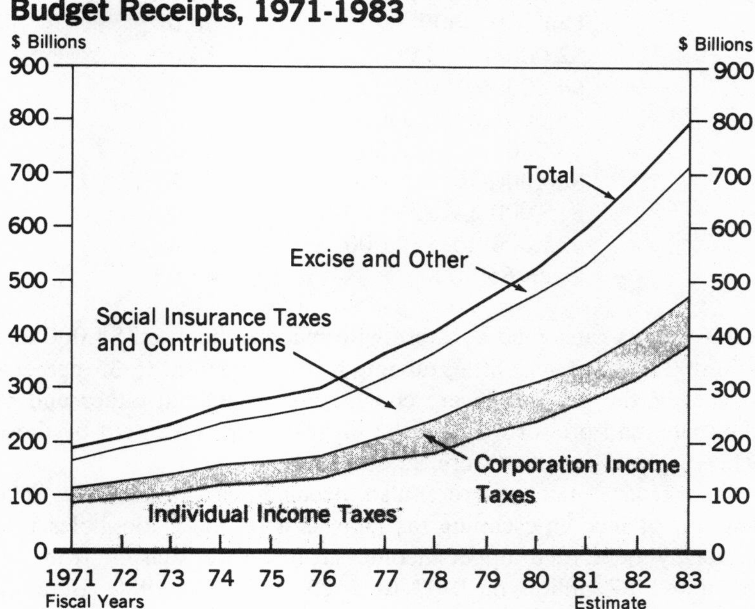

Fig. 12.1. **Budget Receipts, 1971–1983.** In current dollars, not adjusted for inflation. In this period, the proportion of federal revenue raised by personal and corporation income taxes declined, while the proportion raised by social insurance and excise taxes rose. (Office of Management and Budget, 1980)

Furthermore, liberals maintain, the federal income tax should be progressive in order to offset the regressive nature of the tariff, excise taxes, and most state and local taxes. A poor man spends a larger share of his income than a wealthy man on goods subject to a consumer's sales tax, and thus a sales tax takes a bigger bite out of low incomes. In 1979, Social Security taxes took twice as high a percentage of a $22,900 income as of a $45,800 income. According to a member of the President's Council of Economic Advisers, even when the income tax is included the tax burden as a whole is "not progressive, but surprisingly regressive, and becoming more so over the years."

The Herriot-Miller study found that in 1968 the following income groups paid these percentages of their incomes in taxes of all kinds—state, local, and federal:

Income Group	*Per Cent of Income Paid in Taxes*
Under $2,000	50.0
$2,000 to $4,000	34.6
$4,000 to $6,000	31.0
$6,000 to $8,000	30.1
$8,000 to $10,000	29.2
$10,000 to $15,000	29.8
$15,000 to $25,000	30.0
$25,000 to $50,000	32.8
Over $50,000	45.0

Thus the tax rates paid by those with incomes between $4,000 and $50,000 differed very little, ranging from 29 percent to 35 percent. However, the tax rates were considerably higher at either end of the scale, and proportionately the highest rates were paid by those whose annual incomes were $2,000 or less.

The federal tax structure also became less progressive. The amount of income escaping taxation as a result of loopholes that primarily benefitted upper-income groups rose sharply from an estimated 37 billion in 1967 to $125 billion in 1980. Between 1960 and 1975, according to a Brookings study, federal tax receipts from the corporate income tax dropped from 23 to 15 percent of federal tax receipts, while receipts from regressive Social Security taxes rose from 16 to 30 percent. The tax changes enacted between 1970 and 1974 raised taxes on families with income below $3,500 and cut taxes on incomes above $13,000.

Despite differences in their points of view, most conservatives and liberals agree that many inequities have crept into our tax structure. Every exemption won by one group places a heavier tax burden on others. The knowledge that some men do not pay their fair share of taxes causes others to seek ways to avoid taxes. If not corrected, tax inequities could undermine the principal factors which make our tax system work so well—public confidence and the voluntary reporting of income by good citizens.

FEDERAL EXPENDITURES

Including payments from Social Security and other trust funds, President Carter's budget proposed federal spending of $616 billion in the year ending in June 1981. This was approximately $2,800 for every man, woman, and child in America.

Government spending did not reach this high level until recent years. The largest pre–World War II budget was only $9 billion. The Second World War moved spending onto a higher plane: in four years of war we spent twice as much as the total of all federal expenditures in America's previous history. The 1945 budget exceeded $100 billion. Federal spending dropped as low as $33 billion in the postwar period, but then rose again. In 1977–78, spending was fifty times higher than the largest pre–World War II budget. Even allowing for both inflation and population growth, federal spending per capita more than quadrupled in thirty-seven years.

For years the largest rise in spending was for defense. The War and Navy Departments spent only $2 billion in 1940, or 20 percent of the federal budget. In 1980, the Defense Department took $138 billion. Interest on the national debt, 90 percent of which was incurred in war, cost $57 billion. Also associated with defense were expenditures of $21 billion for benefits to veterans, $5 billion for space research, $14 billion for international affairs and foreign aid, and an estimated $1 billion for the CIA. Thus war spending took approximately half of the budget.

Contrary to a popular impression, federal per capita spending for items that could be classified under "welfare" did not rise in most of the postwar period—in fact, allowing for inflation, it declined in the twenty-eight years between 1940 and 1967. However, after 1967, led by a rapid increase in Social Security, spending on civilian programs grew to half of the budget. Among the larger nondefense items in the 1980 budget were $115 billion for social security retirement and disability benefits; $53 billion for Medicare and other health programs; $30 billion for education, manpower, and social services; $31 billion for public assistance food stamps and family assistance; $19 billion for aid to transportation and business; $12 billion for unemployment compensation; $14 billion for civil service retirement; $7 billion for community and regional development; $7 billion for rivers, dams, and natural resources; $7 billion for revenue sharing; $8 billion for energy development; and $5 billion for pollution control.

The National Debt

When the government spends more money than it collects in taxes, it meets the resulting deficit by borrowing. It gives the lender a government bond, which is its promise to repay the loan plus interest at a specified time. Most government bonds are bought by our own citizens—the largest purchasers are the nation's banks.

Before World War I the national debt held by the public averaged between $1 and $2 billion. World War I and the Great Depression raised it to $43 billion by 1940. During World War II it soared to nearly $300 billion. It fell slightly after the war and then moved irregularly upward to nearly $900 billion in 1980, when interest on the debt cost $66 billion.

The debt is huge and is still rising, but in some respects it is less burdensome than it appears. It rose little more rapidly than population, and per capita debt changed little, from $1,902 in 1946 to $1,923 in 1971. Meanwhile, the value of the dollar fell, reducing its burden much more. The national debt fell from 83 percent of the GNP in 1950 to only 37 percent of the GNP in 1979.

WATCHDOGS OVER FEDERAL SPENDING

The federal budget, an estimate of expected income and expenditures for the coming year, is prepared by the Office of Management and Budget, part of the president's staff. The process begins when various government departments and agencies submit estimates of their needs for the coming year. These requests always total more than expected income, and the Budget Office, under the guidance of the president, trims them down and consolidates them into a general plan of expenditures.

In January of each year, the completed budget, a document of more than a thousand pages, is sent to Congress. There it is referred to the House Ways and Means Committee and the Senate Finance Committee. The committees split into subcommittees to study and hold hearings on different parts of the budget. Then they recommend a series of bills to appropriate the money. Of course the items and amounts in the budget may be changed by Congress. The president must accept such changes or veto the entire appropriations bill, which might cripple the functioning of the government. It has been suggested that it would be better to give the president the power to veto some items while accepting others. Many state governors have this *item veto*. President Nixon sought to achieve much the same result by impounding and refusing to spend approximately $8 billion appropriated by Congress for health, education, and welfare purposes; but the courts ruled that he was required to spend it.

The Office of Management and Budget supervises spending by

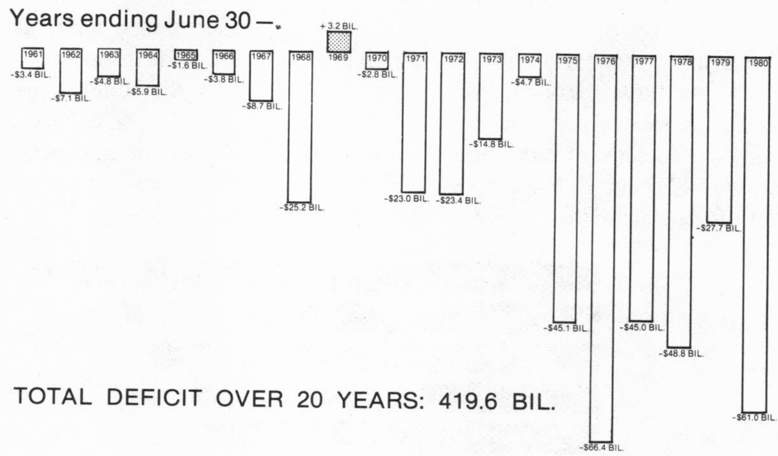

Fig. 12.2. **Budget Deficits, 1961–1980.** (Office of Management and Budget, 1980)

federal agencies and guards against overspending, waste, and theft. Congress also has a watchdog organization, the General Accounting Office (GAO). The GAO is headed by a comptroller-general who, in order to insure his independence, is appointed for a fifteen-year nonrenewable term. He investigates government agencies to determine if they are spending money for the purposes intended by Congress and to uncover and correct wasteful practices. However, this strict supervision does not extend to spending by the Defense Department.

Is Federal Spending Too High?

No one enjoys paying taxes, but we cannot reduce taxes much unless we are also willing to reduce government services. Historically, efforts to reduce government "waste" and "extravagance" have produced rather small savings. Therefore the question of whether taxes and spending are too high is really the question of whether the government is furnishing too much service.

If federal services are excessive, which services should be reduced or eliminated? The answer depends partly on individual preference. Many conservatives want to reduce spending for welfare, for such things as education, housing, assistance to the needy, and public health. Apart from the Social Security system, such spending accounts for only a relatively small part of the budget, and tax savings would not be large. Many other items, such as interest on the national debt, are fixed and cannot be reduced.

As we have seen, approximately 40 percent of the federal tax dollar is spent for purposes relating to the military. Large tax savings would require reductions in this area. This raises the questions of whether our defense forces are too large, and whether we attempt to defend too much of the world.

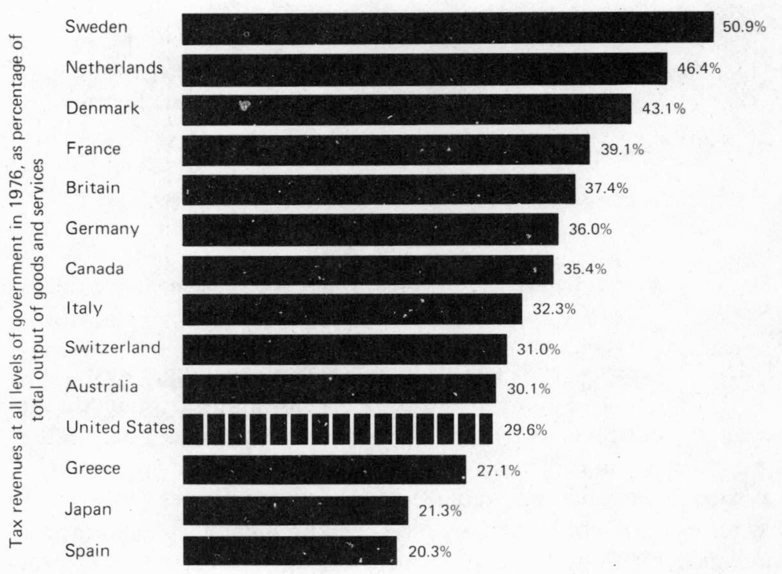

Fig. 12.3. **Tax Revenues as Percentage of Total Output of Goods and Services.** United States taxes are comparatively low.

Taxes have risen rapidly in recent years. In 1902, the average American paid a total of $18 in federal, state, and local taxes; this figure rose to $377 by 1948 and to $1,925 by 1974. Taxes rose from 11 percent of our GNP in 1929 to 30 percent in 1978. This was still a relatively light tax burden when compared to Sweden's 53 percent of her GNP, France's 39 percent, West Germany's 38 percent, Britain's 36 percent, and Canada's 33 percent.

Tax policy is also social policy, and the way a nation spends its money demonstrates its goals, values, and priorities. A question that has been much debated in recent years is: Which is America's most urgent need—more private spending or more public spending? Should we give a higher priority to more automobiles, television sets, clothes, and entertainment, or to better schools, medical care, crime prevention, and cleaner rivers and air?

Because the answers to these questions are value judgments, different individuals will give different answers. Many people maintain that taxes are too high, that government is too big, and that both should be reduced in order to leave more money with individuals for private spending. On the other hand, some economists describe America as a nation of private affluence and public poverty which enjoys the highest standard of living in the world but does not have the best education or medical care, nor the best protected environment. They insist that we are wealthy enough to afford high quality education and medical care, a clean and beautiful environment, and continue to raise private income at the same time.

In conclusion, the American people, through their elected representatives, have called on the federal government to perform certain services which they, acting as private individuals, could not perform at all or as well for themselves. To pay for these functions they levy taxes upon themselves. Collecting taxes involves far more than simply raising funds to pay for government. It involves questions of fairness, social justice, and economic impact. The way tax money is collected and spent largely determines the nation's distribution of wealth, speed of economic growth, and quality of life.

Questions

1. What three kinds of taxes bring in the most revenue to the federal government?
2. How high is the tariff? What percentage of federal revenue does it produce?
3. What is meant by "an excise tax that serves as a user's charge"? Give examples.
4. What is meant by "progressive taxation"? What is meant by "regressive taxation"? Give examples and arguments for and against each.
5. Why is the income tax less progressive than its rates indicate?

6. List the major loopholes in the tax laws. What are some undesirable effects of these loopholes?
7. Compare the consumer sales tax and the income tax in respect to (a) who pays them and (b) their effect on the market.
8. On what major activities does the federal government spend its money? What aspect of federal spending has grown the most since 1940?
9. Has the federal debt become more burdensome or less burdensome than it was in 1946? Explain.
10. Is government spending excessive? Why or why not?
11. Define: indirect tax, reciprocal trade treaty, surtax, sales tax, capital gain, depletion allowance, minimum standard deduction, item veto, General Accounting Office, welfare spending, incidence.

Suggested Reading

Barnett, Richard J. *The Economy of Death*. New York: Atheneum, 1969.

A readable account by one with experience in the State Department and the Pentagon. He argues that military spending absorbs most of the tax dollar and is eroding democracy in America.

Galbraith, John K. *The Affluent Society*, 2d rev. ed. New York: Houghton-Mifflin, 1969.

A brightly written and influential work by a leading economist. Argues that raising production is no longer our primary economic problem and that more of our resources should be devoted to public purposes.

Goldwater, Barry. *The Conscience of a Conservative*. New York: Macfadden, 1960.

The Senator from Arizona, who was the Republican party's presidential nominee in 1964, sets forth the case against progressive taxation and welfare spending.

Heilbroner, Robert L., and Peter L. Bernstein. *Primer of Government Spending*. New York: Random House, 1963.

A short discussion of government spending and its effects.

Maintains that most of our worries about excessive spending and debt are unjustified.

Pechman, Joseph A., and Benjamin A. Okner. *Who Bears the Tax Burden?* Washington, D.C.: Brookings Institution, 1974.
Studies the impact of all taxes on different income groups and concludes that the American tax system is not progressive.

Stern, Philip M. *The Rape of the Taxpayer*. New York: Vintage Books, 1973.
An indignant attack on the tax loopholes that enable many wealthy people to escape paying taxes. Advocates a preference-free tax system.

13
Problems of State and Local Government

What are the chief functions of state and local governments?
How democratic and responsible are state and local governments?
Are reforms in state and local governments needed?

"The powers not delegated to the United States by the Constitution, nor prohibited by it to the states, are reserved to the states respectively, or to the people."

—The Constitution of the United States

"The large freedom of action and broad scope of function given to local authorities is the distinguishing characteristic of the American system of government."

—Woodrow Wilson

"What government is best? That which teaches us to govern ourselves."

—Johann Wolfgang von Goethe

CONTRADICTIONS IN STATE AND LOCAL GOVERNMENT

State and local governments show many apparent contradictions. The remarkable growth of the federal government sometimes gives the impression that state and local governments are fading in importance. Instead, as measured by income, expenditures, and number of employees, they are growing more rapidly. As compared to the federal government, they are closer to the people, but are less understood by them. They are easier for local people to control but often have less democratic policies and tax structures.

Their officials are under closer scrutiny, but are often more corrupt. More of their officials are chosen directly by the people, but often behave less responsibly. Their constitutions have been more amended, but are less well adapted to modern conditions.

The original state constitutions were drawn up by men who were hostile to strong government. Believing that that government is best which governs least, they deliberately designed state and local governments to be weak and inactive. In addition to separating governmental powers among three independent branches, they provided for popular election of most important officials, strictly limited their authority, made their terms short, and often prohibited them from succeeding themselves. They restricted the power of legislatures by putting many matters into constitutions so that they could be changed only by constitutional amendment. Thus it is difficult to adapt state and local governments to new problems.

THE POWERS AND FUNCTIONS OF STATE GOVERNMENTS

The states created the federal government, and they reserved to themselves all powers not delegated to it. These include the police power and the authority to provide for the health, safety, morals, education, common convenience, and general welfare of the people. Some of these powers are exercised from state capitols, and others are delegated by state governments to counties, cities, and other units of local government.

Measured by the amount of money spent, the chief function of state and local governments is public education. In 1974 approximately 39 percent of their spending was for public schools and colleges. The next largest amount, 19 percent, was spent on public welfare (including homes for the aged and orphans; aid to the blind and crippled; food, shelter, and clothing for the poor; and public health). These were followed in order by highways (13 percent), police and fire protection, sanitation and sewage, conservation of natural resources, urban renewal, and parks and recreation.

The people of each state have the power to adopt a constitution of their own making, and no two state constitutions are exactly alike. However, all reflect a common historical experience, and all were modeled on colonial charters or on the United States Constitution and, in consequence, share certain basic features. They divide power among three branches of government and provide each with checks and balances on the powers of the others. They include bills of rights which emphasize freedom of religion, property rights, free speech and individual liberty. All except Nebraska provide for two-house legislatures. All provide for practical methods of amending the constitution and for local self-government for counties and cities.

State constitutions were written in less favorable circumstances than those surrounding the framing of the federal Constitution, and many state constitutions have serious shortcomings.

Political scientists agree that a constitution should have certain characteristics: (1) It should be short. A constitution is basic law and should confine itself to setting forth the basic principles and framework of the government. It should not attempt to specify the details of government operation or include regulations that are more properly left to ordinary laws. (2) It should clearly define the responsibilities of officials and should give them ample powers to fulfill those responsibilities. (3) It should provide a method of amendment that is neither too easy nor too difficult.

The federal Constitution meets all of these requirements, but most state constitutions do not. (1) Most of them are much too long and detailed. The federal Constitution contains only seventy-five hundred words, but Georgia's constitution contains more than 500,000. Powerful groups have succeeded in putting guarantees of their special privileges into constitutions in order to prevent their repeal by state legislatures. (2) They require too many officials to be elected. This makes them independent of each other and splits responsibility to such an extent that it is hard for the people to know whom to blame or credit for government failures or successes. (3) They give state legislatures too little authority. They put many matters beyond their reach and set limits on the frequency and length of their sessions. (4) They give governors insufficient powers to enable them effectively to direct the state administration.

How can state constitutions be modernized? It is very difficult. To draft a new constitution requires election of a special constitutional convention, and the resulting constitution must then be ratified by a vote of the people. Many obstacles stand in the way. The groups that benefit from special provisions in the existing constitution combine to oppose change. If unable to block the calling of a constitutional convention, they get themselves elected to it and join with other special interests to put new special privileges into the new constitution. Many people do not take the trouble to study a new constitution enough to understand it, and they fear what they do not understand. States have held constitutional conventions and drawn up improved constitutions only to have the people refuse to ratify them.

A method that has been used to avoid some of these pitfalls is to give a constitutional convention the authority to revise only certain parts of the constitution. This arouses fewer fears and makes it easier for the people to understand the changes that are proposed. Another method is for the state legislature to submit one amendment at a time for ratification. However, these procedures do not arouse as much popular interest and, even when successful, bring only patchwork improvement, when a complete overhaul may be needed. Despite these difficulties most states have amended their original constitutions repeatedly and several of them have adopted entirely new constitutions at least once.

STATE LEGISLATURES

State legislatures vary in size from Delaware's 58 to New Hampshire's 424 members. The typical legislature has 100 to 150 members in the house and 30 to 40 in the senate. Representation in the lower house is based on population. Until recently each county or district, regardless of its population, had an equal number of senators. In many states this meant that the senate became increasingly unrepresentative as people moved from rural counties to cities. This often gave control of state senates to rural areas that blocked measures desired by most of the people to meet the problems of urban areas. In 1964 the Supreme Court ruled that such unequal representation violated the democratic principle of "one man, one vote," and that representation in both houses must be based on population. This reduced the difference between the two houses.

The need for two houses has been questioned. Many reformers have long argued that a unicameral (one-house) legislature would be more efficient, less expensive, would attract better qualified members, and would make it easier for the people to follow the activities of their representatives. Nebraska has a unicameral legislature of only 49 members which is generally considered to have lived up to expectations. Nevertheless most people want to retain the two-house system. They argue that the requirement that a bill be acted upon by two houses assures more debate and deliberation and helps to prevent enactment of hasty or ill-considered laws.

Perhaps too we are still influenced by the tradition that put more emphasis on protecting liberties than on improving the efficiency of government.

The frequency and length of legislative sessions is strictly limited by state constitutions. In forty-two states the legislature meets once a year. Many states also limit sessions to thirty or sixty days in order to save money and to make it possible for busy men to serve. Many reformers believe that this is not enough time to enable legislatures to deal constructively with state problems. In 1968 the Advisory Committee on Intergovernmental Relations recommended that constitutional limitations on the frequency and length of legislative sessions be abolished. The trend is toward longer sessions.

The terms of legislators are short and their pay is low. In four-fifths of the states, senators serve four-year terms and in the others only two-year terms. Members of the lower house serve only two years in all but four states. This means that many legislators scarcely have time to learn their jobs before facing another election, and even experienced legislators have to spend much of their time campaigning. New Hampshire pays legislators only $100 per year, and only eight states, including California, New York and Illinois, pay them more than $15,000 a year. Consequently, a term in the legislature is a heavy expense for most wage earners and businessmen who are less able than lawyers, salesmen, and farmers to leave their jobs for one or two months.

Many people do not take as much interest in state government as in national government. In theory, state government is closer to them, but fewer people know the names of their state representatives than of their United States congressmen. Public inattention or apathy allows lobbyists for special interests to exert great influence on state legislatures, and corruption is more of a problem on the state and local than on the federal level.

Governors

Most state governors have four-year terms, but four states limit them to two years. Eight states limit their stay in office to one term, and nineteen other states have a limit of two terms. They are paid (1975) between $10,000 and $85,000 per year, plus an executive mansion and expenses.

The governor, of course, heads the executive branch of state government. He appoints many administrative officials. He recommends measures to legislatures and may call them into special sessions, which in nearly half of the states can consider only the subjects he specifies. Every state except North Carolina gives him the veto power, and forty-three of them give him the power to veto individual items in money bills. He usually has power to pardon or reduce the sentences of convicted criminals.

Nevertheless, most governors have relatively little power. In the colonial era, when governors were appointed by the king and upheld royal authority, many people feared and disliked them. The first state constitutions gave them little power, and most of the limited powers that they now have were added by later amendments. In every state they are denied the power to appoint a number of the top men in their administrations. State officials who roughly correspond to members of the president's Cabinet are elected directly by the people. The state treasurer, the secretary of state, the attorney-general, and the state auditor are elected in most states, and the superintendent of schools is elected in twenty of them. Governors have no real control over men whom they can neither appoint nor fire. Thus, most states have, in effect, plural executives with several independent officials exercising the executive power. In addition, many states give control of important state functions to semi-independent administrative boards, such as a board of education or highway commission. The governor can appoint some members of these commissions, but they serve for longer terms than he does and cannot be removed by him. Thus, in half of the states the governor is a very weak executive.

When the chief executive lacks the power to exert effective control over his administration the government is likely to be aimless and inefficient. When power is divided among many independent officials the average voter does not know whom to hold responsible when things go wrong. Governors may receive blame for developments over which they have no control, while guilty officials escape criticism.

Reform groups have recommended that the governor, like the president, should be given the power to appoint the heads of the major departments of state government. The only officials that should be elected, they say, are the governor, lieutenant governor and, perhaps, the auditor. They also want governors to be eligible for reelection so that they can be held responsible for the success or failure of their administrations and punished or rewarded accordingly at the polls. These measures, say reformers, would contribute to more effective leadership and also make state governments more responsive to the wishes of the people.

Financial Problems of States

Together, state and local governments collected $175 billion in taxes in 1977. Their largest single source of tax income was the property tax (36 percent) followed by sales taxes (36 percent), and personal income taxes (13 percent). Large sums were also produced by licensing, corporation income taxes, and excise taxes on gasoline, liquor, and cigarettes. Considered separately, state governments got most of their revenue from sales taxes, while local governments got 85 percent of their income from the property tax.

Most state and local taxes are regressive and take a larger percentage of a poor man's income than of a rich man's income. Sales taxes, property taxes, and fees fall more heavily on the poor than on the wealthy. In one state in a recent year state and local taxes took 9 percent of a $1,000 annual income and only 3.5 percent of a $10,000 income.

State and local governments also received large grants from the federal government. In 1980 such grants totalled $90 billion and accounted for 21 percent of their total incomes (up from $3.3 billion and 10 percent in 1955). They were usually made for specified purposes such as public welfare assistance, education, public health, highway construction, community development, housing, and agriculture. Federal grant programs grew up piecemeal over the years and became extremely complex—in 1969 there were 1,050 separate programs. The Advisory Commission on Intergovernmental Relations recommended that they be consolidated and that in some cases the federal government should specify only the general purpose for which the money was given and let the states spend it as they saw fit.

The incomes of state and local governments from taxes and federal grants grew rapidly, from $118 billion in 1968 to $286 billion in 1977, but it did not keep pace with their spending. Their debts rose to $258 billion by 1977. Between 1964 and 1979 the number of state and local government employees soared from 7.2 million to 13 million. Most of the new employees were in education.

One reason for the financial problems of state and local governments is that they were confronted with problems that were larger than their jurisdictions. Some reformers maintained that education, welfare, and highways were not local concerns but were vital to

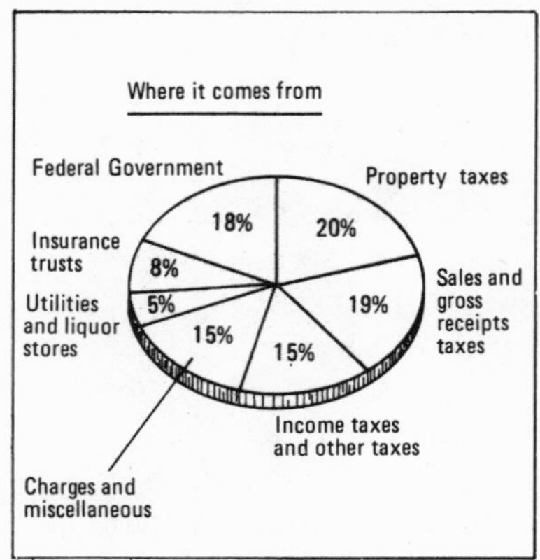

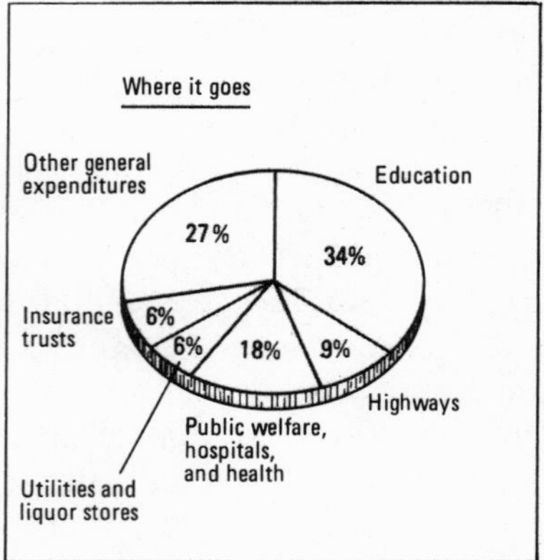

Fig. 13.1. **The State and Local Government Dollar, 1974.** (U.S. Bureau of the Census, 1977)

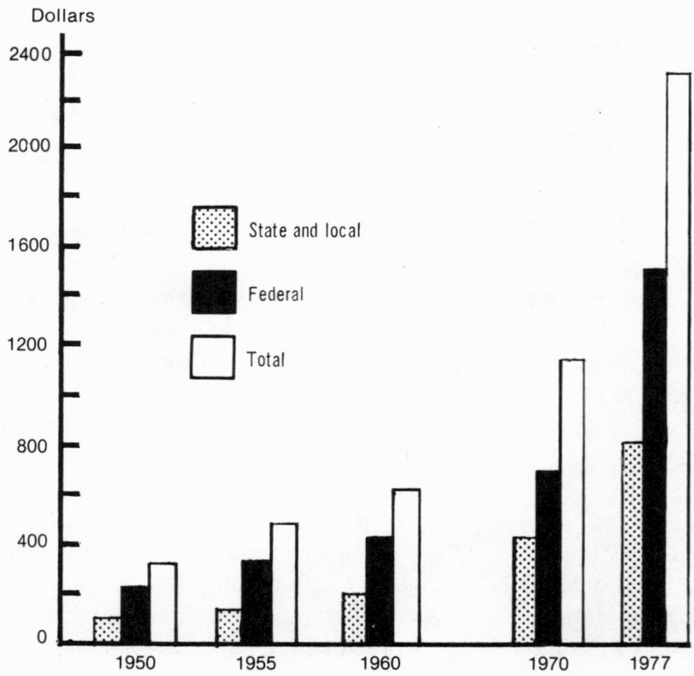

Fig. 13.2. **Per Capita Tax Revenue by Level of Government, 1950–1977.** Between 1950 and 1977, state and local taxes rose more rapidly than federal taxes. (U.S. Bureau of the Census, 1978)

national strength and, therefore, should be federally financed. The National Crime Commission, the National Commission on Violence, and the National Governors' Conference all recommended that the federal government take over payment of all of the costs of welfare and low-income medical care. Others recommended that federal and state governments help take over all education costs from counties. If relieved of these growing costs, they said, state and local governments might be better able to deal with pressing local problems.

In 1971, in an attempt to reverse the flow of power from local and state governments to Washington, President Nixon secured congressional approval of "revenue sharing," a five-year program of turning over more than $30 billion in federal funds to state and local governments to use as they saw fit. One-third of it went to state governments and two-thirds to local governments. The existence of this program was then used to justify cuts in federal welfare grants. However, most state and local governments used the new income to buy equipment, to raise salaries, or to reduce taxes. By function, 75 percent of the $15 billion disbursed in 1973 and 1974 was spent for public safety, mostly police departments, and only 2 percent for social services. In 1978 many states had budget surpluses, while the federal government faced a dismaying deficit of more than $48 billion.

State Courts

One of the powers retained by the states is the police power. The states, in turn, delegate most of this power to local governments. State highway patrols have full police powers in all except twelve states, but usually do not operate within cities. State governments also supervise business and professions to protect the public against possible incompetence and fraud. Corporations and banks are required to meet certain financial standards before they are licensed to do business. Medical doctors, dentists, pharmacists, lawyers, and insurance and real estate brokers must meet state requirements concerning training and competency before being permitted to practice. States closely regulate public utilities such as electric, gas, water, telephone, and railway corporations in the interest of adequate service and fair rates. They regulate wages, working conditions, and child labor.

State courts are far more numerous than federal courts and handle many more cases. They have exclusive jurisdiction over cases involving state law, and the federal government also asks them to try many federal cases, such as civil suits involving less than $10,000.

Courts handle two broad classes of cases: civil and criminal. *Civil law* involves disputes between private individuals, usually over property or damages, for which the courts offer a peaceful means of settlement. *Criminal law* concerns offenses, such as theft or murder, which violate laws and are considered offenses against society. Government takes the initiative in punishing violations of criminal law.

In every state except Louisiana (which originally used the Napoleonic Code) the laws are based on *English common law*. Before the British parliament came into existence, English judges developed rules upon which to base court decisions and they came to be commonly accepted as law. Common law is "unwritten law" growing out of decisions by judges which are used as "precedents" in deciding subsequent cases. It may be either civil or criminal. When legislatures enact laws, called statutory laws, they replace common law. Statutory law has replaced most of the common law involving crimes, but common law is still important in civil cases.

State courts are organized in pyramids much like the federal courts. At the bottom are *courts of limited jurisdiction*. Justices of the peace are found in many rural areas. They are elected and have authority to try minor cases involving small sums, petty crimes, or traffic offenses, and to impose small fines and jail sentences. They are increasingly criticized because many of them have no legal training, and they are paid in fees, a method of payment that makes it profitable for them to decide in favor of those who bring cases before them. Some states have abolished them, but in many areas justices of the peace still offer the only means of settling minor disputes without high expenses and long delays.

In cities, the courts of limited jurisdiction are municipal courts which try minor cases. Often they are subdivided into special courts such as traffic, juvenile, small claims, or domestic relations courts. Far more citizens have contact with courts of limited jurisdiction than with regular trial courts.

Above such courts are the states' *trial courts*. They try important civil and criminal cases. When they serve only one county they are sometimes known as county courts. When they serve two or more counties they are often called circuit or district courts. Each is presided over by one judge who must be trained in the law, is paid an adequate salary, and is elected in most states, usually for a five- or six-year term.

At the top of the system is a *state supreme court* to which defendants who are dissatisfied with the verdicts of lower courts may appeal their cases. It is composed of from five to nine judges, usually elected for terms ranging from six years to life. They are usually highly qualified and well paid. Thirteen states also have *appellate courts* between the circuit courts and the state supreme court to lighten the burden of appeals.

Many reformers have questioned whether popular election is the best means of choosing judges. Persons chosen to represent the people should be elected, they say, but persons chosen for expert knowledge should be appointed. The average voter cannot be well enough informed to make intelligent decisions on the training, experience, and judgment of candidates for judgeships, and political parties often nominate candidates on the basis of political rather than judicial qualifications. In some states judges are appointed by the governor and the legislature acting together. The American Bar Association (a national professional association of lawyers) recommended that governors nominate candidates and then let the people vote on whether to accept them. This plan was adopted by seven states, and in many states if a judge wants to run for reelection, his name alone is placed on the ballot. Thus he runs, not against opposing candidates, but solely on his record. If the people reject him, another election is held to choose his successor.

All states protect the right of an accused person to defend himself against charges of crime. In most states he cannot be put on trial for a crime unless he is first *indicted* by a *grand jury*. A grand (large) jury, usually composed of from twelve to twenty-three members, examines the evidence against accused persons. Such evidence is presented by the prosecuting attorney, usually elected, whose duty it is to seek the conviction of persons guilty of crime. If the grand jury finds that the evidence justifies putting the accused on trial, it so indicts him. In some states a person may be put on trial merely on the basis of a charge by the prosecuting attorney.

At his trial the defendant has the right to employ attorneys, to examine the evidence against him, and to cross-examine the witnesses who accuse him. He also has the right to compel witnesses to appear and give testimony. In criminal cases he has the right to a trial by jury. This means that the state cannot punish him unless his fellow citizens agree that he is guilty.

The jury system originated as a means of protecting citizens against unjust punishment by kings. It has some disadvantages. Members of juries are poorly paid for the time involved, and many have no special qualifications for jury duty. Juries can be misled by emotional pleas or local prejudices into freeing men who have broken the law. Some authorities maintain that it is better to have the verdict rendered by qualified judges, and in most states the defendant may choose to do so. But even in a democracy, the possibility that those in power might violate the rights of others makes the right to trial by jury necessary.

A careful record is kept of every word spoken at a trial and, if convicted, a person has the right to appeal his case to a higher court. If his attorney can convince the appeals court that there is reason to believe that the trial court made an error, the higher court will review the evidence and courtroom procedures and either uphold or reverse the decision of the lower court. If some important point of law is involved, cases may be appealed from a state supreme court to the United States Supreme Court.

One of the most serious criticisms made of our system of justice is that it is so expensive to use, especially appeals to a higher court, that the full protection of a citizen's rights is available only to the wealthy. It does not give an ordinary citizen an equal chance of winning a case against a wealthy man or corporation. Many persons are serving prison sentences who would not be in prison if they had enough money to appeal their sentences. In attempts to meet this problem, some states have provided salaried public defenders, as well as prosecuting attorneys, whose purpose is to insure justice for those unable to defend themselves properly. Legal aid societies, some privately and some publicly financed, offer some legal aid to the poor. However, the scales of justice are still heavily tilted in favor of wealth.

RURAL LOCAL GOVERNMENT

Units of local government are bewilderingly numerous, diverse, and overlapping. Their number is decreasing, primarily as a result of the consolidation of school districts, but according to a recent estimate we still have as many as eighty thousand. They are subdivisions of the states and exercise only the powers that are delegated to them by the states.

The largest unit of local government in most rural areas except New England is the *county.* Counties vary in size from 22 to 20,000 square miles, and in population from 208 to more than 6 million. Their principal governing body is the *county board,* sometimes called a county court or county commission. Typically, it is composed of five members, elected for terms of one to six years, and paid small salaries. Exercising both legislative and administrative powers, it levies taxes, conducts elections, licenses businesses, establishes zoning regulations, and maintains health departments and county roads. The county court, however, does not appoint the other county administrative officials, most of whom are elected directly by the people.

In many counties, particularly rural ones, the best known official is the *sheriff.* He is responsible for maintaining law and order, although he usually leaves actual police work to trained deputies, and he collects taxes unless a treasurer is chosen. A *county coroner* ascertains the causes of deaths, a *prosecuting attorney* seeks to secure the conviction of criminals, an *assessor* determines the value of property for tax purposes, a *county clerk* issues marriage licenses and election certificates, and a *board of education* manages the school system.

All of these and other county officials are elected by the people. When counties were so small that most citizens knew most of the candidates personally, this meant that officials were democratically hired. But many counties have grown so large in population that it is almost impossible for the average voter to know the qualifications of candidates for all county offices and how they stand on the issues. Party labels are not very helpful because party alignments are formed primarily on national, state, and international issues. Nor is a candidate's business or profession a reliable guide. In the city council of which this writer was a member, the progressive faction, which favored municipal parking lots, a sewage disposal plant, public housing, and city planning was led by two Democrats and two Republicans—a retired oil company executive, an automobile repair shop manager, a coal company official, and a professor. The opposition group was led by a Democratic labor union official and a Republican landlord. Only a personal acquaintance with these individuals would enable a voter to know their positions on city issues. Consequently, most voters cast their vote almost blindly among a large number of candidates. This often gives whoever controls a small block of votes the power to choose the officials.

In New England, where early settlers grouped their houses close together for defense against Indians and loneliness, the most important unit of local government is the *town*. The affairs of small towns and the surrounding rural areas were conducted by *town meetings* of all adult males, who elected officials, levied taxes, and enacted laws. This was America's best example of direct democracy. Some town meetings still exist, but when the growth of the population made the attendance of all citizens impractical, they elected representatives to act for them in town meetings, which were then converted into representative bodies. Thus they have come to resemble county governments, except that more officials are elected by the town meeting and fewer by direct vote of the people.

County government has changed less than any other level of government. It has been called "the dark continent of American politics," in which undemocratic policies, inefficiency, and corruption often flourish unpunished. Sometimes sheriffs overlook the illegal activities of political supporters; assessors win votes by assessing property at low rates, thereby depriving schools of proper tax support; and selfish interests block the construction of new roads and public facilities.

Because of such weaknesses, some state governments have taken over a number of county functions, such as property evaluation. Some counties have adopted civil service systems. A few have adopted county manager plans of government. Most counties, however, have resisted change.

WHAT IS THE "BEST" FORM OF CITY GOVERNMENT?

The problem of governing large cities is relatively new in America. At the time of the Revolution fewer than 5 percent of the people lived in towns or cities. Not until 1920 did urban population exceed rural population. In 1980, however, more than 70 percent of Americans lived in cities.

City governments were created by states which gave them limited self-government under state regulation. Because the life of cities is more complex, they must take action on more matters than rural local governments. Their chief functions in 1980 listed in order of amount of money spent were: maintaining public schools, providing protection against crime and fire, disposing of garbage and sewage, maintaining streets, supplying water, providing for the welfare of the poor, safeguarding public health, supplying electricity and gas, clearing slums and building public housing, and maintaining public parks and recreational areas. They also license businesses, register births, deaths, and transfers of property, illuminate streets, and set building and zoning regulations.

A city executive has a complex task. City government is a big business that requires not only political but management skills equivalent to those of the president of a large corporation. Because large cities are relatively new, their governments are more modern than rural governments. The three principal forms of city government now in use are the mayor-council with a weak mayor, the mayor-council with a strong mayor, and the city manager plan.

In almost all cities a city council acts as the city's legislature. In some cities all councilmen are elected "at large" by the city as a whole, but typically a city is divided into sections called wards, and each ward elects one or more councilmen for two-year terms. The councilmen are paid small salaries and meet weekly or every two weeks. They enact the city's laws (ordinances), levy taxes, and approve the city budget. Because few citizens know what issues are under consideration, the strongest pressures on a council come from special interest groups which have a financial stake in its decision.

Under the oldest form of city government, the *council-weak mayo*r form, a mayor and other officials, such as a treasurer, attorney, clerk, and police commissioner, are elected by the people. The mayor is head of the city administration, but, because he does not have the power to hire and fire other officials, he does not control them. He appoints lesser administrators, but only on approval of the council. Thus, control of the city's administration is divided among several officials who are independent of each other. If they are political opponents it is difficult to get the work of the city done. Responsibility is so divided that the voter does not know whom to blame for failures. Furthermore, it is difficult for voters to become well informed on the qualifications of the candidates for so many offices. The number of cities with this form of government is declining.

In the 1880s, cities began switching to a *council–strong mayor* form of government. Reducing the number of officials elected to members of the council and the mayor, they gave the mayor the power to appoint and remove other officials and made him responsible for the conduct of the entire city administration. Most larger cities, and many small ones, now have this form of government. However, the qualities that make a man a good manager of a city's business do not necessarily make him appealing to voters. As a result, voters often elect a man whose talents are political and who may or may not run the city with efficiency. Often he seems more interested in rewarding and punishing his political friends and enemies than in effective administration.

In an attempt to remedy these defects, Americans invented a new form of government, the *city manager* plan. Under this plan the city council hires a professional city manager who tries to stay out of politics and run the city as he would a business corporation. He is given the power to employ persons for city jobs and to operate its many services. Thus hiring and firing, and buying and selling are taken out of the hands of politicians, which reduces the possibility of favoritism and corruption. The council continues to enact ordinances and set broad policies, but the manager conducts the actual administration of the city. The city may have a major, selected by the council, but his duties are limited to presiding over council meetings, appointing its committees, and performing the ceremonial functions of greeting visiting dignitaries and dedicating new public buldings.

Generally, the city manager form has proved to be the most satisfactory form of city government for most cities. Although it originated as late as 1908, it gained popularity and has been adopted by nearly two thousand cities. The evidence is substantial that these cities are governed more efficiently and provide better city services at lower cost to taxpayers than cities with other forms of government.

A major weakness of city manager government is that the head of the administration is not supposed to take part in politics, although he may be subjected to political attacks and removal. Therefore he is not in a position to lay a program of city betterment before the people and to campaign for its adoption. He must confine himself to carrying out policies formulated by the council, and he can influence the council only indirectly through his factual reports on the city's affairs. Consequently, most of the larger cities, some of which have more population than some states, have kept the strong mayor plan.

State and local governments based on "the less government, the better" worked when our population was small and our economy was agricultural. Some of the measures that our forefathers took to protect liberty have become obstacles to popular control of state and local governments today.

Much concern has been expressed by conservatives, and more recently by many liberals, that the federal government is absorbing too much power at the expense of states and localities. Everything could not and should not, they said, be run from Washington. The failure to work efficiently together to solve common problems at the local and state levels is one reason why more control has been assumed by Washington, and this process cannot be halted without improving the effectiveness of state and local government.

Why is the public less interested and informed on state and local government than on the federal government? One reason is that state and local governments are so complex. To make them more understandable would require: (1) Reducing the number of local government units and eliminating the overlapping of city, county, and special districts. (2) Reducing the number of officials to be elected and giving those who are elected sufficient power, including the power to appoint other officials, so that their responsibility for the actions of their administrations is clear. (3) Reducing the size of large legislatures and city councils for the purpose of concentrating responsibility and increasing the visibility of elected officials. (4) Modernizing and simplifying state constitutions and city charters. (5) Shifting more small and medium-sized cities to the city manager pattern of government.

These steps might make it easier for the average citizen to follow the workings of his state and local government, but probably his interest in it will never be as high as it is in the federal government. Local governments deal largely with property questions, most of which affect relatively small numbers of property owners. Most of the issues that come before city councils involve questions of street location, the purchase of equipment, changes in the zoning of land, building permits, enlarging the city's boundaries, and appointment of members of special commissions. The functions of the county board are similarly limited in scope and interest. Separate commissions handle problems relating to schools, water supply, and sewage disposal. Most citizens do not have the time to keep themselves well informed on the activities of many separate bodies. Simplifying local government, shortening the ballot, and clarifying responsibility would help the public to be better represented.

Changes in form and organization of government can help, but they cannot in themselves bring about good government. There is no substitute for alert, interested, and active voters. When average citizens are not informed and active, selfish special interests are able to control affairs for their own benefit at the expense of the public. In a democracy, good state or local government requires the participation of many citizens who understand its problems and support policies in the public interest.

Questions

1. List the chief functions of state government. On which does it spend the most money?
2. How does state and local spending compare with that of the federal government?
3. What characteristics, according to political scientists, should a constitution have?
4. What were the original reasons for having two houses in state legislatures? Which reasons no longer apply? What are the arguments for and against a one-house legislature?
5. What suggestions have been made for improving state legislatures?
6. Why were governors originally given little power? What additional powers do reform groups want to give governors?
7. How should judges be selected? Why?
8. What are the chief sources of state revenue? On what is the most money spent?
9. List two ways in which trial courts and appeals courts differ.
10. What are the arguments for and against trial by jury?
11. What are the leading officials in county government? How are they selected? What criticism has been made of this means of selection?
12. What is a New England township? Why is it called a direct democracy?
13. What powers does a city council usually have?
14. What is the difference between the authority of a weak and

a strong mayor? What are some shortcomings of the strong mayor plan?
15. In what ways is the city manager plan of city government an improvement over other forms? What are its weaknesses?
16. Define: license, civil law, criminal law, justice of the peace, sheriff, grand jury, county board, prosecuting attorney, assessor, zoning.

Suggested Reading

Buechner, John C. *State Government in the Twentieth Century.* New York: Houghton-Mifflin, 1967.
Excellent short survey of state government and how it works.

Committee for Economic Development. *Modernizing Local Government.* New York: Committee for Economic Development, 1966.
A short discussion of a plan for reform.

Committee for Economic Development. *Modernizing State Government.* New York: Committee for Economic Development, 1967.
Describes strengths and weaknesses of state governments and proposes changes.

Halacy, D. S., Jr. *Government by the States: A History.* Evanston, Ill.: McDougall, Littell, 1973.
Briefly outlines the origins of state government and discusses the services they offer, their problems, shortcomings, and prospects.

Johnson, Claudius O. *American State and Local Government,* 4th ed. New York: Crowell, 1965.
A college text that is useful for reference.

Sanford, Terry. *Storm over the States.* New York: McGraw-Hill, 1967.
A former governor of North Carolina discusses the problems and needs of state governments and outlines what steps at the local, state, and national levels he considers necessary to make our federal system more responsive to today's needs.

Index